Development Economics—Nature and Significance

Development Economics—Nature and Significance

Syed Nawab Haider Naqvi

Sage Publications
New Delhi × Thousand Oaks × London

First published in 2002 by

Sage Publications India Pvt Ltd
M-32 Market, Greater Kailash I
New Delhi 110 048

Sage Publications Inc　　　　**Sage Publications Ltd**
2455 Teller Road　　　　6 Bonhill Street
Thousand Oaks, California 91320　　London EC2A 4PU

Published by Tejeshwar Singh for Sage Publications India Pvt Ltd, typeset in 10pt Baskerville Win 95 BT by Unisys Technologies, Chennai and printed at Chaman Enterprises, Delhi.

Library of Congress Cataloging-in-Publication Data

Naqvi, Syed Nawab Haider.
　　Development economics—nature and significance/Syed Nawab Haider Naqvi.
　　　　p. cm.
　　Includes bibliographical references (p.) and index.
　　　　1. Development economics. 2. Economic development.
I. Title

HD82.N245　338.9—dc21　　　2002　　　2001057881

ISBN: 0-7619-9628-1 (US-Hb)　　81-7829-094-4 (India-Hb)
　　　 0-7619-9629-X (US-Pb)　　81-7829-095-2 (India-Pb)

Sage Production Team: *Sam George, Sushanta Gayen and
Santosh Rawat*

Dedicated

To

Saeeda;

our children:
*Andalib, Tehmina, Qurrat ul Ain,
and Neelofar;*

and

grand children:
Akbar, Rohina and Zara

Contents

Foreword

Development economics is sometimes regarded as a branch of economics—a branch that, according to some critics, is withering away. In fact, as Professor Naqvi argues persuasively in this fine book, it is a separate tree. Far from withering away, it is flourishing and blooming. Its subject matter is wider and deeper than economics, drawing on other disciplines and containing a strong ethical component. But it is rooted in the same earth as the main tree of economics.

The author believes, in my view correctly, that development economics should be inspired by a desire to devise a better domestic and international society. He defines development as growth or transformation with equity, and in attempting to achieve this, he sees important roles in a mixed economy for both government interventions and the market—both the public and the private sector.

Professor Naqvi suggests that development economics, now more than half a century old, is a new paradigm. The author sees his task as defending this paradigm, somewhat revised and brought up to date, against more recent attacks.

In the early days of development economics it was thought of as a special field, applicable to the low-income countries of Africa, Asia and Latin America. But two tendencies have been at work to destroy or at least weaken this view. On the one hand, as developing countries have become more differentiated, it has become clear that different principles apply to some countries from those that apply to others. As important difference, for example, is that between economies with unskilled labour surpluses, like those of India, Pakistan, Indonesia or Bangladesh, and those with general labour scarcities, such as Taiwan or South Korea. Among other differences is that between large economies, in which foreign trade plays a comparatively minor role, and which may be able to influence their terms of trade, and small economies, in which trade is very important, and for which the terms of trade are given; or that between land surplus and land scarce economies; or between exporters of manufactures and of primary commodities. Such differentiation points towards the need for a typology of countries, which would depend on the purpose of the analysis and the design of strategies.

On the other hand, it was found that principles initially thought to apply only to developing countries, applied to the whole world community—to advanced and developing countries alike. In the golden days of the 1950s and 1960s, it was thought that the advanced countries knew how to eradicate unemployment, and that it was largely a problem of underdevelopment. But with the rise of widespread unemployment and stagflation in the advanced countries of the North in the last three decades of the 20th century, some of the employment analysis of segmented labour markets that had been conducted for underdeveloped countries seemed to apply also nearer to home. Similarly, the informal sector, first discovered in countries such as Kenya, seemed to have a parallel in the 'parallel', or underground or black economies of Europe and America. One could mention many other ideas that, first elaborated in a development context, found fruitful application in the advanced countries. Small-scale technology, advocated by intermediate or appropriate technologists for poor countries, has acquired a following in the richest countries, and flexible specialization and post-Fordist production methods are replacing Fordist styles. Theories of structural inflation, first formulated for Latin America, found application in industrial countries. Segmented labour markets, though initially formulated in the theory of 'non-competing groups' by John Elliott Cairnes, a contemporary of John Stuart Mill's, were rediscovered by early development economists and later elaborated for the advanced countries. Even the caste system in India has applications to the behaviour of craft and industrial trade unions in Great Britain. To those of us, like Professor Naqvi, who think that neo-classical economics does not apply to developing countries, it should not come as a complete surprise to discover that it does not apply to the advanced countries either. As Professor Naqvi shows, the foundations of neo-classical economics have been shaken by asymmetric information, moral hazard, principal-agent syndrome, multiple equilibria, dynamic external economies, etc. (There has been a similar reunification in the neo-classical camp, in which authors assert that the same principles that apply to the advanced countries also apply to the developing world. This movement has been called the neo-classical resurgence.)

Naqvi wisely warns us against single-remedy solutions such as 'getting prices right.' The statement 'getting prices right' has undergone a curious transformation. In the 1960s it was intended to point to the calculation of correct shadow or accounting prices in the face of 'distorted' market or actual prices. Because market prices reflected all sorts of 'distortions', including those caused by the existing and, from an ethical point of view, arbitrary income and asset distribution, it was the task of the government to intervene and allocate resources according to the 'right' shadow prices. The purpose of government intervention was to correct the distortions caused by the free play of market forces. More recently, the recommendation has been reversed.

It now is that developing countries should get rid of state interventions in order to permit market prices to reflect the 'correct' opportunity costs and benefits. Distortions are now regarded as caused mainly (or only) by governments. Whereas the old, Platonic guardian view of the state said that governments can do no wrong, the currently fashionable view is that they can do no right. Naqvi's sensible view is that they are sometimes right, sometimes wrong, and can by politically judicious action, be pushed in the right direction.

The book discusses well and advocates human development, which is contrasted subtly with various alternative approaches that are found wanting. The treatment is not uncritical, but the criticisms are well taken. In a fine treatment of the impact of globalization, the author shows that it should be focussed on people, and particularly the poor, the deprived and the socially excluded. Talking of the Invisible Hand in developing countries, one may well complain that it is nowhere to be seen.

Some of the neo-classical theories regard the private sector as the source of wealth creation and the public sector as the domain of authority, exercised either benevolently or, more commonly, as a wasteful drain on resources. The distinguishing features of the state, according to this view, are that its membership is *universal*, and that it has powers of *compulsion* not given to other organizations. According to some adherents of this view, many governments in developing countries have usurped the sphere of production, which should be left to the private sector. The remedy lies in the state withdrawing from this area, and confining itself to the protection of its citizens against external and domestic threats.

But it is equally possible to look at the same situation in a different way, with a different division of responsibilities. This way of looking at the two sectors is more akin to Professor Naqvi's approach. We may regard each sector, or better each sphere of responsibility, as creating different forms of wealth, and exercising different forms of authority and compulsion. According to this view, the private sector creates forms of wealth that can be sold for profit, the public sector those that, while also useful, cannot, because powerful externalities and inappropriabilities exist. Public goods, so well discussed by Professor Naqvi, are goods characterized by non-rivalrous consumption, so that one person's use does not detract from another's, and occasionally, though not always, non-excludability from the benefits whose costs are incurred by some. The classic example, given by John Stuart Mill, is a lighthouse (though its construction can, of course, be sub-contracted to private firms, and though it benefits not all sailors but only ships in the region). Armed protection, monetary and employment stability, an efficient market, the administration of justice, and mass education are other examples of public goods, or rather public services. Certain types of infrastructure, such as uncongested roads, bridges and subways, or harbours, dams and irrigation, are non-rivalrous but not non-excludable, for the provider can charge tolls or fees and exclude non-payers. But this means excluding some people the benefits to whom would exceed the costs of supplying them. When price discrimination is impossible, the alternative is for the government to provide these goods and services free and finance them by taxation.

Not all public goods should be produced, provided or financed (important distinctions, often neglected) by the central government. Some can be supplied by the local government, or by cooperatives, clubs or other interested private parties, such as a group of farmers who jointly provide common control over common grazing rights. Others, like a common currency, some observers would take away from government control and put under the control of an independent central bank. Some need no institution or organization and are free goods, like peace, the market, a common language, or trust, loyalty and truth telling in transactions. But given the two characteristics of public goods of non-rivalry in consumption and, normally, non-excludability in charging for their use, the government (central and local) is one of the institutions (among others) that is particularly fit to produce, provide or finance some of these goods and services, particularly if no other institution can or will do so.

On the other hand, there are other reasons for public sector production than the public nature of goods. They include natural monopolies, if their regulation is less efficient, and merit goods, to which the community attaches a high value, but which cannot be afforded by those who need them. Or goods and services, such as the arts or museums or theatres, which are regarded by the community as important, but would not exist if they had to rely wholly on private finance. (There are also merit bads, or demerit goods, such as dangerous drugs, tobacco, alcohol and weapons, whose production or sale the government may wish to restrict or prohibit.)

Production is thus not confined to the private sector. Production of different things can and should therefore occur in both the public and the private sector. And the same is true of authority. The private sector exercises authority through work discipline (hiring and firing, giving and withholding payments), the public sector through the army and the police. And the authority of the state depends on widespread voluntary acceptance by the citizens. A worker can, of course, leave the firm and go to another, but citizens in many countries can also leave and move to another country. States are also constrained by both super-national bodies, like the European Community, and sub-national bodies, like provinces and municipalities.

The question as to whether the private and the public sector use their authority for the benefit of the public or wastefully, predatorily or exploitatively remains to be answered. Such shifts between the two perceptions about the role of the private and the public sector give rise, however, to very different evaluations. They reflect different ideologies, different ways of organizing, filing and evaluating the same observations. The role of profit, of moral and aesthetic considerations and of the use of force, will appear quite different according to which of these two perceptions one accepts.

One of the central themes of this book is the importance of altruism in asking relevant questions and giving proper answers on such vital issues of human existence as inequality, poverty and human deprivation; and to make clear that an uncompromising insistence on self-interest, which neo-classical economics glorifies as the only valid principle of rationality, is both inadequate and counterproductive. Naqvi writes, '[O]ne of the central themes of this book ... is that *the search for value-free or ethically neutral decision rules is both pointless and counter-productive* in evaluating the merits of a successful development policy. It is pointless because ethical considerations do affect economic behaviour so that excluding these from the economic calculus will make the latter incomplete, even misleading, and because no such thing is possible. ... Such an exercise is also counter-productive for the simple reason that keeping ethical norms alive and compelling by internalizing the sense of obligations reduces the cost of policing and monitoring the working of economic systems as well as checking the incidence of free riding in the society.

The point here is that an excessive dose of self-interested behaviour (which is seen to be the hallmark of rational behaviour) weakens "the crucial social underpinnings of market processes" (Hirsch 1977: p. 122). It follows that it is neither irrational to act morally nor immoral to act rationally.'

In an attractive and easy to understand style the author tackles difficult and complex economic, political and philosophical questions. All important development issues are covered and I commend the book warmly for its combination of clear analysis and deep commitment to the poor of our world.

Paul Streeten
New York

Acknowledgements

In preparing this work, which is a sequel to my 1993 book, I have drawn on my own subsequent writings on the subject, especially those published in *World Development* (1995, 1996), ESCAP's *Asia and Pacific Development Journal* (1999) and UNESCO's forthcoming *Encyclopedia of Life Support Systems* (2002). A large amount of development literature that has appeared since 1993 has been consulted. Incorporating these new insights has meant writing a new book, which includes an extensive revision and updation of my earlier work and a net addition of two chapters. In particular, I have included in the present volume some new material on such topical issues as trade and growth, globalization, Sen's capability calculus, economic development and human development. Also, heeding the sound advice of my publisher (Mr. Tejeshwar Singh), and of the many reviewers of my original book, I have tried my best to eliminate repetitions and unnecessary polemics. However, the seeming repetition that still remains is a pedagogical device to relate some of the central ideas to the main theme of each chapter and let them evolve gradually. I try to discuss at length, in each successive chapter, what was only hinted at previously. Some issues which were analyzed in detail in a previous chapter are summarized in a subsequent one in order to keep the narrative in each chapter as self-contained as possible. Thus, the paradigmatic vision of development economics is cited in the second chapter, but it is fully developed only in chapter eight, taking into account the various building blocks of a useful development theory as identified in the intervening chapters. All this then leads to the formation of the vision of the future evolution of development economics presented in chapters nine and ten. Similarly, other themes—import substitution versus export expansion, government versus the market, the Pareto optimality criterion, the Rawlsian principle—have been re-examined from a different angle each time they appear in different chapters so as to throw some fresh light on them gleaned from the surrounding landscape. I hope that this new book—it may well raise a lot of dust, like my earlier one did for joining issue with the stalwarts of our discipline as well as with the agnostics—makes many intricate development issues a little clearer, though not necessarily absolutely clear—such a task is in any case beyond human reach. To this end, I have also tried to make the analysis presented in the book more readable and thus accessible to a wider audience. I hope, however, that this is not achieved by sacrificing the analytical rigour or accuracy of the argument. The review of a large body of literature having a direct and indirect bearing on development economics and the fairly comprehensive reference list placed at the end of the book should be a ready reference guide to students of the subject.

I acknowledge my indebtedness to Mr. Tejeshwar Singh who encouraged me to prepare this book, to Professor Paul Streeten for writing an invaluable foreword, and to Sir Hans Singer and Professor Ismail Sirageldin with whom I have corresponded quite often to seek advice—always given generously and promptly—on some of the ideas discussed in this book. I thank the many reviewers of my 1993 book—in particular, Prof. Lawrence Klein, Prof. Paul Streeten, Prof. Rafiq Ahmed and Prof. Sunat Kumar Saha—and the following scholars who wrote very valuable reviews: Professors Amarendra Sahoo, M.K. Ghadoliya, Basanta K. Sahu, Jagpal Singh, T.A. Mathias, S. Ambirajan, Kalyanjit Roy Choudhury, J. Parmananda Das, M.R. Brett–Crowther, S. Mohan and K.S. Ramachandran. I also wish to express my deep gratitude to the editor, Sage (Sam George) for making significant editorial improvements in the text.

Above all, my gratitude is unbounded to my deceased parents (Syed Mohammed, and Hasan Fatima and Hameed Fatima), my uncle and aunt (Syed Mustafa Hasan and Haidri Begum) whose beneficence continues even beyond their graves, my sister (Nasim Zehra), my immediate family (to whom this volume has been dedicated) and my sons-in-law (Ali Reza and Imran Husain) who enabled me to work on this book in peace and with undivided attention. I also thank my daughter Tehmina Naqvi for helping with the final revision of this book and Mr. Zafar Javed Naqvi for extending invaluable library assistance. However, as always, only I bear the responsibility for the views expressed in this book—especially for insisting uncompromisingly, against the well-meaning advice of some of my reviewers, on the paradigmatic character of development economics around which the raging controversy presented in the ensuing chapters wheels.

Part I

Foundational Issues

1

Development Economics:
A Bird's-eye View

Fifty years after having come into existence, development economics still lacks universal acclaim. Pessimistic evaluations of the subject, which bear an ill-concealed resemblance to obituary notices, continue to appear in learned journals. The academic community has reluctantly granted it the right to exist, though mostly on neoclassical terms, but even this conditional recognition has not been easily won. From the first full-length evaluation of the discipline by Chenery (1965), which regards it as a variation on the classical theme of comparative advantage, to Stern's (1989) sympathetic review of the contributions that the discipline has made to the state of economic knowledge and to the more recent evaluations (Bardhan 1993; Naqvi 1996, 1999; Thirlwall 1999; Todaro 2000) which affirm its truth, development economics has experienced many a vicissitude—both the laurels of glory in its sunny days and the 'arrows of outrageous fortune' in difficult times. Having traversed a tough and tangled territory, it has finally stabilized—albeit, as the agnostics would allege, on slippery ground. As if to prove the ubiquity of the self-interest principle, practising development economics has become an industry in its own right. Not only the social profitability of this industry, but also its 'private' profitability appears to be strictly positive; for instance, the publishing industry continues to patronize it and publish full-length books on the subject.

But the success of development economics, against heavy odds, rests on more solid grounds. As is always the case with the progress of science, both exogenous and endogenous events have contributed to a strong revival of intellectual activity in our discipline. Five decades of a variegated development experience (ranging from economic regress in Sub-Saharan Africa to the remarkable development success in East Asia), the production of massive cross-country and time-series data about a large number of development variables, the construction of large macroeconomic models and fast-running computers and the application of mathematical methods—and, ironically enough, the failure of neo-classical economics to meet the persistent demands for a faster rate of economic development worldwide—have all contributed to rekindle interest in our discipline. The fact is that it continues to enjoy a virtual monopoly in offering an adequate explanation of the nature of development processes and suggesting viable strategies to change the world for the better, a monopoly which is most likely to remain unchallenged in the 21st century as well. All this is good news for development economists, who can now afford not only bread but also some butter for their daily parsnips.

But development economics still has a long struggle before it. As Newton's Third Law of Motion has taught us, 'to every Action there is always an opposed and equal Reaction'. Thus, quite expectedly, the 'liberalists' have stepped up their 'reactionary' activities in direct proportion to the gains made by development economics. They advertise ever more widely the healing touch of the Invisible Hand as a superior alternative to the innate *etatisme* of development economics—implied, for example, by 'balanced (un-balanced) growth', the 'big-push', 'minimum critical effort', the 'centre-periphery' relations and the 'unequal gains from trade and investment'. Thus, even when it amounts to sheer circular reasoning, isolated instances of free-market success or government failure are taken as decisive refutations of development economics as a discipline (Haberler 1988). Not only on the pages of textbooks and scientific journals with conspicuously revealed Paretian proclivities, but also in the real world—for instance, in Eastern Europe, the erstwhile Soviet Union, China, Japan, East Asia and South-East Asia, including India and Pakistan—market forces are seen to be

defeating development economics (Little 1982; Crook 1989).
Spurred on by globalization—which has been praised for causing
unprecedented surges in the wealth of nations as well as reviled for
integrating the rich and disintegrating the poor peoples and countries—there has been a violent kickback of the old-fashioned laissez-
faire market ideology, which extols the virtues of the (invisible)
self-regulating mechanism and makes whatever is privately profitable socially desirable. As a logical corollary, privatization, liberalization and the consolidation of the so-called intellectual property
rights are being emphasized to clear the way for the emergence of
free-trade regimes and integrated capital (*not* labour) markets. Little
surprise, then, that country after country is marching willy-nilly to
the markets (the poor ones more like lemmings) to attain economic
salvation from 'regulatory capture'.

Fortunately, there is nothing to support the prevailing sense of
market-friendly triumphalism—which in most cases amounts to little
more than pandering to the liberalist prejudice—nor is there sufficient warrant to suggest that the demise, actual or predicted, of
our discipline is nigh. In particular, there is not much circumstantial evidence to warrant the charge that 'the poverty of development economics [became] increasingly apparent in the 1970s and
1980s' (Walters 1989: 60). The fact is that there is no solid evidence
to prove that the advent of free markets domestically or globally, in
place of the relatively regulated ones, has ever produced first-best
efficient and socially desirable outcomes anywhere, or at any time
in human history. On the other hand, those developing countries
where development economics has been practiced have grown reasonably fast (for instance, Pakistan, India) and some others have
done so very fast (for example, the East Asian Tigers); while the
crisis-ridden developing countries of Eastern Europe and the former
Soviet Union and the economically blighted Africa have not been
helped at all by the talismanic quackery of free-market economics.
Indeed, free markets have led to a dramatic rise in unemployment
rates, a heavier burden of debt, a further deepening of acute poverty, and tragic episodes of economic *regress*. Also, thanks to it, more
often than not market friendliness has tended to degenerate into
'people unfriendliness'.[2] If anything, the East-Asian meltdown has
highlighted the systemic malfunction of free-market regimes. In
addition to vastly complicating the task of managing viable
exchange-rate regimes, a near-complete freeing of capital movements

(especially of short-term capital) across national borders has destabilized them, notwithstanding their sound 'fundamentals'. Equally unhelpful has been the gross abuse of the TRIPS Accord by the (solely) profit-seeking multinational corporations (MNCs), whose misdemeanour threatens to slow down, even arrest, the accumulation and spread of knowledge, so vital to increasing productivity and rapid economic growth in the developing world. Indeed, in some cases, their activities amount to a 'theft' of the developing countries fund of long-acquired knowledge. 'The new rules of globalization—and the players writing them—focus on integrating global markets, neglecting the needs of the people that markets cannot meet' (UNDP 1999: 30). *Thanks to an unguarded implementation of market-friendly policies which developing countries now have to undertake at the behest of multilateral donors,* the chalice of economic prosperity ever more eludes the grasp of the poor. It follows that there is more, not less, need for a greater role of government nationally and globally to maximize social good and that the time has come to part company with the minimalist government prescriptions.

Thus, development economics, as a discipline in its own right, is in no danger of evaporating under the heat of liberalist ideas. Indeed, in a dramatic reversal of fortunes liberalism, notwithstanding its claims to ubiquitous reach and relevance, withers under the scorn of practical people as it drifts further away from the clamourings of the real world while development economics rises once again in the East! True, in many vital aspects the discipline is not exactly what it was in the fifties, partly due to its endogenous growth and partly in response to the feedback from the fast changing 'reality'; but the point to note is that the hard-core economic logic behind the traditional approach of development economics remains nonetheless valid (UNCTAD 1999).[3] Thus, for instance, while import substitution may have been carried a little too far and not implemented very efficiently in some countries, in others (e.g., East Asia, China) it has led to durable economic expansion on the crest of new knowledge. Thus, partly to guard against the unrequited outreach of neo-classical economics into its domain, it is a worthwhile enterprise—which this volume undertakes—to reassure ourselves about the nature and significance of development economics. To this end, the basic question we seek to answer is: Is development economics a paradigm with a significant territory of its own?

Interpreting the word 'paradigm' broadly as a distinct *Weltanschauung*, the answer to this question must be in the affirmative. This is the central theme of this book. Development economics is presented in these pages not as a deviant branch of mainstream economics, deserving the treatment reserved for heretics, but as a subject performing a useful role. It explicitly seeks to explain the multi-dimensional complexity of the process of economic *development* (*not* just economic growth), which is about the accumulation of physical and human capital, the progress of skills, the march of ideas, the ignition of innovational impulses, the growth of population, and the manner in which the produced and non-produced factors of production are combined and managed to initiate and sustain growth; and it offers sensible remedies to resolve this complexity to everyone's advantage. In all this, it continues to be the sole (though, somewhat melancholy) keeper of the original flame of economics—which Adam Smith (1976 [1776]) referred to as an enquiry into 'The Natural Progress of Opulence'. Also undisputed is its static and dynamic comparative advantage in dealing with the perennial problems of human existence—the myriad insistent inequities, the 'entrenched deprivation' and the extreme poverty of the voiceless underclass—that darken the face of real-life developing societies. An implication of these statements is that because of the 'natural' preoccupation of development economics with such fundamental issues, it cannot afford to be irrevocably and exclusively wedded to the value-neutral engineering solutions presumably produced by the market. The fact is that in the pursuit of its central objectives, development economics is guided by a different set of research priorities which are more problematic than those which define neo-classical economics. While the latter, even when 'dynamised' (i.e., the Harrod–Domar reformulation), remains engrossed—rain or shine—with the existence and manner of 'decomposing' of the sleep-walking, steady-state, long-run solutions that are occasionally awakened by the shock of technological progress, the former is concerned primarily with processes that tend to raise per capita income over time and distribute it more equitably by an overall transformation of the structure of demand, trade, production and employment (Chenery 1981).

With such credentials, an assertion of autonomy by development economics is not illegitimate even when it is seen as sinning against the unity and universality of neo-classical economics. Indeed, this assertion offers a sobering thought about the essential relativity of economics vis-à-vis the nature and the needs of society at various stages of development.[4] It is by no means a decisive argument against the discipline or a final call for it to rejoin neo-classical economics. But a declaration of autonomy is not necessarily a rejection of mainstream economics. Thus, growth theory, which is essentially an intertemporal investigation of the static general equilibrium theory in a positive vein, is by no means entirely irrelevant to development economics.[5] For instance, the dynamics of optimal control is useful in understanding the inter-temporal character of investment decisions, e.g., in determining the optimal size of savings, in estimating the required amount of foreign aid and in making long-term development plans.[6] Indeed, it can be asserted that partly for lack of such an understanding, development economics has tended to overemphasize savings per se—not realizing that eventually, higher savings would raise the capital/output ratio as well, which would thus not be enough to raise the growth of output on a permanent basis—and to neglect somewhat the crucial role of technological change and human capital in the development process. Also, it may be argued that the relative unconcern of its practitioners with achieving rigour, generality and simplicity by codifying their basic ideas in the form of 'internally consistent models' has not helped the growth of development economics (Krugman 1992: 15].[7]

But for development economics to seek intellectual help from neo-classical economics is not necessarily the same as losing its own distinct identity—especially when such a self-sacrifice is both unnecessary and undesirable. This is because by virtue of their broad purpose and basic thrust mainstream economics and growth theory, both of which *assume* optimally structured real-world economies (e.g., an optimal initial distribution of income), do not help at all in fully understanding the nature of the development problem or in diagnosing any meaningful remedial policies.[8] Indeed most of the growth theory is designed to understand what determines growth and *not* to prescribe policies to promote it (Stern 1991). Thus, there is a broad agreement now that even though there are some arresting aspects of the new endogenous growth theory (Romer 1986; Lucas 1988)—its emphasis on technological progress, learning by doing and human (not just physical) capital—it fails to explain the mechanics of development because it assumes a single-sector economy, as if to show its true neo-classical colours! (Naqvi 1995). However, the problem is a general one. It is traceable ultimately to the unquestioning acceptance by neo-classical economics of the Pareto optimality criterion—its philosopher's stone—which accords unifocal priority to efficiency considerations to an 'antiseptic' extent and which for these reasons cannot be exclusively relied upon to comprehend the dimensions of the development problem adequately. This 'alchemic' rule, by its very nature, seeks to maintain the status quo and rests on such defining assumptions as perfect and symmetric information and the existence of a complete set of markets.[9] Therefore, it would not inform us, for instance, that the basic problem of economic development is to manage a growth-promoting synergy between the dual processes of agrarian and structural transformation, to achieve an equitable distribution of income and, more generally, to enhance the economic well-being of the people. It certainly would not help in grasping the importance of changing the structure of private property holdings to improve the lot of the least privileged in the society. Furthermore, the make-believe neo-classical world of self-clearing markets—which is blessed with full employment because it keeps labour markets completely flexible and capital adequately remunerated at all times—does not even recognize the efficiency or moral aspects of the phenomenon of unemployment, let alone offer any meaningful remedies for it.[10] Indeed, there is an intrinsic tendency in the neo-classical tradition to blame it instead on the voluntary actions of wage earners, which allegedly make the labour markets 'rigid' (Haberler 1950). Sometimes, it even dismisses such a life-and-death issue by treating practically any level of actual unemployment as the 'natural' rate of unemployment, about which nothing can or should be done (Malinvaud 1984).[11] Quite understandably (though *not* justifiably), then, state intervention sends neo-classical economists clambering towards the liberalist high ground, where the government can only make matters worse. The result of this hands-off-the-market (non) policy, which neo-classical economics makes look scientific, has been the perpetuation of high rates of unemployment in Western societies (the so-called Euro-11) for more than three decades now. This state of affairs is likely to grow worse as the sprawling multinational corporations—and *not* the textbook atomistic economic agents which populate the mythical regime of pure and perfect competition—come to completely dominate the new-world, 'redder-in-tooth-and-claw' capitalism.

nd yet a full-time preoccupation with self-clearing markets has landed the neo-classical economics of Walrasian vintage—which regards, by virtue of Arrow's Impossibility Theorem and its ordinalist utilitarian convictions, the basic issues of human existence as inescapably arbitrary and intellectually despotic—into a morass of irrelevance. But for development economics to entertain such *anarchic* ideas is simply suicidal, because any such thought would prevent it from comprehending key development problems, let alone making a useful contribution to their resolution. True, under some very restrictive assumptions noted above, free markets may be suitable to optimize output and maximize consumers' welfare. However, an activist role for a non-minimalist state is fairly well defined, especially when a domestic and/or global public good, characterized by non-exclusivity, indivisibility and non-rivalry in consumption, must be consumed and produced, a structural change involving the redistribution of private property rights (for instance, in land reforms) has to be made or when, at the initial stages of economic development, large amounts of investment resources must be undertaken and a vision of the future provided to give a sense of direction to the process of societal transformation. In all these and similar situations, state intervention both at the domestic and global levels could be welfare-raising even if the questions regarding its form and extent remain open to debate.

To assert, as some economists do, that free markets can be fruitfully relied upon even to effect a structural change, provided private property rights are properly defined, is perhaps to stretch one's credulity a little. Indeed, it can be shown that in no case does a Pareto optimal solution necessarily bespeak a market-oriented and a value-neutral ideology (Debreu 1987).[12] Furthermore, if the players in a game-theoretic framework do not possess foreknowledge about each others' utility functions, then such a solution would neither be the most efficient, nor the most equitable (Arrow 1979). The stock argument that 'government failure' is even more severe than 'market failure' ignores nearly all real life situations where, due to the essentially 'asymmetric' and imperfect nature of the information available to rival economic agents and the non-existence of a complete set of contingent markets, the efficiency of market outcomes cannot be guaranteed in advance because it is not Pareto optimal (Akerlof 1970; Malinvaud 1989). When such situations prevail there may be no a priori basis for rejecting government intervention

(Stiglitz 1991). The (correct) argument that the government may also be dysfunctional in such cases should not be construed as a case for the ubiquitous reach and relevance of market solutions; it rather emphasizes the need for an efficient, reform-oriented, nonminimalist government.[13]

If the case for the free, or even freer, markets cannot be substantiated historically, theoretically, or empirically, then why should it be put forward with such an air of Olympian inevitability of its beneficial outcome? The rational expectationist's thesis, that the government thrives only on the occasional lapses in the economic agents' informational faculties, is not universally accepted as a sufficient argument for ending the economic role of the government even in developed countries. There is lesser reason for accepting it in developing countries where, as noted above, 'market failures' are a rule rather than an exception and the problems of structural change require active government intervention. Arrow (1974) has clearly stated that the 'information economy' achieved by the market system is not realized when the relevant markets do not exist to supply this information in the form of prices.[14] Such cases, all too common in the developing countries, warrant 'government intervention, a code of professional ethics or an economic organization with some power intermediate between the competitive firm and the government.' Another apparently more attractive anti-*dirigistic* argument, is that the government should not entertain any ideas of the social good. It should rather be concerned only about protecting the 'negative freedoms' in the society and letting individuals decide, in a non-interventionist environment, what is good for them (Nozick 1974). In this libertarian perspective, free markets are considered the best preservers of individual liberty, which is accorded priority over all else[15] (Buchanan 1986). However, this is not a convincing assertion at all. Since it is decided in advance on ideological grounds that the market does not interfere with individual liberty, while the government does, the superiority of market-based solutions follows by definition. By the same token, the failure of the government is also guaranteed because it undermines (negative) freedoms when it seeks to guard the freedom of the weak against that of the powerful. But such an assertion about the innate superiority of the markets will roll out of every argument on its own circularity.

Whatever be the justification for entertaining such arguments—or tautologies—in mainstream economics, they are not germane to development economics because the process of economic development is too complex to be left to simple unidimensional quick fixes (e.g., 'get the prices right'), which generally fail to produce the desired results. The examples of the erstwhile Soviet Union and that of sub-Saharan Africa may be the most dramatic cases of a monumental market failure, but even the less striking ones point in the same direction. There is now a consensus that a successful development policy employs both the market and the government to promote economic growth with distributive justice (Streeten 1993; World Bank 2000). The point, however, is that while individual liberty must be prized as an absolute value, it should not be to the extent where preserving it means tolerating and perpetuating extreme social injustice and misery for the majority of humankind. This cannot be, even when Buchanan's 'calculus of consent' signals unanimity about such an undesirable state of affairs, or even if the rectification of such injustice offends Nozickian non-consequentialism. This is because the degree of freedom enjoyed by economic agents is relative to the state of the society. Keynes put this point clearly: 'A great deal is at stake... we have to show that a *free system can be made to work*. To favour what is known as planning and management does not mean a falling away from the moral principles of liberty which could formerly be embodied in a simpler system...' (Harrod 1972; italics mine). The task of the modern societies is to find a delicate balance between individual freedom and social organization. A failure to achieve such a balance is to invite a social disaster. This is even more true of the developing countries where basic social institutions are much weaker than in the developed countries, and are less able to check the pulverizing fallout of individual greed on the working of social and economic institutions.

An important reason why a neo-classical prescription fails to help is that—especially in the context of economic development—it becomes more difficult to distinguish between the 'is-questions' and the 'ought-questions'.[16] Answering such a complex set of questions involves making normative judgements. Thus, for instance, the self-interest maximization rule—practiced by heroically selfish economic agents indulging in 'business, as usual' even in the darkest hour—which mainstream economics has created in its own image, cannot be the sole index of rationality in thinking about such issues. Even though it helps to produce neat theoretical results, this rule neither reflects experience nor survives reflection, and it is definitely not a universal description of ideal, or much less, actual human behaviour.[17] The rule, which regards virtue and self-interest as indivisible, becomes even more grotesque when it seeks to drive out of circulation everything that is not self-interest maximization, on the ground that it must by definition be irrational because it is ethical! Such a stance is socially undesirable because an unrepentant insistence on self-interest maximization alone would change the objective reality accordingly (Hausman and McPherson 1993) and, at any rate, it would soon knock human society to pieces. The fact of the matter is that a significant part of our behaviour is motivated by altruism, even by commitment, and we may be willing to sacrifice some of our personal welfare for the benefit of others (Harsanyi 1977a; Sen 1987; Streeten 1989). The collective mind of humankind may rightly regard such an event as economically beneficial, even though it may not be Pareto optimal. What is even more important is that ethical considerations, based on either secular or religious motivations, focus our attention on crucial development and global concerns—such as, poverty, distributional inequities and unemployment—with an urgency that positive economics lacks.[18]

A strictly neo-classical answer to development questions is also inadequate, partly because such an answer professes strict 'neutrality' regarding issues of justice in the economy. According to Debreu (1991), economists would be required to take an 'inhuman stance' when confronted with such a choice.[19] It is in the nature of a positivistic calculus that it cannot even distinguish between a wealthy individual and a poor one, so that a distributive scheme may as well be a perverse one—one that transfers real resources from the poor to the rich.[20] It follows that development economics needs, among other things, to draw on the more capacious social choice rules which explicitly allow normative judgements—for example, 'what would I do if I were in anyone else's shoes?'—to be able to prescribe institutional change where an undesirable status quo exists. Obviously, the distributionally barren Pareto optimality rule, which according to neo-classical economics is the oriflamme of economic forces, is not of help in addressing developmental issues. This is partly because it is inherently status quoist, and partly because it has not been programmed to answer value-loaded questions about vital domestic and global development issues.[21] On the other hand, there are non-utilitarian criteria like the Rawlsian Justice-as-Fairness and Difference Principles, which should be helpful because of their uncompromising insistence on changing social and economic institutions if the existing ones do not perform in a morally acceptable way—especially if they do not satisfy the needs of the least privileged individuals in society by ensuring their prior access to the 'primary social goods' which are a universal need.[22] Similarly, Sen's capability calculus focuses on the centrality of converting resources (or the Rawlsian 'primary social good') for living a better life by taking into account circumstances which are 'internal' to an individual. Needless to say, such choice rules give a distinctly moralistic and reformist edge to economic reasoning. They raise the kind of questions which are helpful in conceptualizing development issues and in suggesting adequate remedies for them. Paying due regard to such moral concerns has acquired greater urgency as the de-equalizing and poverty-enhancing aspects of globalization become more obvious. There is now a widespread demand—which has become impossible to ignore even politically both in the East and the West—that a new set of rules of global governance be codified, based on 'a common core of values, standards and attitudes, a widely shared sense of responsibilities and obligations' (*HDR* 1999: p. 8).

It should be clear to the reader by now that this book is not always motivated by concerns that are universally shared by mainstream economists, or even by some development economists. Indeed, it may stick in the gizzards of both the neo-classical orthodoxy as well the agnostics among the development economists. Development economics in these pages does not appear engulfed in a riot of confusing (and confused) ideas, especially those which are antithetical to its very existence. Thus, it does not take Pareto optimality as its guide; nor does it pretend to be excessively market friendly and recklessly outward oriented, or to be a 'rock of positivity' concerned only with securing value-neutral solutions. Indeed, it is one of the central theses of this book that a development economics accommodating such inaccessible concepts of neo-classical economics will spell the former's decadence as surely as the Trojan horse spelt the doom of Rome! On the other hand, it would be idle to deny the existence of competing development paradigms—the neo-Keynesian, Marxist/structuralist and institutionalist—from which development economics can borrow (and has borrowed) to acquire greater explanatory and prescriptive powers (see Chap. 8). The point, however, is that notwithstanding such inter-paradigm exchange of ideas, development economics has retained its distinctive identity which this book seeks to highlight with a view to providing reliable guidance to development policy. But to this end, development economics should avoid being excessively economistic, remain wedded to a mixed-economy dispensation, seek a middle ground between full fledged import substitution and no holds barred export orientation, and be seen as possessing a warm 'heart' when the need to make explicit normative judgements is too pressing to be ignored even at a theoretical level. Thus, I do not share the pessimistic view of those who have been writing obituary notices for development economics. This is partly because most of its original insights—the balanced growth doctrine, the vent-for-surplus conjecture, the center–periphery hypothesis, a distinct bias in favour of import substitution activities, the pioneers–latecomers syndrome—have stood the test of time. Indeed, some of these ideas have acquired considerable relevance in this 'Age of Globalization'. Similarly, I differ with those who think that to be able to face difficult development problems like poverty development economics should fall in love with the status quo-preserving free market, for that would be virtue paying tribute to vice! At any rate, an uncritical implementation of the so-called market-friendly policies has miserably failed to pave the promised primrose path to economic prosperity. Finally, I reject the viewpoint that development economics is some brand of applied economics, that it is not a discipline in its own right, or that it is blighted by the poverty of ideas.[23] Instead, this book emphasizes the fecundity of our discipline to generate new ideas. It also recommends waiting for a new dawn, like the one that shone on the pioneers of our discipline, in those areas where the illumination of traditional development economics is too faint to be a guide. Even a cursory reading of this book would convince the reader about the presence of concrete ideas helpful for the healthy growth of development economics as an intellectual paradigm. A growth of this nature, in turn, is essential to provide an understanding of the reality in the developing countries and to change it for the better. One does not have to be a Marxist to insist that the essential building block for a useful development theory is an overarching vision of socio-economic change—a change leading to a more just social order in which the needs of the least privileged sections in society are looked after in the best possible fashion; where unemployment, inequitable distribution of income and wealth, extreme poverty, and social degradation are seen as problem areas deserving the highest priority and in which human freedom is incomplete without some measure of equality. In short, following Meade, I believe that development economics, inspired by 'a passionate desire to devise a better domestic and international society' (Meade 1983: p. 268), should aim at fulfilling the progressive design of history by creating a dynamic *and* humane society. I have no doubt that such a vision of a better world cannot be of one ruled exclusively by the free markets; for, however 'natural' such a rule may appear to be, it is not inevitable. This is because history (or, even common sense) does not confer legitimacy on it. As Hirsch (1977) remarked, 'market capitalization (guided by the individualistic calculus) has never been the exclusive basis of the political economy in any country at any time' (p. 118). What is, however, inevitable is that a vision of a better world will be approximated only in a democratic society with a mixed economy, which is duly informed by the 'right' kind of moral values.

According to T.H. Marshall (1950), such a society is simply an extension of the revolutionary 18th-century idea of the rights of the citizen. Such a welfare-oriented society could be labelled Keynesian or neo-Keynesian, involving as it does a restriction of free markets, some restrictions on the institution of private property and the creation of an of effective system of resource transfer from the rich to the poor. On the other hand, the Friedmanite, Hayekian and rational-expectationist visions, which essentially aim to revive the concept of a Natural Order that sees the economic universe as run exclusively by the Invisible Hand, are all examples of misleading ideas. Their libertarianism has made mainstream economics scholastic, making it lose touch with reality and become 'less and less significant for the layman's concerns' (Malinvaud 1991: p. 66). Also, 'growth fundamentalism' (incorrectly attributed to some of the pioneers of development economics) is not a heritage worth preserving in the next cycle of the growth of our discipline.[24] Economic growth is clearly the vehicle of economic development. However, at the same time, an equitable distribution of the fruits of economic progress is necessary to give people an opportunity to lead a minimally acceptable life and to make the entire exercise worthwhile for the majority of humankind.

I firmly believe that the infatuation with unadulterated capitalism, made respectable by the libertarian moral-right philosophy,

and by citing questionable circumstantial and empirical evidence—
the remarkable growth performance of the East Asian countries
and the collapse of the East European socialist regimes—does not
provide such a vision.[25] If anything, the East Asian meltdown of the
late 90s—precipitated by the vagaries of the free capital markets
even in economies with solid economic fundamentals—the growing
inequalities of income and wealth within and between nations, the
rising incidence of poverty and unemployment worldwide caused
by globalization, and the need to provide global public goods to
minimize the incidence of environmental degradation have neces-
sitated greater and well-focused government intervention, duly
informed by moral considerations, at the domestic and international levels. Thus, practising development policy in the twilight of
discredited liberalist ideas, for which artificial demand is being
created in developing countries by the international donor agencies, is against the progressive design of history. These ideas have
done great damage even to Western democracies by robbing them
of their humane character and by making the privileged classes
stronger and more insensitive to human suffering. The rise of unemployment to unprecedented levels in the post-war era is directly
attributable to the intermediation of Hayekian liberalism, Laffer
curves, rational expectations and Friedmanite monetarism. It has
led to social instability in these societies, even though they may
have gained a modicum of economic efficiency, which remains a
doubtful proposition in itself. I am apprehensive that—as the experience of Eastern Europe and the former Soviet Union amply
demonstrates—*the transplantation of such defective ideas onto the fragile
social structures of the developing countries will spell even more undesirable
consequences for equity and growth.*[26] It is a patently unsatisfactory social
philosophy which, in the process of securing individual freedom
for the few, deprives us of our compassion towards the withered
lives of the underclass and which, in the blind pursuit of economic
efficiency, is incapable of providing answers to the obvious questions that the 'voiceless millions' ask. Clearly, a satisfactory social
philosophy would accord centrality to such life-and-death issues,
and emphasize entitlements as much as achievements.

Notes

1. Valuable contribution has been made by the World Bank in the form of several
   yearly analytical and statistical publications. Most worthy of mention among

these are its annual WDR (*World Development Reports*), TIDE (*Trends in Development Economies*), SID (*Social Indicators of Development*), and WDI (*World Development Indicators*). In addition, the invaluable analyses and data presented in the United Nation Development Programme's (UNDP) annual *Human Development Reports* (HDRs) and UNCTAD's annual *Trade and Development Reports* (*TDRs*) are also worthy of mention in this context.

2. Russia has been the hardest hit by the Invisible Hand: its 'economy has shrunk by upto one-third; and income inequality has increased dramatically. Living standards have deteriorated along with GDP, and health indicators have worsened'! (World Bank 2000). Also, the (African) countries, which have integrated most completely into the world system (i.e., with the highest export/GDP ratio) have been marginalized by globalization (UNDP 1999).

3. The observation in the text relates to a re-examination of the by-now entrenched agnosticism about the merits of an active import substitution policy. The argument is that—as also argued in this book—there is a need to keep a balance between export expansion and import substitution strategies in order to maximize growth with a reasonably viable balance-of-payments situation.

4. Deane (1983) has emphasized the 'relativity' of the discipline of economics: 'There is no one kind of truth which holds the key to the fruitful analysis of all economic problems, no pure economic theory that is immune to changes in social values or current policy problems' (p. 11).

5. This opinion, held by Hahn (1987), is not widely shared. See, especially, Goodwin (1990).

6. See Chakravarty (1969) for an example of the application of the theory of optimal control to problems of development policy. However, it may be pointed out that it is by their application to development problems that some of these esoteric mathematical tools have become relevant to economics.

7. On the other hand, the estrangement between neo-classical economics and development economics has also been detrimental to the former. Quite satisfied with its static existence, the former has not alluded frequently enough to its own origins—an understanding of the causes of the growth of the 'wealth of nations'. I agree with Sen (1988) that while promoting fruitful interaction with neo-classical economics, 'development economics...has to be concerned not only with protecting its "own" territory but also with keeping alive the foundational motivation of the subject of economics in general [i.e. development]' (p. 11).

8. Hahn (1987) clearly states the reasons why 'neo-classical growth theory is not...even a theory of growth' (p. 625). As noted in the text, this comment also applies to the recent endogenous growth theory notwithstanding the fact that the concept of the economies of scale is as central to it as it is to development economics.

9. However, the rule could be used to compute shadow prices for evaluating the efficiency of alternative investment plans.

10. This remark does not apply to the Akerlof–Stiglitz version of neo-classical economics. See, for instance, Stiglitz (1988). However, this version is neo-classical only in name, without which it cannot gain recognition in a typical US University.

11. It is unfortunate that the recognition granted to this phenomenon by Keynesian economics—of the possibility of reducing unemployment through

macroeconomic management—has been withdrawn even at the macro level, especially by the rational expectationists.

12. Debreu (1987) clearly states that the Pareto criterion is 'ideologically-free'; and that it could be used to demonstrate the 'unqualified superiority of the market economies', as well as to show that it really supports state intervention because of the 'discrepancies between the theoretical model and the economies they (i.e. economists) observe' (p. 402).

13. It has been argued in the literature that, since the government ultimately serves the vested interests, it is incapable of bringing about reforms of the kind noted in the text (Becker 1983). This is, no doubt, true to some extent—for instance, the relative failure of the governments in Pakistan, India and the Philippines to carry out meaningful land reforms. But there are also instances where the more development-oriented governments have succeeded in bringing about such structural reforms (for e.g., those of South Korea, Taiwan and China). There is nothing inherent in the government per se that makes it incapable of promoting structural change; it depends on the type of government in question and the manner of implementing a reformist agenda—one that wins popular acclaim. Furthermore, it needs to be pointed out that all democratic governments—indeed, even undemocratic ones—are subjected to constant public pressure to display 'concrete' achievements for the benefit of the poor. In many cases such pressures do succeed. In Pakistan, where the government has generally failed to root out feudalism, the first relatively effective land reforms were carried out by the military regime of Ayub Khan (see Naqvi, *et al.* 1989) which, however, is not an argument against democracy because similar reforms had earlier succeeded in Bangladesh (then East Pakistan) in an essentially democratic set-up.

14. The problem of the non-existence of markets, which is an extreme form of market failure, is especially acute with respect to 'future goods'.

15. It may be interesting to recall Titmuss's (1971) case against those *laisser faire* economists who in their obsession with individual freedom and the free markets would even commercialize the supply of blood in England where, as opposed to the US, it is given on a voluntary basis: In saying this we recall that Keynes once expressed the hope that one day economists 'could manage to get themselves thought of as competent people on a level with dentists. This day has not yet dawned for some of the order who, after taking oaths of ethical neutrality, perform as missionaries in the social welfare field and often give the impression of possessively owning a hotline to God.'

16. For details, see Putnam (1990).

17. Thus, for instance, the profit maximization rule, based on self-interest, is empirically non-verifiable (Machlup 1956).

18. In the United States, the Pastoral Letter (1985) highlighted important economic issues on moral grounds. Interestingly enough, highbrow economists like Tobin (1985) and Klein (1985) have supported the Letter: 'The Catholic Bishops have put the present economic debate on a new plane' (Klein 1985: p. 364). More recently, The World Summit on Social Development, 1995, specifically focused on issues of poverty, employment and social cohesion. On the importance of adhering to a set of moral principles to devise a fairer basis of international cooperation, see Streeten (1989).

19. Debreu (1991) advocates such an 'inhuman stance' because economists 'must be impartial spectators of a play in which they are the actors' (p. 8).
20. This is because the ordinalist calculus underlying much of mainstream economics does not allow interpersonal comparison of utilities, while insisting that welfare be measured exclusively in terms of the metric of utilities.
21. The distributive neutrality of the Pareto optimality rule is not in the least diminished by the possibility of making lump-sum income transfers from the potential gainers to the potential losers. This is partly because the loss suffered by one (poor) person cannot be morally justified by the gain enjoyed by another (rich) person, and partly because such transfers are *not* required to be actually made but are merely an index of what could potentially be done in such a situation.
22. It is instructive to note that the apparently 'secular' Rawlsian criterion is directly related to the Judaeo-Christian ethical principle of helping the 'powerless' (see the Pastoral Letter 1985). Incidentally, Islamic ethical principles also accord priority to the needs of the 'oppressed' and the 'deprived' (see Iqbal 1936; Naqvi 1981, 1993).
23. One of the evaluations of the subject refers to development economics as a 'branch of applied economics' (Bell 1987: p. 825).
24. In a latter day review of his work Lewis (1984b) dismissed the charge that development economists in 1950 did not care about distribution as completely 'off the mark'. On the other hand, he reminds us that 'we were all in favour of land reforms, for reasons of equity as well as output' (p. 130). In particular, Tinbergen (1959, 1977) was very explicit on the egalitarian content of development economics. More recently, this point has also been made by Drèze and Sen (1995).
25. Heilbroner's (1990) recent evaluation also falls in this unacceptable category. He asserts: 'with few exceptions, socialism has experienced a public de-legitimization… whereas capitalism, despite its failures, has enjoyed… a rising degree of internal political support' (p. 1097). In my opinion it is too soon to infer from the break-up of the Soviet Union an unbounded love for unfettered capitalism. Indeed, the growing disenchantment with globalization and with the overly market-friendly policies of the international donors (e.g., the IMF), as the fires at the 'Battle in Seattle' highlighted, is a vote against the latter. Also, the rapid growth of China, an avowedly socialist regime, should be a sufficient refutation of Heilbroner's hypothesis.
26. Galbraith (1991), opposing the imposition of a market economy on the Soviet Union, recounts that in reply to a question asked at the end of his lecture, as to why he did not recommend Hayekian economics for Eastern Europe, he said, 'this was not a design which in its rejection of regulatory, welfare and other ameliorating action by the state, we in the United States or elsewhere in the non-socialist world would find tolerable' (p. 45).

2

Who Wears the Emperor's New Clothes?

As we enter the 21st century, development economics is well set to take back the territory it lost to neo-classical economics. We, therefore, propose to take a closer look at our intellectual heritage in the context of the new realities in this Age of Globalization. The central question we should ask here is: Are the development economists indeed wearing the 'emperor's new clothes' as some market-friendly economists assert? If the answer is in the affirmative they are in danger of losing their identity as intellectuals armed with a cause, technique, and a special message for sustaining high rates of economic and human development. If that be the case, being rational profit-maximizers, development economics had better return to the fold of the neo-classical economics of Walrasian vintage, or at best function as a branch of applied economics.

However, this is fortunately not the case. As one would expect, there are many economists—Sen (1983a), Lewis (1984a, 1984b), Singer (1984), Stiglitz (1986), Chenery (1988, 1989), Khan (1989), Stern (1989), Streeten (1993), Naqvi (1996), Todaro (2000)—who emphasize the existence of a distinctive development economics with a research programme of its own. This chapter and the following ones in this volume show that the prevailing doubts about the future of the discipline are unjustified.

Obituary Notices for Development Economics

It would be instructive to begin by disproving Schultz's (1964) antithesis, which denies not only the existence but also the very need for a 'separatist' development economics. In his Nobel Lecture (Schultz 1981), he claims that 'standard economic theory is as applicable to the scarcity problems that confront the low-income countries as to the corresponding problems of the high-income countries' (p. 4), for the simple reason that 'poor people are no less concerned about improving their lot and that of their children than rich people are' (p. 3). Besides, he points out, 'the early economists dealt with conditions [in Western Europe] similar to those prevailing in low-income countries today'. The failure to see such a simple point has been, according to Schultz, the 'original sin' of development economists. Since history, logic, and simple common sense are against development economics, it would only be rational for its practitioners to give up and opt for mainstream economics, both for a better conceptualization of the development problem and for offering sensible policy advice. This opinion is shared by Haberler (1980), Bauer (1972), Little (1982) and Walters (1989), to name a few, and it also forms the basis of the weighty 'Washington Consensus'.

Giving in to extant intellectual agnosticism, Hirschman (1981c) wrote what could be regarded as an obituary for our discipline. Somewhat wistfully, he declared: 'I cannot help feeling that the old liveliness is not there, that new ideas are ever harder to come by and that the field is not adequately reproducing itself' (p. 1), so that 'the decline of development economics cannot be fully reversed' (p. 23). Accordingly, he counsels fellow economists to bear the passage of our discipline philosophically because 'we may have gained in maturity what we have lost in excitement' (p. 23).[1] In order to think clearly about the nature and significance of development economics, I have examined both these arguments in the present chapter. To set the stage for subsequent discussion, I start the proceedings by evaluating the claims made by Schultz and Hirschman.

Schultz's Iconoclasm

The difficulty with Schultz's argument is that his case against the existence of development economics rests entirely on the assertion that farmers are rational decision makers who respond positively to monetary and non-monetary incentives.[2] Now, it is clearly unsatisfactory to define rationality in a simplistic and mechanistic way (i.e., in terms of the 'correct' price response of the farmers). This is because even cases of apparent irrationality may simply contain rationality of a more complex kind, which reflects the interplay of structural constraints formed over the years by the dynamics of class relations. Bardhan (1988) points out that 'The plausibility of the assumption of maximization [i.e., rationality] is not independent of the market structures or even the mode of production' (p. 41). Furthermore, Schultz's criticism is not even logically coherent. To reject development economics on the basis of a single refutation is not good logic because, in the stochastic world of economics, the improbability of a hypothesis does not imply that it is false. Even the demonstration of the falsity of just one element in a doctrine, which is a collection of hypotheses, cannot invalidate the entire doctrine. To put the same point positively, the mere demonstration that *one* assumption of the standard economic theory does hold for developing countries is not to imply that *all* its assumptions must also hold. At any rate, it has never been seriously claimed that irrational decision making is a regular feature of economic agents in underdeveloped economies—not even when development economics was still a new discipline. Indeed, the rational concern of the poor people about improving their lot in the present day developing countries is precisely the reason for development economics to respond positively to such concerns—especially because neo-classical economics seems to have forgotten the Smithian preoccupation with increasing 'universal opulence which extends itself to the lowest ranks of the people' (cited in Heilbroner 1980: p. 60).

The historical part of Schultz's argument is also questionable. The fact that West European countries in an earlier stage of their development experienced problems similar to those of the underdeveloped countries of today does not necessarily invalidate the case for development economics.[3] Even if it is assumed that the nature of the economic challenge then was the same as it is now, it does not follow that the quality and intensity of the response of the Third World today must be identical to that of the developing countries of the West in the 19th century. Nor does it follow that the prescriptions of modern development economists must be identical to what the economists might have prescribed earlier to bestir the underdeveloped West. In other words, the historical development experience of the West is not likely to have current relevance in today's developing countries because the surrounding circumstances, institutions and international environment are totally different in the two time periods.

It is for this reason Gerschenkron (1962) jeered at the Rostowian thesis that 'the process of industrialization repeated itself from country to country lumbering through his [i.e., Rostow's] pentametric rhythm' (p. 355). He insisted on the multiplicity of growth paths, leaving enough 'room' for a healthy diversity in development policies born of the special circumstances, policies, institutions and ideologies of different developing countries. Indeed, one of the central lessons of development experience in the past 50 years is that different countries have differed significantly not only with regard to the speed of development (the rate of industrial growth), but also with regard to the productive and organizational structures of industry which emerged from those processes. A dramatic manifestation of such growth differentials over space and time has been the rising inequality between the wealth of nations—the Gini Coefficient rose from 0.40 in 1900 to 0.48 in year 2000 (IMF 2000a: p. 155).

Hirschman's Obituary

According to Hirschman (1981c), when it all began in the early 1950s, development economics was essentially based on the simultaneous rejection by development economists of the 'mono-economics' claim and the assertion of the 'mutual benefit' claim.[4] The alleged rejection of the mono-economics claim by Nurkse (1953), Rosenstein-Rodan (1943), Lewis (1954), Leibenstein (1957) and many others, and their insistence on the need for a new development economics, was based on the existence of rural underemployment in developing countries. They believed that these countries, suffering from the latecomer's syndrome, needed shock treatment in the form of a 'big push', 'great spurt', 'minimum critical effort' and 'take-off' by igniting the 'backward and forward linkages' of the 'engine of growth' (i.e., the manufacturing sector). On the other hand, the alleged acceptance of the mutual benefit claim may have rested on the belief that there existed an essential harmony of interests between the developed and the developing countries.

The former felt capable of helping the latter rise out of underdevelopment through financial assistance, provided that the latter organize their production and trade structures according to the 'universal' principle of comparative advantage. According to Hirschman, since these two claims are no longer acceptable, it is necessary to resolve the seeming stalemate between the thesis put forward by the founding fathers of the discipline and the neoclassical antithesis by presenting a grand new synthesis. However, as he asserts, 'no new synthesis appeared' (p. 20). Hence the obituary notice which, however, appears to have been somewhat premature. This is because the development of a science in response to endogenous growth and exogenous shocks involving a reformulation, even rejection, of some of its original hypotheses is not a sign of its decay. On the contrary, such transient stillness may simply presage a new flowering of ideas when the 'right' wind blows. This is exactly what is happening to development economics, which like a thriving subject knows exactly what the next crucial questions are—and which even the neo-classical economists must respond to positively. Helped by a large collection of theoretical and empirical literature, it has entered a new cycle of regeneration and growth. Indeed, partly under its influence, a fairly integrated social science approach to development problems has taken shape.

The main problem with Hirschman's argument is that he has put development economics in a typological cell in which it may not belong. The fact is that with the honourable exception of the inveterate 'agnostics' (e.g., Viner 1952; Haberler 1950; Bauer 1972), the mutual benefit claim has never been widely accepted by development economists.[5] Indeed, such could not have been the case in view of the inherent conflict situations arising from the brutal disproportion of power between the rich and the poor nations and peoples—the economic and social consequences of which were first seen by development economists. Thus, Prebisch (1950) and Singer (1950), discerning the rising income and wealth inequalities between nations because of the perverse working of free trade when it is based on static comparative advantage, rejected such a claim. As noted above, these inequalities have grown steadily over the last century and worsened in this 'Age of Globalization'. They insisted that the two sets of countries have, instead, been engaged in an antagonistic zero-sum game in which the rich countries get 'the best of both the worlds'. Further, Myrdal (1956b) saw the mechanism of international trade as contributing to the growth of inequality between nations through the so-called 'backwash effect'. Lewis (1955) held that, without appropriate state intervention, the developing countries with surplus labour would lose out to the developed countries, where the share of labour tends to rise with the growth of national income. Since then, the doctrines of 'dependency' and 'unequal exchange', advocated by Cardoso (1972), Emmanuel (1972), Amin (1976) and others of the neo-Marxian band have questioned the veracity of the mutual benefit claim. Instead, they emphasize the inherently exploitative nature of world capitalism as the *cause* of underdevelopment in the 'periphery' countries.

There is an undeniable element of truth in the neo-Marxian thinking which should be acceptable to development economists who do not like to be labelled neo-Marxian. For instance, Baran's (1957) pessimism about the beneficial effects of foreign capital, though a little bit too excessive, explains rather well the destabilizing effects of foreign (especially short-term) capital even on developing countries with strong fundamentals (see Chap. 9). Also, the Kemp-Ohyama model (Kemp and Ohyama 1978) highlights the fundamental asymmetry in the working of the international economic system, which works against the South and is much more lenient to the North. This truth is in no way invalidated by claiming to have disproved the Singer–Prebisch thesis about the uneven distribution of the gains from trade and investment between the (rich) lending and (poor) borrowing countries on the basis of 'evidence' that the alleged movement of terms of trade against the South is mixed (Spraos 1980) or that many of the countries of the South now produce and export both primary goods and manufactured products (World Bank 1999). The fact of the matter is that the basic truth of the Singer–Prebisch thesis has been widely endorsed by the Pearson Commission Report, 1969, the Brandt Commission Report (Brandt 1980) and the recent experience of globalization (Streeten 1998).[6] Also, the terms of trade for non-oil exports have become increasingly volatile, having declined steadily, secularly and persistently since the 1980s (Borensztein *et al.* 1994; UNCTAD 1999). The conflict of interest also arises from the pursuit of power and its enjoyment by the modern corporate and management controlled enterprises (i.e., the MNCs) at the expense of the host governments. None of this should be surprising when market power matters most; those who have more, gain more from trade than those who have less. Thus, the challenge before development economists and social philosophers 'is not to show areas of common or mutual interest or benefits, but to show how conflicts, when they arise, can be resolved' (Streeten 1984: p. 342).

Search for New Foundations

Lewis's (1984b) thumb rule—'development economics is a subject which deals with the structural behaviour of economies where output per head is less than 1980 US $2000' (p. 1)—is helpful in getting a hold on the reach and salience of development economics. But a more revealing way of understanding its nature and significance is to look at it in terms of the methodology of the philosophy of science developed and applied, of late, by Popper (1980), Kuhn (1962) and Lakatos (1970). In this spirit, the questions to ask are: Does development economics amount to doing 'normal science'—elaborating, refining and applying existing principles of the ruling neo-classical economics—or does it constitute a new 'paradigm' requiring some basic changes in the way that economists view the real world? Or more accurately, is it a new 'scientific research programme' in the sense that it comprises a distinctive set of metaphysical beliefs about how the economic universe hangs together and works in reality as well as offers a number of refutable hypotheses about the motivations, aspirations and behaviour of economic agents in this universe? Furthermore, assuming that such a scientific research programme does exist, is it theoretically and empirically 'progressive', in the sense of having a greater 'empirical content' than neo-classical economics claims to possess? And, finally, does the new research programme predict 'novel facts' about developing countries?[7]

The present book gives, though only heuristically, an affirmative answer to these questions. Here we highlight the paradigmatic character of development economics with reference to its innate capacity to respond creatively to the searing facts of human existence, which include an unacceptably high rate of unemployment, a lack of sustained economic growth at a moderately high rate, rising inequalities of income and wealth within and between nations, the failure (with few exceptions) of the developing countries to catch up with the developed, the lengthening shadows of poverty, the persistence of social injustice and economic deprivation, all of which weigh heavily on the developing countries. True, these problems are also found in the developed countries, but this is not a denial of the truth of development economics. If anything, it shows that the writ of development economics extends to these societies as well. This is a desirable state of affairs, because neo-classical economics does not address these problems for the simple reason that it presumes pre-existing, well-ordered societies where many of the key developmental issues remain within socially acceptable limits.

A Paradigm Shift

The main assertion made in this book is that development economics constitutes a positive paradigm shift from neo-classical economics in that it challenges the latter's unbounded faith in the unimprovability (Pareto Optimality) of the competitive market solutions which are inconsistent with a non-minimalist state, and the 'rationality (i.e., the amorality) of human behaviour which takes the self-interest principle as its guide. These matters will be discussed in some detail in the rest of the book, but the following remarks should be suggestive of their essence.

1.   To study the problems of developing countries there had to be a change in the focus of analysis from a nearly full-time obsession of general-equilibrium economics with the study of the properties of the stationary state, and that too, in a closed economy context. But on what Marshall (1920) referred to as the 'high theme of economic progress' (p. 461), he or his neo-classical successors accomplished next to nothing.[8] This task has been achieved by development economics which, by the very circumstances of its birth in the late 1940s, has been devoted to the issues relating to the problems of economic *development* in an open economy context. It aimed at a better comprehension of the working of economic reality, especially of the asymmetric working of the world trading system, and at offering sensible policy advice to change this reality for the better.[9] The theory of economic development, which Lewis (1955) initiated, deals explicitly with comprehensive, widely shared economic progress—something that cannot be analysed with the tools of standard neo-classical economics.

To some extent, the standard growth theory did help to clarify some key aspects of the central problems that developing countries faced, though not without breaching the narrow static confines of neo-classical economics. These insights relate basically to the role in the growth process that the Harrod–Domar model assigns to such variables—the propensity to save, the capital/output ratio and the growth of labour force (population)—and, even more fundamentally, to its emphasis on 'treating technical progress as a built-in propensity in an industrial economy' (Robinson 1973: p. 98). Nevertheless, the growth theory, notwithstanding such invaluable insights which have only come in fits and starts (there was a complete lack of interest in the subject for almost 20 years from 1964 onwards!), 'has in many ways missed the crucial issues for developing countries' (Stern 1991). Indeed, it has been concerned with esoteric issues which are not very relevant even to developed countries. In particular, its unifocal preoccupation with elegant proofs of the existence and stability of steady-state growth paths has no operational content in it. A single example should suffice to illustrate this point. According to an estimate made by Sato (1963), the time taken by an economy which is off the steady-state path to get back on to it is about 100 years! This is a literal example of the Keynesian long run in which we shall be dead. This stricture also applies to the theoretical and empirical studies initiated by Solow (1957) and others. It is for such reasons Hicks (1976) remarked that growth theory reflected no more than 'the shadows of the real problems'. While the neo-classical endogenous growth does come a bit nearer to these problems, it too fails to provide 'a powerful framework for thinking about the actual growth phenomenon' (Pack 1994: p. 55; Naqvi 1996).

2. Extending the analytical canvas from economic growth to economic development has also meant focusing on the moral character of our discipline as opposed to the unadulterated positivism of mainstream economics because 'people's economic behaviour is influenced by their moral beliefs, and it [is important] to see what impact these beliefs have on economic outcomes'. (Hausman and McPherson 1993: p. 679). This aspect of development economics has led to a fundamental revision of the inviolability and rationality of the self-interest principle. The rationality aspect of this principle has been breached by the introduction of such important concepts as asymmetric information, moral hazard, strategic behaviour, the principal-agency syndrome, dynamic external economies, increasing

returns to scale, multiple equilibria, etc., all of which have given economics new challenges to respond to (Stiglitz 1986; Eatwell *et al.* 1989; Bardhan 1993). Also, the new advances in public choice theory, mainly informed by the problems of developing countries, have made it usable for analyzing the problems of inequality, poverty and 'entrenched deprivation' by granting admission rights to the interpersonal comparisons of utilities (Sen 1999).[10] For the same reasons, the Benthamite pleasure–pain utility calculus has given way to more tangible measures of economic well-being. The most important of such measures are:

(a) The Rawlsian 'theory of justice-as-fairness' (1971), which measures individual advantage in terms of his/her possession of 'primary social goods'; and

(b) Sen's capability theory (1992), which takes into account circumstances internal to a person in converting resources into his/her capability to live a good life (see Chapters 6 and 7 for details).

3. Released from the artificial confines of the basic neo-classical assumptions noted above, development economics explicitly focuses on the problem of reconciling economic growth with improving the distribution of income and the eradication of the worst forms of poverty in a manner that is socially and politically acceptable. The initial de-equalizing conjecture, due to Lewis (1954) and Kuznets (1995), has of late been modified by the finding that, if properly managed, growth can be equalizing and poverty-reducing, especially if per capita income grows at a fast enough rate of over 3 per cent. Conversely, it is also true that a reduction in inequality and poverty helps growth (Naqvi 1995; World Bank 2001). For both these reasons it is essential that high rates of growth of per capita income are sustained for long enough periods to finance a significant redirection of the flow of income and wealth from the rich to the poor, such as Tinbergen (1959) demanded. This is because, as Dutt (1985) shows, a regressive income distribution tends to depress consumption demand and, through the accelerator, adversely affects the rate of investment and also pulls down profits and growth. A perfectly viable strategy to promote economic growth with distributive justice would be to keep the rate of capitalist profit, adjusted for the share of wages in net output, at a level that could be realized in the production of wage goods. This level should then set the

ceiling for the rate of profit in the rest of the economy. This is the essence of Sraffa's (1975) generalization of the Ricardian theory of determination of the rate of profit on investment. It is of special relevance for developing countries because they cannot ignore the dictates of social justice in their bid to secure high rates of economic growth for political, economic and moral reasons. Such concerns have underlined the UNDP's 'human development' strategy.

4. However, the issue of distributive justice brings to light that economic development entails, above all, a restructuring of the basic institutions of society which, among other things, involves a redistribution of assets and private property, particularly of landed property. This is not only morally right, but also efficient. For instance, Berry and Cline (1979), and Naqvi *et al.* (1989) show that agricultural productivity is negatively related to the large size of farm holdings, which symbolize a feudal structure. The Marxist emphasis on the historically determined class power and alliances which occupy most of the space in the production–distribution chain, is here worth highlighting. Thus, Baran (1952) emphasized that in order to release the forces of socio-economic change the existing power structure, which represented a symbiosis of the worst elements of the two modes of production, must be redesigned. In his words:

> *This superimposition of business mores over ancient oppression by landed gentries resulted in compounded exploitation, more outrageous corruption and more glaring social injustice. [What resulted from this superimposition] was an economic and political amalgam combining the worst features of both the worlds—feudalism and capitalism—and blocking effectively all possibilities of economic growth (Agarwala and Singh 1963: p. 76).*

These observations are a fairly accurate description of the conditions prevailing in many developing countries where the feudal–capitalistic structures compromise their growth potential and, at the same time, perpetuate inequities in income and wealth and restrict the flow of goods and services to the poor. It is interesting to note that every developing country which has achieved great development success, such as Japan, South Korea, Taiwan and China, freed its economy from the chains of feudalism in the initial conditions.[11]

5. Yet another element of the new research programme is its recognition that 'the primary sources of development are learning and knowledge and accumulation' (Bruton 1998: p. 903). This is also one of the main messages of the endogenous growth theory which, though not a theory of economic development (see Chapter 9), does make the valuable point that low human capital endowment is one of the primary impediments to growth. It follows that public policy should mainly focus on human capital formation and knowledge acquisition to put the economy on a high growth (and development) trajectory (Romer 1986; Lucas 1988). The importance of knowledge in the context of economic development is also highlighted by the fact that where knowledge is an essential part of the system, the knowledge about the system changes the system itself (Boulding 1966). This is particularly true of the developing countries, where the initial stock of knowledge about the existing economic systems is small to begin with, and the rate of economic progress is directly related to an increase in knowledge about the dynamics of growth. Thus, the objective reality cannot be assumed to have remained unchanged as information inputs are injected into the system.[12] As such, development economics not only takes into account the objective reality on the ground but also recognizes the change that occurs in the people's perception of this very reality due to the development process (Sen 1988). The recognition of knowledge as a factor in economic development also leads to an emphasis on the role of the state in the creation and distribution of knowledge, which, being essentially a public good, cannot be optimally produced in response to market signals alone (World Bank 1999).

6. The scientific research programme that development economics represents cannot coexist with the assumptions of unchanging tastes and independence of the individual's utility functions.[13] The restrictive nature of such assumptions, which are routinely made by neo-classical economists, should become transparent when it is remembered that the process of economic development itself represents, in the words of Samuel Johnson, 'the wild vicissitudes of tastes' and the preferences of the various strata of society in developing countries. Similarly, as Veblen (1973) and Duesenberry (1952) observed fairly long ago, consumption functions are typically

interdependent. This is particularly the case in developing countries. An interesting example of such interdependence is the Hirschman–Rothschild (1973) conjecture that growing inequalities of income in the early stages of development are tolerated by the poor only in the hope that they too will ultimately receive a due share of the increase in the nation's wealth, and that this tolerance of inequality diminishes sharply once the poor perceive that their expectations are not likely to be fulfilled.

7. An important defining element of development economics is its international dimension, which has featured the 'unequal exchange' relationship between the developed and the developing countries (Singer 1950; Prebisch 1950). This aspect of the North-South relationship has become even more important as the star of globalization rises on the economic horizon—it is now recognized as the dominant force in the 21st century (UNDP 2000: p. 25). True, it has drawn the world together into a 'global village', which promises to be exhilarating for the rich, but by and large it has been suffocating for the poor. Yet another de-equalizing factor, also related to globalization, is the emergence of the new 'red-in-tooth-and-claw' capitalism, which is essentially run by about 1,000 powerful multinational corporations (the 'notorious' MNCs), of which 85 per cent reside in the OECD countries (*The Economist* 2000a). This factor has only made the exchange between the rich and the poor countries even more unequal. This is inevitable because, as Joan Robinson pungently remarked, there is only one thing worse than being exploited by the capitalist, and that is *not* being exploited by him!

The Empirical Content of Development Economics

The preceding brief discussion strongly suggests that development economics constitutes a viable scientific research programme, which sets it apart from the value-neutral and distributionally insensitive neo-classical economics. It remains to be shown that this programme is also 'progressive' in that it has 'ample empirical content' and that it predicts 'novel facts' about developing countries. The following aspects of this research programme should strongly suggest its empirical fecundity.

1. The most important theoretical and empirical advances in development economics have indeed been made in the process of examining and responding to the reality in the developing countries, and by an intense desire to change it for the better. Indeed, its direct concern with policy-related issues sets it apart from neoclassical economics, the important accomplishments of which belong to the realm of 'economic metaphysics' with no relation to real world issues—for example, the 'beautiful' Arrow's Impossibility Theorem, the two elegant Fundamental Theorems of welfare economics. Perhaps the most fundamental piece of research, which development economics has encouraged, is related to a study of the stylized facts of economic development, especially those which refer to the universal phenomena of agrarian and structural transformation. The focus has been on the consequences of the migration of labour from agriculture to manufacturing and of the shifts in the composition of demand, production, government revenue exports, etc. (Syrquin 1988; Chenery and Syrquin 1975; Chenery *et al.* 1986). This research goes back to the earlier work by Clark (1940).

2. But even more to the point, the recognition of surplus labour in rural areas as the key factor in developing countries had led to the formulation of the two-sector model by Lewis (1954, 1955), which was elaborated on by other economists like Fei and Ranis (1963). Later, the models of 'migration and unemployment', developed by Harris and Todaro (1970) and elaborated on by Khan (1980a, 1987a), focused instead on urban unemployment, which is caused by rural-urban migration and a politically determined urban wage.

3. An important aspect of this recognition is that free-market equilibria are not unique. More significantly, in real-world situations these are rarely Pareto optimal, and are almost always improvable by state intervention (Greenwald and Stiglitz 1986). Yet another example of the fecundity of development economics is the spate of empirical work that has been generated on the relation between economic growth, income distribution and unemployment. These studies have resulted in the generation of new knowledge about the process of economic development, inspired solely by the actual problems of developing countries—for example, those by

Kuznets (1955); Chenery *et al.* (1974); Ahluwalia (1976); Adelman (1978); Naqvi (1995); Aghion *et al.* (1999); World Bank (2001).

4. Yet another example of the theoretical and empirical progress that has been made as a consequence of studying the real-life situations in the developing countries are the numerous empirical studies conducted with regard to the relative merits of import substitution and export expansion processes—(Singer (1950), Edwards (1993), Bruton (1998), WTO (1998)—and the equally large literature about the real domestic resource cost (DRC) entailed by a dominant import substitution strategy in the form of the estimation of effective rates of protection. This theory has spanned a large body of empirical work, which, with the help of such 'operational' concepts as explicit and implicit effective rates of protection and domestic resource cost, throws new light on the industrialization strategies of developing countries—Johnson (1969), Little *et al.* (1970), Bhagwati (1978), Balassa (1971), Corden (1966), Naqvi and Kemal (1991), and many others. Also worth noting are the works by Krueger (1978), Bhagwati (1982) and Srinivasan (1985), among others, which explore the adverse consequences of state intervention in the form of the proliferation of rent-seeking as opposed to profit-making activities. This invaluable research has added to the empirical content of development economics, even though it has been more successful in explaining the failures of government-sponsored industrialization than its splendid successes (for example, the East Asian Miracle).[15]

These are just a few examples of the manner in which development economics has explored and predicted novel facts; many more such examples can be cited. To this end, the econometric revolution engineered by Tinbergen, Klein, Malinvaud and others has been more fully reflected in our discipline than in neo-classical economics.[16] It should be clear, then, that our discipline is by no means a 'black hole' of the economic universe but that it has made vital contributions to neo-classical economics. Therefore, there should be little doubt that development economists, far from wearing the mythical 'Emperor's new Clothes', have presentable clothes to dress themselves in. In any case, the important question to discuss is: What should development economists, including those in India and Pakistan, be doing in their distinguished raiments? This is the question we address in the subsequent chapters of this book.

Notes

1. Much later, Krugman (1983) handed down a much harsher judgement. He stated: 'Once upon a time there was a field called development economics..., that field no longer exists' (p. 15). However, as if to refute such off-hand remarks, a two-volume *Handbook of Development Economics* (Chenery and Srinivasan 1988, 1989) has been published by Elsevier Science Publishers, which runs to an impressive length of 1773 pages. It includes comprehensive surveys in as many as 32 areas, including such important matters as trade and development, fiscal policy, project evaluation, processes of structural transformation, migration and urbanization and the economics of health, nutrition and education, to name only a few. An extensive bibliography is appended to each of the surveys, which is enough proof that our discipline is alive and well.

2. The empirical part of Schultz's thesis, that the surplus labour theory is a 'false doctrine', has also been shown to be rather weak. Sen (1967) points out that the empirical test performed by Schultz to test the strength of the 'surplus labour' hypothesis is based on data relating to Indian agriculture before and after the influenza epidemic of 1918–19. Even otherwise, surplus labour simply means that, as Lewis (1954) clearly noted: 'The supply of labour is, therefore, unlimited so long as the supply of labour at this price [in agriculture] exceeds the demand!' (quoted in Agarwala and Singh [1963]: p. 403)—a formulation with which it is hard to disagree. Furthermore, this phenomenon signifies a transitory phase of economic development, and development problems will still be there once labour becomes relatively scarce. By the same token, development economics can peacefully coexist with the relative scarcity of labour as well as with a surfeit of it.

3. Reynolds (1977) also shows excessive reverence to the classical writers and pleads that they be not considered 'relics of a bygone era'. We may accept his plea and yet disagree, for reasons given in this book, with his judgement that 'the classical economists wrestled with problems that confront economists in India, Nigeria, or Brazil' (p. 20). Be that as it may, it certainly does not follow from Reynolds's judgement that development economists should hold exactly the same theories and views as held by the classical economists more than 200 years ago.

4. As a variation on the mutual benefit claim, globalization has been singled out by the World Bank (along with urbanization) as one of the defining characteristics of 'development thinking' in the 21st century (World Bank 2000). However, the *WDR* has been careful to point out some areas of essential disharmony between the developed and the developing countries.

5. Indeed, Lewis described a mutual conflict situation between the underdeveloped and developed countries in his Nobel Lecture (Lewis 1980). However, it should be noted that, in Lewis's presentation, the mutual conflict situation is set out not as an inexorable law of nature, but as a result of the slower growth of world trade relative to the growth during the two decades before 1973.

6. Using UNDP data, Streeten (1998) shows that the global distribution of wealth has moved against the developing world. While the share of the developed countries increased from 67.3 per cent in 1960 to 78.7 per cent in 1994, that of the developing countries declined from 19.8 per cent to 18 per cent during

the same period. According to UNDP (1999), the income gap between the fifth of the world's people in the richest countries and the fifth of the people in the poorest countries increased to 74:1 in 1997 from 60:1 in 1990 and 30:1 in 1960!

7. A rigorous answer to these questions requires an explicit description of the new paradigm in terms of a 'hard core', a 'positive heuristic' and a 'protective belt'. But in economics, much less in development economics, such a description may look somewhat artificially structured. See Blaug (1976) for a discussion of some of these issues.

8. Looking at what mainstream economics should become in the 21st century, Baumol (1991) remarks that 'a return to the wealth of nations [should be] a leading focus for economic research', and that the 'pertinent theory still has a long way to go to learn from the experience of the LDCs (p. 7). It may be noted in this context that the dynamic optimization exercises of luminaries like Koopmans (1965) did not make an impact on real policy problems (Stern 1991).

9. Meir (1984b) points out: 'Development economics did not arise as a formal theoretical discipline, but was fashioned as a practical subject in response to the needs of policy-makers to advise governments on what could and should be done to allow their countries to emerge from chronic poverty' (p. 4). But in this respect mainstream economics is also to a great extent exogenously driven—Keynesian economics in response to the Great Depression, neo-classical economics in response to 'excesses' of the European Welfare states, monetarism inspired by the inflation of the 1970s and finally, the current disarray of the 'Arrow-Debreu Consensus in the face of the ubiquity of informational and market imperfections mainly observed in the developing countries!

10. The ban on the interpersonal comparisons imposed by Robbins has been accepted as an integral part of welfare economics. Thus, Arrow (1951) stated that "interpersonal comparison of utilities has no meaning". This denial is one of the basic reasons for Arrow's famous Impossibility Theorem. However, this impossibility result is resolved once interpersonal comparisons of utilities are allowed (Sen 1999).

11. The importance in this context of carrying out land reforms in the initial conditions has also been emphasized by Adelman (1978), and Adelman and Morris (1973).

12. The remark in the text is an application of the Heisenburg Principle, which lays down that objective reality changes as we learn about it. However, this is generally true only in the theory of *large* games.

13. There have been significant recent attempts made in mathematical economics to replace such an assumption. For instance, see Khan and Sun (1990). But, in general, the state of neo-classical economics is as I have indicated in the text.

14. Schmalensee (1991), reviewing the state of economic science, observes: 'The average [neo-classical] academic's willingness to supply policy relevant research has probably declined' (p. 117).

15. The source of the problem with these theories, however, is the use of a non-observable Pareto optimality criterion as a reference point for measuring the loss incurred due to the adoption of second-best policies. This has compromised the usefulness of the policy recommendations coming out of this work,

which sometimes degenerates into an ideological advocacy of competitive markets and free trade and a denunciation of state intervention in general.

16. Baumol (1991) has emphasized that to make mainstream economics more useful for its practitioners the future curricula should feature more of econometric analysis and less of things 'like indifference maps and Slutsky Theorem, etc.' (p. 5).

3

The Liberalist Counter-revolution and Development Economics

The analysis presented in the preceding chapter would convince the reader that development economics has a definite place under the sun. And yet policy-making and, to some extent, academic research activity in developing countries are held in thrall by the simplicity of free-market logic (or shall we say, magic), even though repelled by its adverse consequences for the economic well-being of the people. It is ironical that this is the case at a time when the liberalist counter-revolution of the 1970s has fizzled out because the Arrow-Debreu neo-classical synthesis which sustained it has been undermined by its own success (Eatwell, *et al.* 1989). It has now been established that, even at the theoretical level, market-based solutions are generally neither efficient nor equitable and that, to make matters worse, these are largely irrelevant to real-world problems. Ever since the advent of liberalism in the 1970s, the incidence of unemployment, poverty, crime and suicide has risen dramatically. As a result, more and more peoples and governments, even in Western Europe, are turning away from unfettered market regimes to the 'left-of-the center' economics and politics—also referred to as the 'Third Way' (*The Economist* 2000c). The recent East Asian crisis of the late 1990s, spurred on by the MNCs, and the built-in instability of the free capital markets has only added to the current sense of disillusionment with the Hayek–Friedman extreme 'rightism', which prioritizes individual liberty to the exclusion of all else, confines a minimal state to guarding the negative freedoms (of the rich), and solves the problem of distributive justice and poverty by taking it off the reformist agenda!

A natural corollary of these 'events' should have been to lay as few hostages as possible to the vicissitudes of the liberalist's economic philosophy and revive the embers of faith in development economics. On the contrary, the liberalist counter-revolution is being fortified by pointing to the 'potential' long-run benefits of market-friendly policies, including those flowing from (market-driven) globalization, while its risks for the development process are being underplayed. Apparently taken in by this thinking, but in fact under duress, most developing countries, including India and Pakistan, have accepted to be ruled by the market. The results so far have not been encouraging. A more damaging aspect of the Liberalist counter-revolution is that it has created a chasm between development economics and development policy. Under the new dispensation, the latter now pays homage to the unregulated markets and 'right' prices—and to the defunct economist.[1] Unfortunately, the development economists of neo-classical persuasion, especially those who have been attracted to the discipline by their profit-maximizing instincts rather than out of conviction, are doing no better. The neo-classical political economy, according to which the 'Invisible Hand' is not allowed to work by the so-called 'Invisible Foot'—that is, the forces that prevent competition from working for the larger good of society (Collandar 1984)—seems to give a bit more respectability to the defunct economist. To suit the liberalist's ideology, the success of developing countries like Singapore, South Korea, Taiwan, Hong Kong, Malaysia and China has been misinterpreted as a positive proof of the success of market-friendly policies.[2] This is especially true of South Korea and Taiwan—the 'original' Tiger economies—which have been misleadingly advertised as the paradise of free traders.[3] But surely, this must have been a gross misreading of the ground realities because the existing markets in these 'miracle economies have been noticeably regulated' (Sen 1981b), and new markets have been created by 'picking winners' among the potential producers through carefully crafted and flexible government intervention (for example, the directed credits)

(Stiglitz 1996b).[4] It is now widely accepted that development success has been secured there by the same protectionist instruments used in the countries where development has been, relatively speaking, somewhat lacklustre (for example, in South Asia). The main difference between the two seems to be the 'manner of implementation and monitoring rather than the policies themselves' (Bruton 1998: p. 924).

To shed light on the impact of the liberalist counter-revolution on development economics, we have to first identify its main actors—the defunct economist, the policy-maker and the development economist—and their interaction,[5] and then trace the twists and turns in development thinking, not all of which represent scientific advance. The basic themes, alluded to here somewhat informally and rapidly, are developed more carefully in the subsequent chapters of this book.

The Rise of the Defunct Economist

A comparison of the teachings of development economists and the practices of policy-makers shows that, apart from the ascendancy of the liberalist thought, there is yet another cause for the increasing reliance of the latter on the defunct economist with the passage of time. This is the aversion of the policy-maker to anything which looks complicated. Thus the ideas of living (development) economists were quite faithfully reflected by the policy-maker in the Five Year Plans, as long as the unifocal pursuit of economic growth remained the objective of development policy. However, this happy equation changed once it became obvious that economic development is a more complicated matter in that it denotes a 'widespread, widely shared, sustainable economic growth accompanied by significant structural change ... and a generalized improvement in the living standards' (Adelman and Morris 1997: p. 831), and that it takes redesigning the structure of property rights by land reforms, etc., to make it irreversible. This being a little too complex for the policy-maker, the liberalist emphasis on letting the 'Invisible Hand' do the job for them must have come as a welcome change. This welcome has, however, proved rather costly for economic development. For instance, not fully understanding the logic of the structural transformation (denoting a rising share of manufacturing output in total GDP), development policy has not aimed at securing a dynamic equilibrium between agriculture and industry, or at making industrialization sufficiently employment-creating, or at making both more productive. Also, because of an undue reliance on the 'Invisible Hand', the crucial role of technological progress and knowledge creation as the major driving force of progress has been neglected and the need to produce a literate and skilled labour force in order to accelerate the rate of human (as opposed to just physical) capital formulation was not felt. Some of this is changing now, but with the benefit of hindsight it can now be stated that the neglect of these ideas of the development economists by the policy-maker has been responsible for a less-than-vibrant agriculture where about 70 per cent of the total population still resides, for depressing labour productivity and for sub-optimal industrial progress.

The explanation we have just given for the rise of the defunct economist and for the policy-maker falling for him is that the latter invariably opts for simple answers to difficult questions.[6] We have here a case where, by a variant of the Gresham Law, the defunct economist drives the living one out of circulation. This has been unfortunate because managing economic development is too difficult a business to be left at the mercy of obsolete ideas.[7] And, yet it needs to be stated that the policy-maker is not the only one to be blamed for this revealed preference for the defunct economist.

However, while such 'arguments' may *explain* the policy-maker's preferences for the defunct economist, these are not a satisfactory *justification* for it. The fact is that development policy now does not get clear-cut guidance from much of market-oriented research— for example, policies on the rent-seeking phenomenon and directly unproductive profit-seeking (DUP) activities by Krueger (1974), Bhagwati (1971) and Srinivasan (1985). This work, though most valuable in itself, fails to explain the development success achieved by efficient governments. It also does not follow from these studies that state intervention should be eliminated altogether and that things should instead be entrusted to the 'Invisible Hand'.[8] A better focus for development policy is to recognize that there lies a whole territory between the opposing poles of the market and the government where these characters can, and should, meet in friendly embrace to accelerate the development process.[9] But this brings us back to the fold of development economics.

Development Economics as a Guide

The above-mentioned discussion should not, however, lead one to surmise that policy-makers have always been averse to the thinking of the (living) development economist. The fact is that while the development process was still guided by the principles of development economics—which is referred to below as the 'Age of Chivalry'—such a relationship remained strong enough to keep the defunct economist in hibernation. And, though somewhat atypically, policy-makers regularly paid homage to the 'living' economists—for example, Rosenstein-Rodan, Harrod, Domar, Lewis, Rostow, Kaldor, Hirschman and Mahalanobis—in the dusky dawn of development economics.

The Age of Chivalry

The central idea of development economics, which gained currency in the policy-making circles, was that achieving rapid rates of economic growth holds the key to igniting the process of widespread development. (This has been incorrectly dubbed by some as 'growth fundamentalism' for its unifocal emphasis on growth). True, this insight had been presaged by many historical studies of the England of 1776, of Communist Russia after 1917 and of Japan during the Meiji period, all of which emphasize the supporting (not just extractive) role of agriculture in the process of economic development, with the industrial sector cast as the star performer—a subject central to the discipline of development economics as well.[10] However, the idea became dominant only when development economics was formally inaugurated by Rosenstein-Rodan (1943). Writing about the experience of the Eastern European countries, he thought of industrialization as the principal engine of growth. Then came the growth equations of Harrod (1939, 1970) and Domar (1946, 1957), and their subsequent reformulation by Solow (1957) and many others. These were essentially dynamic extensions of Keynesian economics, but they did nevertheless help the development economists understand the key factors of the growth process. These equations state the fundamental relationship that the 'warranted' rate of growth (which in equilibrium equals the rate of growth of labour supply or the 'natural' rate of growth) is exclusively a function of the marginal savings rate and the capital-output ratio.

Notwithstanding the extreme restrictiveness of its underlying assumptions (for example, a one-good economy) and the esoteric nature of its 'exploits' (i.e., a study of the steady-state behaviour of these variables), these ideas have provided much food for thought to a whole generation of development economists and policymakers, even though the point of attraction for the latter must have been their apparent simplicity and manageability. Not surprisingly, therefore, the development plans in developing countries have sought to achieve a fast rate of economic progress by accelerating physical capital formation, by raising the saving rates significantly and by lowering the average capital-output ratio to achieve greater economic efficiency. Also, inspired by these ideas, Lewis (1954) placed raising the saving rate to finance (physical) capital formation firmly at the center of the development process.[11] He declared: 'We cannot explain any industrial revolution ... unless we can explain why saving increased relatively to national income'. To this end, a necessary condition for economic development to occur in Lewis's model is that the share of profits in total national income rise to finance capital accumulation. He states candidly:

> *We are interested not in the people in general, but only say in the 10 per cent of them with the largest income, who in countries with surplus labour receive up to 40 percent of the national income.... Our problem then becomes [sic] what are the circumstances in which the share of profits in national income increases (Agarwala and Singh 1963: p. 416).*[12]

Assuming that the demand conditions are the right ones, the growth of the manufacturing sector—which is regarded as the engine of growth—will be accelerated so long as labour is transferred from the agricultural sector without eliminating the gap between the agricultural wage and the manufacturing wage—the former staying significantly lower than the latter. At least initially, this one-way transfer of labour (and capital), and the speed at which this transfer takes place, is determined by the rate of capital accumulation in the manufacturing sector.[13] By the classical saving function, profits are entirely saved and readily invested, while wages are normally consumed. In contrast to Harrod's formulation, in which the saving ratio is constant, Lewis postulated that the key to rapid economic growth is the raising of the saving ratio to a high enough level to finance the required rate of investment through a process of structural transformation—the share of manufacturing steadily rises in the GDP. As pointed out by Chenery (1983), the central feature of this structural transformation is the growth-generating reallocation of labour from the low-productivity to the high-productivity sector, as opposed to the neo-classical growth model in which the sectoral composition of growth is irrelevant because it assumes a one-sector economy. Furthermore, also as a consequence of assuming a neo-classical saving function, Lewis painted a scenario in which a widening inequality of income is a necessary (though, presumably, not a sufficient) condition for rapid economic growth.[14]

Subsequent empirical studies by Kuznets (1955) conferred some respectability on this line of thought by showing that income distribution follows an inverted U-shaped trajectory—it first worsens and then improves as economic growth proceeds apace. Kaldor (1955), and Galenson and Leibenstein (1955) laid the foundation of a theory that supported the policy of generating investible surplus in the (corporate) manufacturing sector. Kaldor also assumes that the wage-earner's marginal propensity to save is nearly zero, and that of the capitalist close to one, so that growth equilibrium is determined exclusively by the savings rate of the capitalist. Similarly, Galenson and Leibenstein require that to make the 'critical minimum effort' savings be placed in the hands of those who are inclined to invest most of it, namely, the capitalist. In the same vein, Hirschman's theory of unbalanced growth (1958), and that of Perroux (1955), laid emphasis on the growth poles from where, through the trickle-down effect, the benefits of growth were assumed to spread throughout the economy. (Myrdal (1956a) also spoke of the 'spread effects' of growth.) That these growth poles could enfeeble the periphery of their growth potential was, however, not sufficiently emphasized.

In India, the Mahalanobis–Feldman hypothesis—formulated within the context of a closed economy and on the assumption of complete non-shiftability of capital stock from the consumption-goods sector to the investment-goods sector—argued for first setting up a capital-goods base to achieve high rates of saving, capital formation and economic growth by imposing suitable constrains on 'initial' consumption. Bhagwati and Chakravarty (1969) inform us that at about the same time in India the alternative Brahmanand–Vakil hypothesis (1956) assigned to the production of wage goods, especially food, the key role in the promotion of economic growth. This would be done mainly by mobilizing the disguised unemployed, who were seen as the bearers of substantial (potential) savings. Apparently, this reasonable hypothesis got overshadowed by the brilliance of the Mahalanobis model, which formed the basis of India's Second Five Year Plan.[15] Yet another theme current in this period was that, especially in the balanced-growth scenario sketched by Rosenstein-Rodan (1943) and Nurkse (1953), the course of economic growth must be consciously guided by the state.[16] Taking a leaf from Pigou (1932), there was a near-consensus among development economists that, in view of the 'failures' of the market that presumably occur more frequently in the developing than in the developed countries, economic development could not be left entirely (or even mostly) to the magic of the ('missing') markets.[17] Singer (1950) and Prebisch (1950), echoing the same distrust of the free markets, advocated that an overly export-oriented policy, based on static comparative advantage, is more likely to weaken the growth impulses in developing countries than strengthen them because this would mean their specializing in primary goods and simple manufactures. In this milieu, even the flow of foreign investment into these activities will only exacerbate these immiserizing tendencies. Hence, they argued that an essentially 'inward-looking' pattern of industrial development must be deliberately engineered in order to initiate the development process and 'find' the dynamic comparative advantage of the developing countries through learning-by-doing. This prescription, coupled with the general notion that the main constraining factor in the developing countries came mainly from the supply side and not from any deficiency of effective demand, was used as a justification for the policy bias of protecting domestic (infant) industries through import licensing and capital-cheapening policies—the focus of which has been the target of much liberalist criticism.[18]

However, it was soon realized that the rate of growth, as also its composition and quality, is a function not only of physical capital but also of human capital. True, this insight came, at least explicitly, from the neo-classicals. However, its importance became evident only through the empirical studies of the East Asian Miracle economies. According to this line of thought—first formulated in 1962 by Schultz (1962) and Becker (1962), and most recently emphasized by the endogenous growth theory—such diverse activities as education, health, job search, migration and in-service training are rational acts of investment in human capital which link present decisions to future returns. A related idea, much emphasized in a large number of studies pioneered by Solow (1957) and Denison (1962), but also clearly perceived by Harrod and Domar, is that the most important determinant of growth has been technological progress, which again is mainly a function of knowledge accumulation in the society. Also recognized by the development economists, as noted above, was the central importance of effecting structural change (in the sense of changing the pre-existing structure of private property holdings), and not merely of accelerating the growth of output, as a means of raising the economic well-being of the poor. In this context, the question of an egalitarian redistribution of assets—in particular, of land holdings—holds the key to an orderly growth process, which also contributes to resolving the problem of poverty.[19]

This then is the paradigm that the majority of development economists subscribed to and the policy-makers heeded during what I refer to here as the 'Age of Chivalry'—that is, when they did not yet have the benefit of an empirical verification of the basic statements of development economics. The predominant sentiment among development economists was one of optimism—of slaying the dragon of poverty by the 'simple' manoeuvre of raising the rate of saving and capital accumulation along a 'balanced' or 'unbalanced' growth path. The industrial sector was the engine of growth, propelled by import-substituting industrialization. As the resource constraint was the only binding one, this objective could only be achieved by a combination of a critical minimum domestic saving effort to finance the ever higher investment requirement, with the difference being made up by the more or less assured inflow of foreign aid, on the assumption that these resources will be efficiently invested.[20]

The Evolution of Development Policy

Finally, we look at the changing shape of development policy, reflecting the initial influence of development economics, and then that of liberalist thought. This discussion is motivated mainly by the development experiences of Pakistan and India, which is, however, not atypical of other developing countries as well.

Growth Fundamentalism

The structure of development policy in India and Pakistan during the 1950s and 1960s—with important differences that can be attributed to some extent to the diversity of their respective value premises, and cultural and political environs—has broadly consisted of the elements discussed below.

In Pakistan, any explicit commitment to the socialistic ideology was ruled out, though it was greatly emphasized in India. In practice, however, both countries set out to evolve a capitalistic pattern of production, following growth fundamentalism. True, as Bhagwati (1984) informs us, there was some talk in India about growth 'not being an objective in itself but a way of making a sustained assault on poverty'. But in fact, though it remained somewhat infructuous until the mid 1990s, growth fundamentalism was followed relentlessly. The need for heavy investment in the capital-goods-producing sectors at the initial stages of planning was emphasized with a view to maximizing the consumption of such goods over the planning period. The purpose was to accelerate the growth rate to attain self-sustaining growth in the shortest period of time—which remains the overarching, though unfulfilled, objective of planning in both the countries. In sharp contrast, the light-industry option was exercised in Pakistan with apparently better results in terms of realized growth rates. However, exercising this option has meant much weaker 'fundamentals'—that is, lower saving and investment rates and a significantly less diversified industrial structure than what India has been able to achieve (Naqvi 2000).[21]

To pursue the commitment to growth, the policy-makers in both the countries allowed the fruits of economic progress to grow in the immediate neighbourhood of the growth poles in the hope that these would become available to all—rich and poor—through some kind of a backward or forward locomotion of the engine of growth. Since industrialization was 'universally' adopted as the engine of growth, a pre-existing thriving agriculture was milked to support the nascent industrial sector—which tendency, however, has proved to be a costly mistake. Simultaneously, driven by a desire to increase the size of the domestic market, the industrialization process in Pakistan was initiated by import-substituting consumer goods, especially luxury goods—the imports of which had to be curtailed partly for balance-of-payments reasons and partly because of the ready domestic availability of raw materials (such as cotton and jute) and a plentiful domestic supply of cheap labour. Similarly, India, following Mahalanobis (1953), initiated the import-substitution process with investment in heavy industries—on the implicit assumption that factor prices (especially the wage rate and the exchange rate) have little effect on the choice of production techniques. Turning the rate of the investment in heavy industries into a policy variable was expected to help the growth of 'downstream' consumer-goods industries and increase total output when compared to exercising the 'light-industry-first' option. True, attempts were made to encourage exports through special schemes in both the countries—for example, the Export Bonus Scheme in Pakistan. However, the net result was still to preserve a significant margin of protection for the import-substitution activity as compared to export expansion (Bhagwati and Desai 1970; Naqvi 1971).

Since the economy could not raise itself by its own bootstraps, foreign aid was accepted as a supplement to domestic savings, which were supposed to rise over time. The 'aid-to-end-aid' rhetoric was freely used, presumably in all sincerity, in both Pakistan and India. Foreign aid was accepted, rather light-heartedly, to finance economic growth with a view to relieving the domestic-resource constraint. True, the goal of self-reliance was explicitly spelt out in successive development plans, but in this respect the deeds seldom matched the words. Foreign aid, which started as a tiny trickle, soon assumed the proportions of a vast torrent drowning all hopes of self-reliant growth—more so in Pakistan than in India—plunging both countries, especially Pakistan, into a swamp of indebtedness.

There was also a consensus among the policy-makers that the task of achieving economic growth, balanced or unbalanced, required direct and indirect state intervention. As elsewhere in the developing world, including the (very) fast-growing East Asian economies, the planned route to development was accepted in both Pakistan and India, who launched their own Five Year Plans which directly determined the size of public investment (savings), and indirectly regulated private investment (savings) by a set of fiscal, monetary, credit and trade policies. These policies, acting in unison as well as at cross purposes, had the effect of literally providing a captive market to the domestic (private) producers by removing the threat of foreign competition. It also sought to maximize investible surplus in the hands of the capitalists with the aim of achieving high rates of private investment and industrial growth. That such policies introduced widespread inter-sectoral and intra-sectoral inefficiencies has been competently reported in the development literature (Bhagwati 1978; Krueger 1974 etc.). What, however, would have been the state of development in the developing countries in the absence of such interventionist policies (that put a premium on import institution with a view to eventually helping export expansion) has only been conjectured, if at all. Such conjectures have, however, simply restated revealed liberalist preferences for free-market solutions, which, as subsequent events have shown, have been more a part of the problem rather than of the solution.

The Emergence of a New-old Religion

Through a curious process of learning and unlearning from recent history, the policy-makers were persuaded to agree on a new-old structure of economic policy. The main elements of the policy were:

1. The maximization of growth, but with a substantially larger allocation than was made in the past for such 'basic needs' as clean water, housing, electricity and education.[22] The main point of this new-old strategy was to deal *directly* with the problems faced by those who live below the 'poverty line', rather than leave them to the care of the trickle-down effects of a high rate of economic growth—a set of ideas which have found a fuller development in the UNDP's annual *Human Development Reports (HDRs)* (see Chapters 6, 7 and 9).

2. Far greater emphasis was accorded to agriculture than in the past though, quite appropriately, not as the engine of growth.[23] The emphasis of economic policy has been on increasing agricultural production mainly by enhancing per-hectare productivity by the use of improved variety of seeds and a more ample supply of key agricultural inputs like fertilizer at a subsidized rate. Yet 'structural reforms' in the agricultural sector that could change the

extant imbalance of economic power and yield considerable gains in per capita productive efficiency have been postponed, most pointedly in Pakistan.[24]

3. Conscious export promotion was pursued, mainly by dismantling the exchange-control regimes and by a downward adjustment of the par value of domestic currencies. This was done to balance the earlier preoccupation with import substitution, which was shown to have led to allocative inefficiency in the industrial sector, and also to have lowered its employment-generating content and the share of wages in total national income. Furthermore, the earlier export pessimism was found not to be entirely justified as export-promotion measures did pay off to some extent, if not a great deal. The extraordinary growth of world trade has also been interpreted as having helped to erode the earlier export pessimism (WTO 1998).

4. Government intervention in economic activity has been minimized in order to give market forces a free rein by privatizing government-controlled activities. This was done in the belief that the private sector should be encouraged—with all the incentives that it takes—to eliminate the alleged wasteful rent-seeking activities due to government activities, by unleashing the forces of the market, even though so far the actual outcome of such efforts has not measured up to expectation.[25]

5. The goal of independence from foreign aid and loans need not be pursued actively because, as in the past, aid is required to bridge the investment–saving gap. Breaking a time-honoured tradition can be a risky affair, much more so now than in the past. At any rate, more aid is needed to service and pay off old debts as well. Also, considering that Official Development Assistance (ODA) comes at only nominal rates of interest—implying negative real interest rates—it has been mistaken as a gift.

Notes

1. Keynes (1936) explicitly assigned a prominent role in the conduct of economic policy to the defunct economist who keeps being reincarnated to satisfy the excess demand for his services whenever new ideas are in short supply. However, it is safe to conjecture that if the iconoclast of the *General Theory* were a development economist he would have exorcised the ghost of the

defunct economist from its realm, even if that meant setting up a few stuffed shirts to be shot down. No worshipper at the temples of Adam Smith and David Ricardo, Keynes did not believe in the unlimited magic of the market, the ubiquity of self-interest in human affairs, or in the institution of (unlimited) private property.

2. As if to make the liberalist cause look scientific as well, the neo-classical economists have finally secured Adam Smith's message for posterity by proving the First and Second Fundamental Theorem of Welfare Economics. (For a careful statement of the theorem see Khan (1987b), Feldman (1991), and Chapter 6 of this book).

3. While this Gang of Four and the other East Asian latecomers achieved great success by any standards, one important contributory factor to their success must have been that, for strategic reasons, their defence needs were fully met by the United States.

4. Sen (1983a) has argued, 'if this is a free market [in South Korea] then Walras's auctioneers can surely be seen as going around with a government white paper in one hand and a whip in another.'

5. A promising approach to the problem of identifying the defunct economist is to look for one who is an active practitioner of what Lakatos (1970) calls a 'degenerating' Scientific Research Programme (SRP), as opposed to a 'progressive' SRP, the practitioners of which are the living economists. Another approach is Hick's (1976) philosophical-cum-historical explanation, which should be especially to the liking of the policy-maker. He opines that, unlike a natural scientist for whom 'old ideas are worked out [and] old controversies are dead and buried', an economist cannot throw overboard the deadweight of the past. This explains why 'neo-classical succeeds neo-mercantilist; Keynes and his contemporaries echo Ricardo and Malthus; Marx and Marshall are still alive'. That may well be so, but, in my opinion, in economics like in other sciences, old ideas do get worked out with the passage of time, making way for new and more relevant ones, especially when their context and the institutional structure get profoundly transformed. In contrast to the widely held view that the basic ideas of economics have remained unchanged since Adam Smith (Schmalensee 1991), the fact is that there have been genuine 'revolutions' in it in the sense that a 'progressive' SRP with excess empirical content has replaced a 'degenerating' SRP, even though not always in the Kuhnian (1962) sense of a 'discontinuous jumps' from one ruling 'paradigm' to another with no conceptual bridge between the two. One of the most recent of such revolutions is the emergence of development economics!

6. However, Lewis offers a somewhat offhand answer to this question, which is exactly the opposite of what we have suggested in the text. He thinks that most problems in the developing economies seem to be amenable to the time-honoured tools of economics, viz., supply and demand and the Quantity Theory of Money and, one may add, Say's law. 'This is why', Lewis (1984a) asserts, 'there are so many good untrained economists, and also why some of our most high-powered colleagues perform no better than a good undergraduate' (p. 2). With this interpretation, the defunct economist is twice blessed! If the intellectual endowment of many developing countries in fact consists of little besides the talents of good (or bad) undergraduates, the simpler views of the

defunct economist on economic matters should enjoy an exalted status in the eyes of the policy-maker.

7. As if to prove the strength of their Pavlovian reflexes, the development economists have continued to consult these (defunct) predecessors from the past, namely: 'The physiocrats for agriculture; the mercantilists for export surplus; the classicists for free market; the Marxists for capital; the neo-classicists for entrepreneurship; the Fabians for government; the Stalinists for [heavy] industrialization; the Chicago School for schooling; and econometricians like E.F.Denison for a large residual'. (Lewis 1984a: p. 7)

8. An interesting example of the contention made in the text is provided in a study of wheat markets in Pakistan by Naqvi and Cornelisse (1986), which shows that the policy of procurement of wheat by the government, even though defectively implemented, has been useful in preventing the private traders in the wheat market from becoming exploitative.

9. This has been recognized by the World Bank: 'Markets cannot operate in a vacuum—they require a legal and regulatory framework that only government can provide. And markets sometimes prove inadequate or fail altogether in other regimes as well. The question is not whether the state or the market should dominate: each has a unique role to play' (World Bank 1991).

10. For an excellent study of the Japanese example of agriculture as a sustainer of industrial development and for the relevance of this example for developing countries, see Okhawa *et al.* (1970), especially Chapter 4.

11. Nurkse (1953) also stated: 'the problem of development today is largely a problem of capital accumulation' (p. 1).

12. It is interesting to recall here that the 'bloody-mindedness' about economic growth and the seeming lack of concern for income (and wealth) distribution displayed by Lewis and some others like Galenson and Leibenstein (1955) in the 1950s (which Lewis hotly denies in his 1984 paper), and even earlier by Schumpeter (1934), parallels the sentiment of Adam Smith in 1776 when he set out to explore only 'the nature and causes of the wealth of nations'. He was followed by David Ricardo who too was only secondarily concerned with distribution. It was left for John (Stuart) Mill to emphasize the primary importance of distribution. The stage was thus set for Marxian distributive socialism, which equated capitalist surplus with capitalistic exploitation. True, the leaders of the 'marginalist revolution' did try to explain away the capitalist exploitation by reference to the imaginary episode of each factor of production receiving its just reward, but this defence, based on a confusion between the sources of income and the factors of production, was by and large ineffectual, (Robinson 1979).

13. But Lewis (1955) emphasized that the rising share of the manufacturing activity is *not* inconsistent with the strong growth of the agricultural sector.

14. However, Lewis was careful to point out that this does not mean that the inequality of income per se is essential to growth; it is rather 'the inequality which goes with profits that favours capital accumulation and not the inequality which goes with rents' (Agarwala and Singh 1963: p. 420).

15. On this, see Malenbaum (1962). A brief history of Pakistan's first two Five Year Plans is given in Haq (1963). Bhagwati and Chakravarty (1969) provide a comprehensive analysis of India's first three Five Year Plans. A general account of

planning experiences in developing countries is given in Waterston (1965). For an early account of the government-sponsored private capitalism in Pakistan, see Papanek (1967) and Lewis (1969).

16. On the other hand, Hirschman (1958) argues unconvincingly that even without a planned effort an unbalanced growth strategy will draw into the open, somewhat mysteriously, the hidden entrepreneurial and other resources, which will respond to the challenges posed by economic growth.

17. Haberler (1950) and Viner (1952), however, emphasized the importance of relying on free trade and free markets—an opinion that was generally ignored when it was expressed, but has now been brought back to life by the 'liberalists'.

18. The 'distortionary' effects of such policies have been extensively studied by Naqvi (1964, 1966), Bhagwati and Desai (1970), Bhagwati (1978), Krueger (1978), etc.

19. The central importance of a 'radical structural change' for achieving 'equitable economic growth' has been brought out in sharp relief in the work of Adelman and Morris (1973). However, Lewis (1984b) claims that land reforms were actively advocated by the founding fathers of development economics as well. Sen (1981a) has set out a theory of 'entitlement', according to which a person's entitlement consists of his 'ownership' and his exchange possibilities, which together determine his overall endowment, and which the process of development should seek to expand.

20. The question as to whether aid helped or hindered economic growth has been extensively debated. The agnostic view is given in Griffin and Enos (1970). On the other hand, Papanek (1972) has been the vanguard of the defenders of the faith. He has shown that the agnostics' case (that foreign aid tends to supplant domestic saving instead of supplementing it) is mistakenly based on the assumption that saving equals investment minus foreign-aid inflows, from which it followed that 'as long as the effect of an additional unit of foreign resources on investment is less than one, its effect on savings will appear to be negative'.

21. Quite expectedly, therefore the growth rate markedly accelerated in India and decelerated in Pakistan during the 1990s.

22. Inspired by the Sri Lankan experience, such a line of thought has been advanced by many economists, See, for example, Sen (1983a).

23. Lewis (1984) observes that 'given the range of possibilities, the search for "the" engine of growth must be foredoomed' (p. 8).

24. For an interesting account of the effect of structural reforms and other factors on Pakistan's agriculture, see Khan (1983); some special aspects of Indian agriculture are analyzed in Krishna (1963).

25. For a good account of the experience with privatization, see Bennet (1997), and the chapter on India (by Mahnot) and Pakistan (by Naqvi and Kemal). In Pakistan's case privatization has, at least so far, meant lower outputs and higher prices of the goods produced by the privatized public enterprises, a higher unemployment rate, and lesser job security for the workers. Simultaneously, the reduction of development expenditure has lowered total investment and the growth rate of the economy.

Part II

The Mixed-economy Route to Development

4

Where the Visible and Invisible Hand Meet

The damaging role of the government in the economic universe has been emphasized ever since modern economics was founded by Adam Smith. Little surprise, then, that it has also come to dominate development debates. What, however, *is* surprising is that free-market and minimalist-government philosophy, safely anchored in the Washington Consensus, could gain currency even though it is now well-known that markets are seldom, if ever, free in an absolute sense, that the government is required to supplement them to maximize social welfare, and that in some cases (externalities and public goods) the need for it will be quite substantial. Empirically as well, the development experience of the last 50 years has convincingly shown that government intervention has, by and large, succeeded in initiating and sustaining higher-than-historical rates of economic growth throughout the developing world, including the 'miracle' economies of East Asia. And yet, somewhat illogically, it is still claimed that the liberalist philosophy has been vindicated by real-world events—*both* by the development failure of the centrally planned economies of Eastern Europe and the former Soviet Union because they did not rely on free-markets, and by the financial crisis that engulfed East Asia in the late 1990s because of their governance failures. The policy advice in *both* cases is to rely even more on the free markets (especially by freeing the capital markets) even though in both cases such a policy has entailed slower economic growth, a worsened human development and greater financial instability. It may, therefore, be useful to look at the market-versus-government issue rather closely in this and the next two chapters.

It is argued in the present chapter that the liberalist assertions about generalized government failure (and generalized market success) are essentially wrong-headed. The Keynesian middle-of-the-road economic philosophy, advocating a judicious mix of the market and the government—which development economists have adopted by common consent—is founded on sound economics and supported by hard empirical evidence about the episodes of development successes (and development failures) in the last 50 years. It is common knowledge now that the mixed-economy route to development is inevitable because free markets lead to a Pareto optimal constellation of production and consumption (i.e., a state in which not everyone's welfare can be increased simultaneously, so that if someone is to gain, others must lose) only under certain stringent conditions, and only if supplemented with an appropriate mechanism to bring about some desired distribution of income and wealth. However, if any of these conditions are not satisfied (which in the real world is almost always the case) then free markets cannot yield an optimum (efficient) solution, and appropriate government intervention will unambiguously improve the market outcome (Stiglitz 1991). Furthermore, the claim that the self-interest principle coordinates the individual actions of the economic agents to work for the social good is by no means universally true. This is illustrated well by the parable of the Prisoner's Dilemma—that is, when individual rationality diverges from collective rationality. In this situation both the prisoners ('rational' utility-maximizers) get the worst of all the possible worlds because they opted to act selfishly rather than in concert[1] (Rapoport 1991).

The Anatomy of a Mixed Economy

The Evolution of a Development Consensus

A near consensus evolved among development economists during the 1950s and 1960s around a philosophy of economic development that incorporated the basic features of the Harrod–Domar growth theory and the Keynesian theory. While economic growth is assumed to be a function of (physical and human) capital formation, the problem of inadequate effective demand is also recognized, though not always adequately emphasized. As noted in the previous chapter, the central theme of this philosophy is 'balanced growth', which was made prominent by Nurkse (1953), but was first spelled out in the form of Rosenstein-Rodan's (1943) 'big-push' conjecture. While these hypotheses envisage a balanced growth of various components of the industrial sector—initiated and sustained by 'a wave of capital investments in a number of different industries'— their basic message is that the key sectors of the economy should grow harmoniously, in proportion to their respective output and income elasticities, in order to internalize inter-sectoral feedbacks for the purpose of accelerating economic growth.[2] Lewis's dual-economy model sets up a mechanism to achieve a dynamic balance between key sectors of the economy by a growth-promoting re-allocation of labour from the agricultural sector to the industrial sector. This is because the marginal productivity of labour is assumed to be higher in the latter sector than in the former. This process continues as long as the wage rate in the industrial sector is higher than in the agricultural sector and the price of capital services in the former remains both high and positive. One of the most fruit-ful generalizations of the balanced-growth hypothesis has been suggested by Chenery (1965). According to him, the key problem is that of 'balancing supply and demand for different commodities and factors of production'. This approach, using input-output analy-sis, has the added attraction of providing a check on the consist-ency and feasibility of specific development plans. It allows the computation of 'shadow prices' associated with the given invest-ment programmes and, utilizing them, permits an explicit analysis of the requirements of inter-sectoral balance and consistency.

The basic point in the present context is that a balanced growth of various components of the industrial sector, or of different sectors of the economy, cannot possibly be brought about by free markets alone. Nurkse explicitly stated: 'Economic progress is not a spon-taneous or automatic affair. On the contrary, it is evident that there are automatic forces within the system tending to keep it moored to a given level'. Rosenstein-Rodan (1984), in the review of his earlier work, is equally candid on this point:

The programming of investment in a developing country is necessary to correct for such distortions as indivisibilities, externalities, and information failures. 'Programming' is just another word for rational, deliberate, consistent, and coordinated economic policy (p. 216).

Hence the need for taking a planned route to development with a view to changing the structure of the economy in the 'initial' period. However, this prognosis was never confused with the centrally planned route to development which communist countries advocated and practiced—a route explicitly rejected by development economists quite early in the debate. It would, therefore, be fallacious to cite the 'failure' of central planning in the former Soviet Union as a refutation of development economics, which has emphasized—from the very beginning of the discipline—the essentially complementary roles of the government and the market in managing the process of economic development without rejecting the information and allocative economies that free markets achieve at a minimal cost (Waterston 1965). Prebisch (1984) clearly envisaged 'an active role' for the state in development planning, which was needed to induce 'structural change' and to 'intensify the rate of internal capital formation'. Rostow's 'take-off' (1956) is generally preceded by a 'sharp stimulus', which requires, among others, radical changes in production techniques and consumption patterns. Both these opinions clearly imply government intervention if and when the free markets do not deliver all by themselves. Mahalanobis's model for India (1953) envisaged an initial concentration on the development of heavy industries in the belief that it would lead to a higher rate of economic growth by diversifying the structure of production, generating 'forced savings', accelerating capital formation and inducing technological improvements. Mellor (1986) and many other writers have noted, in respect of promoting a balanced sectoral growth, that real income of the rural poor should be raised by keeping the price of food lower than would prevail in the free market. A similar line of reasoning appears in World Bank's (1986) study. That policy-makers dutifully accepted this advice is evident from the large number of medium-term (indicative) plans that have directly guided the public-sector development efforts with a view to 'crowding in' private investment in developing countries.[3]

The Dissenters: There have been dissenting voices against the reigning development paradigm from its very inception. Schumpeter (1934), writing before the formal 'inauguration' of development economics by Rosenstein-Rodan in the late 1940s, viewed the process of economic development as essentially a *market* response to the shock of entrepreneurial initiatives (innovations). From the initial 'circular-flow' configurations, the economy moves to a 'new and higher equilibrium' through the pursuit by lesser mortals of monopoly profits created by the pioneer entrepreneur. There is no room here for the government to act as an entrepreneur and/or signal profitable investment opportunities. Following him, among the founding fathers of our discipline, Hirschman (1984) calls himself a 'second generation dissenter' who fought a 'major battle' in his *strategy* against the widely alleged need for a 'balanced' or 'big-push' industrialization effort (p. 96).[4] Hence, his 'unbalanced growth' hypothesis is a search for 'hidden rationalities' in the 'processes of growth and change already under way'. With the help of backward and forward linkages, unbalanced growth would, by 'creating tensions' at strategic points in the producer-to-producer chain, somehow enlist latent entrepreneurial talent to energize an otherwise dormant economy. Galenson and Leibenstein's (1955) advocacy of the 'critical minimum effort thesis' put the capitalist at the center of the development process. They, and subsequently Kaldor (1955), assert that since a wage-earner's marginal propensity to save is nearly zero, and that of a capitalist close to unity, the growth equilibrium would be determined exclusively by the savings rate of the capitalist.

But the dissenters never went so far as to dispense with the role of government in economic management altogether. Hirschman (1958) remains skeptical about the efficiency of the free markets, especially when their signals remain invisible to the investor. His idea of a 'strategy' implies an effort by the government to call forth and enlist 'development resources and abilities that are hidden, scattered, or badly utilized' because the markets can hardly be expected to deliver them in the required sequence and amount. What he was fighting against, and justifiably so, was the 'myth of Integrated Investment Planning', such as was practiced in former Soviet Russia—which, at any rate, never found favour with development economists. Also, in the Galenson–Leibenstein scenario, the state is supposed to support capitalist accumulation through fiscal and monetary policies, and guide this process through specific investment techniques and criteria. The point is that the prevalent consensus in favour of government intervention when markets do not exist, or when they function inefficiently because of a lack of enough information to the economic agents, was never seriously questioned by such dissenters.

The Loyal Opposition: The problem for the first group of development economists belonging to the opposition is not to deny government intervention but to worry about its optimal 'form', depending on the source of 'distortion'. When it is shown that the distortion in question lies in the foreign-trade sector and is caused by quantitative trade restrictions, then the recommendation is to replace such restrictions by tariff restrictions. However, if the distortion in question is domestic, then optimal tax-cum-subsidy policies are preferable to import tariffs. The main thesis here is that distortions in the domestic sector and the foreign-trade sector should be removed by directly impacting the locus of distortion, with a view to avoiding the 'excess burden' imposed on the economy by allocative inefficiencies (Bhagwati 1971; Naqvi 1969; Johnson 1964a, b). The effect of these 'reforms' in many cases is to lower the overall incidence of government intervention, but their main point is to make it explicit (for example, tariffs as opposed to quotas) and amenable to market solutions. There is yet another train of thought which links government intervention to unproductive rent-seeking (Krueger 1974), or to directly unproductive profit-seeking (DUP) (Bhagwati and Srinivasan 1982). In each case, the 'unproductive' part flows from the deviations of a real-life economy *with* government intervention to an imaginary Pareto optimal economy *without* any government intervention. This approach, however, becomes clearly objectionable when it amounts to making out a case, on the basis of such essentially non-empirical comparisons, for generalized market success—which, needless to point out, is not even a logical position to take. At any rate, the whole point of this rent-seeking literature is lost once it is noted that rent-seeking activity is at least as widespread in private organizations as in public enterprises! (Milgrom and Roberts 1990).

The Rebels: Finally, there are those who oppose all government intervention on ideological grounds. The fact of 'market failure', according to such arguments, does not mean that the government will also not fail in similar circumstances. Further, because the latter eventuality is *inevitable* rather than *probable*, it is worse than the former. One of the earliest rebels in this class is Bauer (1972), who remains to this day a model agnostic; who accepts *nothing* that development economists say or do, *because* of their innate interventionist inclinations. To quote his recent summing up of his own work: 'I noted then that comprehensive central planning was certainly not necessary for economic advance; it was much more likely to retard it' (Bauer 1984: p. 42). Of course, he forgot to note that development planning in most developing countries has been mostly of the indicative type and that it has mostly succeeded, not failed, in encouraging higher-than-trend economic growth and development. He remains convinced that, just as in the plantation economies of the then British West Africa which he visited and wrote about in the 1930s, economic development in the developing countries of today will come about, as before, owing to 'the individual voluntary responses of millions of people to emerging or expanding opportunities created largely by external contacts and brought to their notice in variety of ways, primarily through the operation of the market' (ibid: p. 32). Then, there are those economists who, in their proselytizing zeal, condemn all forms of government intervention as sinful. For instance, Lal (1983) concludes that 'the *dirigiste* policies... have led to outcomes which ... may have been worse than a *laissez-faire*' (p. 16). He, therefore, explicitly rules out, like Bauer, the possibility of steering 'a middle course between *laissez-faire* and the *dirigiste* dogma' (p. 109). Buchanan (1986) pleads to restore the economic universe to the Smithian natural order, run entirely by the Invisible Hand in which problems of inefficiency *and* inequity cannot arise (see Chapter 6). That being the case—so the argument goes—the developing countries will be better off in the company of free markets rather than in the protective custody of the government. According to him, even the theoretically justifiable forms of government intervention are harmful because these tend to work perversely in practice and, even more importantly, stifle individual freedom. Hence, a one-way journey from government control to free markets, with no provision for a stopover at some intermediate station, is the only way to achieve both economic growth *and* equity for the simple reason that government intervention itself is responsible for the less-than-complete realization of these policy objectives. The implication is that the market *always* succeeds, even in cases where its failure has been duly acknowledged—for instance, in the case of public goods and externalities of various kinds (see Chapters 5 and 6).

But where do these agnostics and dissenters draw their inspiration from? To answer this question, let us have a look at the development economist's backyard, where neo-Keynesianism (favouring a mixed economy) is found at odds with a resurgent monetarism and rational expectationism (favouring free markets).

The Development Economist's Backyard

Neo-Keynesianism and Monetarism

Bell and Kristol (1981) suggest, though not entirely convincingly, that the 'house that Keynes built' is in disarray, and that the neo-Keynesian synthesis—elaborately forged by Hicks, Samuelson, Klein, Tobin, Modigliani and many others in order to reconcile Keynesian macroeconomics with the classical microeconomics and to give the former an empirical content—is about to disintegrate. Here we try to perceive the connection between the reported sense of crisis in neo-Keynesian economics and the prevailing lack of confidence in development economics. The connection is important because both share common ground (a mixed-economy perception and an ethical predilection). Further, they also face a common adversary (neo-classical economics) which is irrevocably wedded to the inviolability, the universality and the positivity of free-market solutions.

The conflict between the monetarists and those who call themselves 'rational expectationists' (or 'ratex'), on the one hand, and the neo-Keynesians, on the other, revolves around the appropriateness of government intervention in the conduct of economic policy. Klamer (1984) notes that the basic question being addressed by the two adversaries is: 'Can the government help to stabilize the economy through active interventionist policies?' Modigliani (1977) states that while the neo-Keynesians advocate an active interventionist policy for stabilizing the economy through fiscal and monetary policies, the monetarists and the rational expectationists say the opposite. According to this latter group, the efforts to stabilize the economy are more likely to increase instability than decrease it.

Their recommendation is, therefore, to let the market do the job in its own inscrutable ways.

The Neo-Keynesians: The neo-Keynesians are unambiguously persuaded that a mixed economy, which is the common characteristic of *all* the economies outside the former communist bloc, requires redirection and control by the government. Tobin neatly summarizes the neo-Keynesian position: 'I think the basic issue there is the question of whether there are any deadweight losses or market failures of a macroeconomic nature in a market economy (cited in Klamer 1984: p. 101). Neo-Keynesians think that there are, and that the government can do something about them. Associated with this vision of a mixed economy is a deep (moral) concern about promoting a socially desirable income distribution that the free market, if left to its devices, is ill-equipped to take cognizance of. Hence, according to Tobin, 'a neo-Keynesian seems to be more concerned about employment, jobs, and producing goods than people who have great faith in market processes' (cited in Klamer 1984: p. 101). These social and political considerations provide an independent justification for government intervention in capitalistic economies which are *not* inherently self-equilibrating and where income and wealth are, as a rule, unequally distributed. Such situations grow only worse without a proactive public policy. Fundamentally, the neo-Keynesians hold a relativistic view of individual freedom, which must be constrained significantly to maximize social welfare.[5]

The Monetarists: In sharp contrast, the monetarists reject such a world view. According to Friedman (1968), the real-world economy is inherently self-equilibrating and self-regulating. He maintains that the apparently rigid wages are really not rigid, with the result that the Keynesian involuntary unemployment is not possible. Instead, the Hicksian mechanism, powered by the 'required' changes in the real money supply, ensures full employment. Friedman views a competitive economy, 'disturbed' by a government-induced demand stimulus, as adjusting itself to a 'natural' rate of unemployment *entirely* by the voluntary actions of wage-earners and producers. In this competitive wonderland, replete with optical illusions, wage-earners initially do not 'see' the inflation-induced fall in their real wages, but producers do get a higher price for their produce and 'see' higher profits coming. Thus, unemployment is reduced in the short run. But that is only a temporary phase, which is eventually undone by the *voluntary* actions of wage-earners who reduce the additional supply of their services at a lower real wage and contract for higher wages. To make matters worse, inflation rises even as the 'over-heated' economy settles down to the 'natural unemployment rate'.

The Rational-expectationists: In Friedman's Adaptive Expectations Model, there is still room for the government to operate effectively along a short-run, negatively sloped Phillips Curve. But, according to Lucas (1972) (also see Lucas and Sargent 1978), the government cannot succeed in manipulating the economy to its advantage even in the short run.[6] Friedman's adaptive expectations are, in these models, replaced by 'rational expectations', according to which it is only rational to banish Keynesian 'animal spirits' from the world of expectations once and for all. Once the mechanism through which economic agents form expectations is saddled with a rational structure, 'revolutionary' results will follow. Thus, for instance, if the government decides to increase money supply on the basis of some (privileged) information, the individuals come to know about it (presumably through the 'private eye') and alter their behaviour instantaneously. Thus there is no room for the government, even in the short run, to alter the course of events, which makes economic management (even, mismanagement) an impossibility! It is, therefore, only in moments of transient informational lacuna, when individuals randomly make mistakes that, according to the so-called Sargent–Wallace proposition (1975), (unanticipated) monetary shocks can produce at best short-run, tangible effects on real macroeconomic magnitudes.

As if to make sure that the successive errors of expectations are not significantly serially correlated, the smart actors in the rational expectations models learn very quickly from their moments of informational blockage and use up *all* the information that the government has access to. Since the government cannot systematically fool them about its intentions, they are well set to take the economy, all by themselves, to a long-run equilibrium about which they form accurate estimates. Thus, systematic, monetary or fiscal policies will have no effect on output or employment. Government intervention, according to Lucas, is irrelevant because 'this (U.S.)

economy is going to grow at 3 per cent a year, no matter what happens. Forever'[7] (cited in Klamer 1984: p. 52). Here, at last, we have a vision of economic processes that is the closest possible approximation to the physicist's vision of an 'autonomous' universe. In conformity with the First Law of Motion—according to which physical bodies keep moving in the same direction and at the same velocity until something stops them—the economy is seen by the 'ratex' group as driven by some mysterious, invisible economic law of motion unless that visible 'something', called government, stops it. We may note that in this Galilean vision of real-world economies no ethical issues arise from the fact that unemployment prevails because, given the labour market rigidities, it results from the *voluntary* actions of wage earners themselves. There can also be no social injustice in such a self-equilibrating economy for the simple reason that the government itself is the source of all injustice. Hence, Lucas discounts any role for the government in resolving social injustice: 'I can't think of explaining the pharaohs as being in existence to resolve social injustice in Egypt. I think they perpetrated most of the injustice in Egypt' (cited in Klamer 1984: p. 52).

Thurow (1983) examines in detail the policy nihilism of the monetarists and the rational expectationists. First, rational expectationists would not allow any possibility of improving economic performance by government intervention, except by mistake. For if there were any such opportunities, economic agents in Lucas's model would already have acted upon them and eliminated them. Second, the policy nihilism of the rational expectationists, if carried to its logical end, would immobilize policy-makers for ever. This is because if economic agents knew everything that the government knows and does, not only would government intervention be unfruitful, but all attempts to end government intervention would also be equally unfruitful. By virtue of the omniscience of Lucas's economic agents, the government's decision *not* to intervene would also be counter-productive, even though the decision to intervene was unfruitful in the first place. Hence, as Thurow observes, 'policy-makers should continue to make the decisions that they were making as if the rational-expectationist hypothesis were not true'. Thus, the Visible Hand, if it exists already, can, by the sheer logic of the rational expectationist's reasoning, continue to live happily ever after!

Modigliani (1977) also discounts the nihilistic message of the rational expectationists: 'We must, therefore, categorically reject the monetarist appeal to turn back the clock forty years by discarding the basic message of the *General Theory*. We should instead concentrate our efforts on an endeavour to make stabilization policies even more effective in the future than they have been in the past'. Klein (1994) regards the rational expectationist thesis 'as totally unrealistic, lacking in predictive power and contrived to reach preconceived conclusions'. There are many others who express similar views. Thus, while acknowledging the great beauty of Adam Smith's creation, Samuelson (1976) would 'not go to the other extreme and become enamored of the beauty of a pricing mechanism, regarding it as a perfection in itself, the essence of providential harmony, and beyond the touch of human hands' (p. 43). But there is an even more fundamental flaw that both the monetarists and the rational expectationists share. As Hahn (1991) points out, both disregard the importance of learning by the economic agents: 'but the large multiplicity of such situations as well as the possibility that some of these allowed agents to live in an essentially fictitious world (sunspot equilibria) has convinced pure theorists (though not all macroeconomists) that the learning stage cannot be skipped' (p. 49).

The Mixed-economy Route to Economic Progress

This brief review of the state of the art in mainstream economics should make clear, among other things, the (neo) Keynesian connection of development economics—both are explicit that there *is* a place under the sun for the Visible Hand as well as the Invisible Hand to work for the good of society. The 'accommodating' attitude of development economists has been broadly consistent with, though not identical to, the neo-Keynesian prescription. The difference is that unlike the latter, the former offer primarily supply-side stuff, so that *aggregate demand kept at the desired level* to propel the development process does not figure prominently in its policy prescriptions. For this reason macro-stabilization policies (those which tend to retard growth in the short to medium run) are implemented primarily under the influence of neo-classical notions. However, the former's emphasis on the government's role is very neo-Keynesian. Also, unlike the communist countries, development economists do not downplay the importance of the market mechanism as an information gatherer. Since such information is not always complete, and sometimes is altogether missing, it cannot be unquestioningly accepted as the sole basis of public policy. Furthermore, markets do not operate in a vacuum but within a wider institutional and historical framework. Thus, 'if we want an Invisible Hand to bring everything into some kind of social consonance, we should be sure, first, that our social institutions are framed to bring out our better selves, and second, that they do not require major sacrifices of self-interest by many people much of the time' (Simon 1983). Also, there are many important cases of 'external economies,' those not captured by market prices, which vitiate the argument that government interference with the working of the free market is mostly, if not always, counterproductive (see Chapters 5 and 6).

As this is the happy middle-of-the-road philosophy that most development economists recommend and policy-makers accept by common consent, why should liberalist opinion try to disturb such (near) consensus among development economists about the relative, and beneficial, roles of the government and the market? If, by calling government intervention counter-productive, it is meant that developing countries where the government has significantly intervened have fallen behind economically rather than gone forward, then this claim is patently false because there is *no* developing (or even developed) country which has been successful without government intervention! Indeed, as Bhagwati (1985) reports, there is nothing in the three decades of development experience to suggest 'increasing immiserization or even stagnation in the living standards of the poor.' In fact, a look at the successive World Bank's Annual *World Development Reports* (*WDRs*) would show that the rates of growth of per capita income in many developing countries have been quite respectable by 'historical' standards, and that the intensity of poverty there has also been alleviated to varying degrees.[8] For instance, the East Asian miracle economies, and now China, have scored resounding development successes, all using the mixed-economy approach—indeed, in the latter, the economy has been primarily run by the government. Nearer home, the actual per capita growth rates achieved by Pakistan and India, though relatively modest, would have appeared like a fantasy at the time of their independence from colonial rule. Clark (1984) reports that, in 1947, there was a consensus among economists that the Indian economy would at best achieve a long-run growth rate of 0.5 per cent. Pakistan's growth possibilities were considered to be much worse. However, as Maddison (1970) has shown, India and Pakistan, which had grown at rates of only 1.2 per cent during 1913–50 period, recorded a much better growth of 3.7 per cent and 2.7 per cent respectively during 1950–60. This is the period when interventionist policies were widely practiced by both the countries!

True, as Meier (1984a) points out, some 'disappointments' have also been experienced by some developing economies. Zero and even negative growth rates of per capita income, a fairly high level of absolute poverty, and visibly large differences in income and wealth continue to darken the face of the societies in many developing countries, especially those located in the economically blighted Africa (*IMF* 2000a). But we know now that these regressing economies are the ones which were never subjected to the allegedly distortionary development policies (for example, import substitution) that have been practiced more or less successfully by other developing economies (Riddell 1990). Indeed, these have also been the economies where the Invisible Hand's writ has remained practically unchallenged (UNDP 1999)! It is, therefore, a gross misreading of reality to still declare the free market as a panacea for all, or even most, development problems—including those involving structural change. In particular, it would be naive to think that the elites in developing countries, whose economic interests are served by the existing institutions, would voluntarily accept substantial changes in those institutions. A decisive government action is required to make a dent in the status quo, which is not to deny that vested interests in developing countries, especially those governed by undemocratic regimes, often prevent the government from acting in the national interest (Naqvi 2000).

A stocktaking of past failures and successes should convince us that, for all its shortcomings, the 'traditional' development strategy has served the developing countries well. This, however, does not mean that it is unimprovable. The fact that there are possibilities of improving a strategy is by no means a convincing reason for its total rejection. If, in the words of Lewis (1984a), 'the viability of LDCs in normal times, like the 1950s and the 1960s, is now beyond doubt', the credit for pulling off this extraordinary feat must go to the time-tested mixed-development strategy. This strategy should remain an integral part of development policy as we enter the 21st century in order to ensure that the society does not continue to let only (or mostly) the poor shoulder the major burden of economic development all the time. Without such an institutional bulwark against social exploitation, economic progress will not be meaningful for the majority of humankind. These matters are explored in greater detail in the next two chapters.

Notes

1. When such a possibility is generalized to more than two players, the Prisoner's Dilemma case becomes a version of the so-called 'Tragedy of Commons' (Hardin 1968).
2. Balanced growth does *not* imply a policy of a simultaneous expansion of all sectors to the same extent and at the same time. Rather, it means that faster growth will occur—according to this strategy—where the output and income elasticities are relatively high, while the industries and sectors where these elasticities are lower would grow more slowly (Scitovsky 1987).
3. It is interesting to note that the World Bank and the United States not only did *not* object to planning but actively encouraged it in developing countries *as a condition* of receiving aid and loans. The planned route to development was indeed seen then as ensuring the success of the development effort (Bruton 1998).
4. Among the dissenters, it is important to distinguish the economists whose main concern is about an appropriate form of government intervention from the agnostics who would totally reject the government just because it is one!
5. To dramatize the point made in the text, Samuelson (1976) points out that in a free economy, where slavery is prohibited, 'a man is not even free to sell himself: he must *rent* himself at a wage' (p. 52).
6. Even a hard-boiled neo-classical like Haberler (1980) signals his disapproval of this new nihilistic school, which 'is best known for the startling conclusions... to wit, that macro-economic policies, both monetary and fiscal, are ineffective *even in the short run*... it is the extreme antithesis of orthodox Keynesianism.'
7. This is not the consensus now. Infact, the (new) U.S. economy, which has grown robustly for eight years has seen some leaner days in the past, and is again threatened with a downturn. The important point is that even the new-found strength of the U.S. economy is not by any means due to the alleged rule of the unfettered markets; nor is it a correct reading of the ground reality to claim that the U.S. (or any real world) economy is now free from any macroeconomic management!
8. The first *World Development Report*, 1978 explicitly stated that, on the basis of the evidence extant then, growth effort during the 1950s and 1960s was 'a substantial improvement of the historical record' (World Bank: p. 3).
9. For all his hesitation on this account, Lewis (1984a) notes that 'what development economists cannot leave out of their calculations is the government's behaviour' (p. 4).

5

Efficiency, Equity and Markets

The preceding chapter questions the validity of the arguments which seek to dramatize instances of government failure as costlier than those of market failure, whether measured in terms of its efficiency cost or by its adverse effect on economic freedom. Such comparisons are generally invalid because we are thereby cast on a barren no man's land where nothing grows or works efficiently—neither the government nor the private sector, because *both* are inefficient rent-seekers! Thus, barring a vote for anarchy, the only logical option left for development economists (as well as neo-classical economists) is to tread the mixed-economy path to address development issues. This chapter broadens the scope of these arguments by exploring its global dimension, and by relating these to such important goals of economic development as efficiency, equity and social justice.

A central theme of the analysis presented here is, while it would be unwise to suppress markets if and when they function efficiently, the dictates of equity and dynamic efficiency require government intervention when they do not. This may be due to external economies of various kinds, when public goods (including the Rawlsian social primary goods and global public goods) must be supplied, or when institutional constraints created by the pre-existing inequitable patterns of asset ownership and the mode of property relations need to be suitably eased. These, in turn, comprise the necessary conditions for achieving dynamic and static efficiency as well as equity in resource allocation. An implication of this analysis is that the standard liberalist corrective medicine, which is always to get the prices 'right', does not work in all circumstances. Indeed, in an absolute sense, (market) prices are seldom right in *any* conceivable circumstances. Instead, given the conditions in the developing countries, a set of ('shadow') prices must be invented as 'duals' of a linear program to make market prices right! Thus, the advocacy for unregulated markets is ill-founded both in theory and practice, and the frequent appeals to the 'first-best' competitive outcomes are outrageously misplaced because such outcomes are *not* guaranteed to be Pareto optimal or efficient if *any* of the circumstances regarding market failure hold—which is almost always the case in the developing countries and, indeed, also in the developed countries.

Free Markets and Efficiency

The essence of the neo-classical cure for various 'distortions', frequently encountered in real-world situations, is a strict adherence to the first-best rules of competitive efficiency—that is, to satisfy the equality between the domestic marginal rate of substitution (in consumption), and the domestic marginal rate of transformation and the foreign rate of transformation (through foreign trade) which, in turn, is equated to international prices (Naqvi 1969). The implication is that since competitive equilibrium will surely lead to an efficient allocation of domestic and global resources, provided that certain stringent conditions are met, state intervention is both redundant and counter-productive—redundant because market outcomes in such cases are regarded as unimprovable, and counter-productive because it imposes an avoidable excess cost in the form of various domestic and foreign trade distortions (discussed below) on the economy. A remarkable result cited in support of market-oriented efficiency solutions is the 'duality' property of an efficient resource allocation. Every maximum welfare problem has embedded in it a set of (shadow) prices, which correspond to optimal input prices—that is, wages, rents and interest rates. The desired distributional outcome can also be secured through the market if lump-sum transfers are made and if certain restrictions on the production and utility functions, noted in Chapter 6, are satisfied. But for that to happen, in both static and dynamic (uncertain) contexts, a perfect, self-policing competition must obtain in all markets. This, in turn, requires that (contingent) markets exist for all situations, that all economic agents face the same degree of uncertainty and that these markets 'clear' at all times. The resplendent world where all this happens is referred to as the 'state of bliss', secured by all-round convexities and multi-market Walrasian equilibria.

'Price Rightism'

Does it follow, then, that a policy of freeing the markets from government regulation and 'getting the (relative) prices right'—which nearly always means the 'right' exchange rate and/or the 'right' wage rate—will actually lead a real-world economy (which, for example, following the liberalist prescription, is made supplicant to price signals by large-scale privatization) to the state of bliss promised in the standard economics textbooks? Unbelievable as such a claim may seem, this is exactly what some economists seriously believe should, in fact, be the case in the real world as well. For instance, Lal (1983) thinks: 'The Utopian theoretical construct of perfect competition then becomes relevant as a reference point by which to judge the health of an economy, as well as the remedies suggested for its amelioration' (p. 15).

This line of thinking is erroneous, both theoretically and empirically, as the following points show:

1.   The proponents of the Neo-classical Political Economy school consider the Pareto optimal state as an observable counterfactual, distortion-free state, by reference to which the policy-induced (potential) waste of real resources can be measured—and corrected—by restoring the writ of the Invisible Hand in the economic universe. However, such a 'revisionist' (to borrow a Marxian phrase) strategy can be operationalised only if all the producers and consumers are reborn as selfish profit and utility maximizers and face the same price, and if all sources of market failures (externalities, public goods, etc.) are foreclosed. But, as soon as these and other conditions attached to a successful return to the free market are explicitly stated, the unrealism of this entire project becomes abundantly transparent. In other words, a return to free markets need not necessarily mean

greater competition (as the experience with privatization and glo-balization amply illustrates) if for one reason or another noted in the literature—incomplete and asymmetric information, adverse selection, moral hazard, etc.—markets are missing, non-universal, or prone to complete collapse. And since in such cases the link between competitive equilibrium and Pareto optimality is broken, such a strategy will not lead to efficient solutions either.

2.   The liberalist plea for a return to the free markets is misleading because the existence of the Pareto efficient configuration of prod-uct and input prices tells us only the rules which 'sustain' a bliss configuration that is *already in place*. As Bator (1958) points out, in the bliss situation 'we shall be concerned only with the prior prob-lem whether a price-market system which finds itself at the maxi-mum welfare point will or will not remain there.' *It does not tell us how to get there.* Thus, even theoretically, whether or not a 'market friendly' policy of 'getting the prices right' will in fact land an economy with the 'wrong' prices in a state of bliss endowed with the 'right' prices is not a sure thing. Indeed, it can as well lead into some bewildering 'people-unfriendly' diaspora.

3.   Obedience to the rules of allocative efficiency does not neces-sarily mean a shift from the government to the free market and greater competition. This is because, to quote Bator (1958) again, 'the necessary conditions of decentralized price-profit calculations (hold) both in *laissez faire* and in a socialist setting of Lange–Lerner civil servants.' Also, the situations of the failure of the basic duality property—that is, 'failure by existence,' 'failure by signal,' 'failure of incentive' and 'failure by enforcement'—apply as much to 'laissez faire markets with genuine profit and satisfaction seekers' as to the 'decentralized efficiency of a Lange–Lerner type of (socialist) or-ganization scheme'. The only difference is that the conditions re-lating to a 'self-policing' competitive economy, characterized by very many producers in every market, will not be relevant in a so-cialist economy. However, it is possible for central planning to mimic the competitive equilibrium process so that it too can lead to a Pareto optimal outcome (Hurwicz 1960). Further, as if to turn the tables on the liberalist, the competitive game can even be played *better* through a planned process than by the market (Lange 1936–37). This is *not*, however, to argue that market outcomes are always

inferior to centrally planned ones, which development economists have seldom, if ever, sought. Nor does it matter at this level of analysis, whether the Pareto optimal solution, which is assumed to maximize social welfare, is attained by the 'Invisible Hand' or calculated electronically by a computer. All that is asserted is that 'an appropriate price system is associated with an efficient state' (Malinvaud 1969), and that these are not *market* prices, but are, strictly speaking, the unbargained for Lagrangean multipliers which are mathematically equated with (shadow) profits, wages and rents. However, note that these shadow prices may or may not equal market prices. Indeed, as has been widely noted in the development literature—for example, Little, Scitovsky and Scott (1970)—in all cases (most of which originate in the developing countries) where external economies obtain, this equality seldom holds.

4. An important implication of these observations is, there is no *a priori* presumption that privatization will improve the situation with respect to efficiency. Indeed, the Fundamental Law of Privatization, due to Sappington and Stiglitz (1987), shows that the conditions required to ensure that privatization does lead to efficient (and equitable) outcomes are *at least* as restrictive as those required for Pareto optimal solutions (for example, symmetric information, zero transaction costs, a complete set of markets, etc.). Hence, 'privatization has to be justified on a case-by-case basis to ensure that the increase in efficiency is sufficient to outweigh the disadvantages of privatization' (Stiglitz 1996a). It follows from these arguments that the specific cases of rent-seeking behaviour—noted by Krueger (1974), Bhagwati (1982) and others—lack generality. Not unexpectedly, therefore, whatever empirical evidence there is shows that the efficiency performance of privatized public-sector units has seldom improved—in many cases, it has actually deteriorated. For instance, in Pakistan, output has declined, product prices have increased and unemployment has risen in nearly all the privatized public sector units (Naqvi and Kemal 1994, 1997). Further, there is much rent-seeking in the private sector as well. Indeed, as also noted in the preceding chapter, the existence and importance of rent-seeking in modern managerial capitalism is an established fact (Schleifer and Vishny 1989; Edlin and Stiglitz 1992). Thus, it is not an uncommon sight when an 'agent' in the free market commits 'fraud' against the 'principal' by misrepresenting the information

to misguide the latter into doing things he would not have done otherwise. In this case, real resources are diverted to the provision of unnecessary services (Karni 1989). In all such cases, the government may have to intervene to reduce essentially wasteful private rent-seeking (Streeten 1993; Naqvi 1999). Much worse, the primary objective here is not profit maximization; it is, rather, the pursuit and the enjoyment of power (Galbraith 1991).

5. South Korea and Taiwan have been cited as showcase economies run according to the (Pareto optimal) efficiency rules, and which have grown very fast for that very reason. It has been asserted that 'apart from the creation of [these neo-classical conditions] it is hard to find any good explanation for the sustained industrial boom in Taiwan' (Little 1982).[1] However, most competent observers of the South Korean and Taiwanese miracles plead innocence of their Paretian proclivities. Bardhan (1988) observes: 'the favourite neo-classical showcase of South Korea is not predominantly one of market liberalism but of aggressive and judiciously selective state intervention' (p. 62). The fact is that the miracle economies have heavily used illiberal compliance mechanisms of selective command and administrative discretion, thereby restricting imports for industrial promotion, disciplining the private sector through control over domestic credit, forex as well as underwriting foreign borrowing, and enabling public enterprises to lead the way in many areas (Stiglitz 1996b). Similarly, all developing countries which have grown less spectacularly (for example, Pakistan, India) have also rebelled against the first-best rules of market efficiency (and Pareto optimality) in every possible way, with state intervention being used in its qualitative as well as quantitative manifestations. Findlay (1988) points out that 'the experience of all the NICs has been marked not only by a strong reliance on world market forces, but also by very far-reaching and pervasive intervention and control in all segments of the economy.'[2] On the other hand, the countries that did *not* practise such distortionary policies (for example, Sub-Saharan Africa) have regressed!

The preceding discussion shows that the equitable state of bliss of the economics textbook may not even be approximated, let alone actually achieved, in the real world for more than one reason—the lump-sum transfers from the gainers to the losers from a change are not actually made, (involuntary) unemployment may coexist with market equilibrium, an equitable redistribution of property and asset holdings cannot be brought about by the market, and 'free riding' may prevent the consumers and producers from acting competitively. Also, in the absence of perfect information, which is almost always the case in the real world, especially in the developing countries, competitive market equilibrium will not be Pareto efficient, leaving ample room for improving such outcomes without making anyone worse off. The fact of the matter is that inherent (generalized) government failure cannot be asserted in the same sense as the Marshall–Pigou type of (selective) market failure, partly because government policies, for better or worse, set the parameters within which markets function. The utility-maximizing calculus, based only on the consumption of the (private) goods by the individual, cannot take him far without the availability of public goods. At any rate, the process of economic growth and the painful structural adjustment required for this process to continue unhindered cannot be propelled by the utility- or profit-maximising economic agents alone. A sovereign state must initiate 'policy action and institutions are required to minimize the costs of, and resistance to, the structural shifts implicit in, and required for, a high rate of growth' (Kuznets 1971). Indeed, vigorous and strategically targeted (*not* necessarily minimal) state intervention is required to provide a framework for 'conflict management' and entrepreneurship—and a 'vision of the future in a period of transformation' (Chang 1994).

The picture that emerges from this analysis is not one of a non-interventionist, minimalist state doing no more than guarding the 'negative freedoms' of the (rich) individuals and leaving all the rest to an invisible auto pilot! Of course, one could still persist with the anti-*dirigiste* thesis and maintain that 'it is not outlandish to believe that South Korea, and other NICs especially, would have done even better if its government had intervened less...' (Crook 1989). But rather than being a scientific statement, this is simply an assertion of a metaphysical belief in the superiority of free markets.

Free Markets and International Trade

There has been a sharp difference of opinion between the development economists and the neo-classical (also classical) economists on the trade-and-growth nexus. The neo-classical economists insist on the superior merits of a free-trade policy, which is mostly seen as an export-led strategy. The role of the state is, therefore, simply to eliminate (or, at least, greatly reduce) the barriers to trade and capital flows to maximize each country's—and total world—welfare. The development economists, on the other hand, emphasize the perverse effects of international trade and investment—reflected in the terms of trade of the developing countries—on their growth possibilities by a misdirection of real resources from high-productivity to low-productivity sectors. Thus, the gains from trade and investment will not be equitably shared between the developing and the developed countries. In effect, developing countries (the 'periphery') would, on balance, be financing the rapid growth of the developed countries (the 'center'), with the latter reaping the best of both the worlds at the expense of the former. This is the essence of the Singer–Prebisch thesis. The export-led growth is, therefore, *not* likely to work to the advantage of the developing countries, especially when taken as a group. This is because, by the 'fallacy of composition', 'what is possible for one or some of the LDCs or newly industrializing countries cannot work if all, or the great majority of, developing countries seek to pursue export substitution [export-led growth] at the same time' (Singer 1984: p. 294). Let us now consider these matters in some more detail.

The Neo-classical Orthodoxy

The neo-classical position is that, by comparison with a free-trade regime, a regime of tariffs, quotas and exchange controls implies high effective protective rates (ERP's) for the import-substitution activity and a net disincentive for exports. The outcome is to reduce growth and worsen the functional distribution of income between capital and labour. This is because, by the Heckscher–Ohlin–Samuelson Theorem (Heckscher 1933; Ohlin 1933; Samuelson 1947), trade restrictions would lower wages, increase the unemployment rates, raise the rental on capital and increase the underutilization of capital. But, by the Stolper–Samuelson Theorem (1941), such a policy would lower (raise) the relative and absolute rewards of the abundant (scarce) factor in all the trading countries. The first-best (neo-classical) answer to the problem is, therefore, simply to liberalize trade, remove restraints on imports—especially the quantitative restrictions (for example, quotas) which subvert the market—replace these by 'tariff-equivalents' and then gradually lower (even abolish) the latter as well. Simultaneously, it is recommended that the multiple exchange rates be 'unified' by an appropriate devaluation of the domestic currencies of the developing countries vis-à-vis the US dollar and the unified exchange rate allowed to find its 'own level' in the market—as if going down (the drain) is their currencies' appointed fate! That done, the government should leave the rest to the Ricardian Law of Comparative Advantage and the Heckscher–Ohlin–Samuelson Theorem to sort out such intricate issues as repositioning (even relocating) the production structures of each trading country according to what each can produce best (at least cost), ensuring an equitable sharing of the gains from trade (and investment), and apportioning factor rewards (between labour and capital) in the fairest possible manner.

Thus, trade-liberalizing reforms are expected—as surely as the light of the day follows the darkness of the night—to usher in the 'first-best' configuration of production and consumption along the lines of each (developing) countries' comparative advantage, to increase the real wages and employment rate and to reduce the rental on capital by encouraging labour-intensive exports activity at the expense of the relatively more capital-intensive import substitution activity. True, trade liberalization opens up the inefficient domestic manufacturing activity to the wintry blast of foreign competition, but it eventually makes it more efficient, encourages exports, and attracts foreign capital to fill in the gap between domestic saving and investment. An important property of this first-best result is that it entails only minimal, well-focused state intervention in the domestic sphere and lets free trade flourish in an environment where a 'thousand flowers bloom'.

However, the neo-classical position is seen by development economists as resting on thin ice. This is illustrated by the examples given below. First, the first-best result will, for instance, not hold if there are unexploited opportunities to exercise monopolistic/monopsonistic powers in trade, in which case the optimal solution is to set tariff exports/imports at the 'right' rate. Second, this result will also not hold if the implied assumption of perfect tradability is relaxed to envisage a realistic situation in the developing countries where goods are only imperfectly tradable. The apparently second-best remedy for this scenario—import-substituting industrialization to achieve 'dynamic comparative' advantage—is essentially the optimal one, given the initial imbalances in their economic position vis-à-vis that of the developed countries. Thus, *selective* state intervention would let developing countries garner the long-run benefits of increasing returns to scale in the information and human-resource intensive industries, which promote growth by encouraging learning-by-doing and larger R&D expenditures (Grossman and Helpman 1994). Here is an example where first-best policies, which let the time-honoured principle of (static) comparative advantage work unhindered, are likely to be positively harmful because these expose developing countries to the enervating 'Dutch disease'—one that forces developing countries into a growth-reducing Hechscher–Ohlin low-equilibrium trap so that they continue to specialize, even if not exclusively, in a handful of labour-intensive industries. Such policies may be helpful initially, but are more likely to promote 'immiserizing growth' through an adverse movement of the terms of trade (Bhagwati 1958). They also inflict a permanent damage on these economies by 'decoupling' them from technological progress, and by preventing the production of high-productivity industries. In other words, it is no longer true that free trade is always (or even mostly) superior to sophisticated state intervention (Krugman 1987; Naqvi 1999).

Export Expansion versus Import Substitution

Knowing all this should lead one to question the liberalist emphasis on implementing the first-best policy prescription which, according to multilateral agencies (i.e., the IMF, World Bank and WTO), invariably means 'big bang' structural reforms that help export expansion, liberalization of trade and capital inflows, devaluation. Now, it is true that excessive protectionism, in the form of heavy tariff and non-tariff import restrictions, has to some extent imposed significant domestic resource cost (DRC) on developing economies—especially in India and Pakistan during the 1960s and 1970s—by fostering inefficient industrialization, including industries with negative value added through overvalued exchange rates, supported by stiff exchange controls. The net effect of such import restrictions has been to preserve a margin of protection for the import-substitution activity by keeping the domestic prices of imported goods significantly higher than the c&f prices and to impose a welfare loss on the society (Little, Scitovsky and Scott 1970; Naqvi 1971; Bhagwati 1978; Krueger 1978). Worse still, a continuation of these policies, well past their announced goal of letting 'infant industries' grow, has led to the opposite result. Large-scale smuggling, induced by high import restrictions and heavy export subsidies, has had the paradoxical effect, at least in Pakistan, of *lowering* the domestic prices of imported goods below the duty-paid import prices. This, in turn, has adversely affected the growth of domestic industries (Naqvi and Kemal 1997).[3]

These results suggest that, rather than favouring export expansion at the expense of import substitution, the logical recommendation should have been a neutral trade policy to minimize the foreign-trade distortions and promote a first-best allocation of domestic resources (Bhagwati and Ramaswami 1963; Johnson 1964; Naqvi 1969, 1971). Yet, the most recommended liberalist policy has been vigorous export expansion, implying that the incentive structure should be reversed in favour of export expansion and against import substitution industries. This is because the welfare cost of excesses in export expansion activity are much less than those in import substitution activity (Krueger 1978), greater exports lead to a higher GDP growth (Michaely 1977; Balassa 1978) and the profits made by exports are a surer indicator of efficiency than those earned on domestic sales (Stiglitz 1996b). This reasoning is, however, faulty for the simple reason that a *correlation* between the rate of growth of export shares and the growth rates of GDP does *not* decide the issue of *causation*. Is it the faster GDP growth that causes greater exports, or is it the other way round? A 'diplomatic' answer to this question has been that perhaps it works both ways (Harrison 1975) and the empirical evidence here *may* be read as favouring export-led strategy! The fact, however, is that it is simply not possible to resolve this (statistical) problem in a simple straightforward fashion, because the amounts countries trade in are not determined exogenously. As a result, 'correlations between trade and income *cannot* identify the effect of trade'. True, there may be other complicated ways of determining the positive effects of GDP growth on exports by spurring the accumulation of physical and human capital, by increasing output and by increasing factor productivity (Frankel and Roemer 1999). Yet the fact is that the issue of causation still stands unresolved.[4]

However, even assuming that export expansion is invariably growth-promoting, the question is, should development policy be biased in favour of export expansion and against import substitution? Further, does the creation of such an export bias 'prove' that it maximizes growth, and, for that reason, can free markets be deemed superior to state intervention? The second question can be quickly answered in the *negative* because such a policy reversal simply shifts the locus of state intervention; it does not aim to lower or abolish it! At any rate, circumstantial evidence has shown conclusively that the import substitution syndrome has generally been associated with higher-than-trend growth rates in India, Pakistan and China, not to speak of the East Asian Tigers (Bruton 1998). It has also proved that 'unbridled competition particularly among unequals has never, by itself, delivered faster growth and shared prosperity even in today's developed countries, and it has at times been destructive' (UNCTAD 1999: p. 1). This evidence also confirms the reasonableness of the Singer–Prebisch hypothesis cited above.

The first question will be explored in detail in Chapter 9. At present, it is sufficient to note that the empirical evidence on this issue is not even suggestive, let alone decisive. The fact of the matter is that 'export fetishism' hurts more than it helps (Rodrik 1997). On the other hand, the countries which have import substituted *first* and exported later have generally done better than those (for example, the African countries) which ventured directly into exports (Linder 1961). Moderately outward-looking and moderately inward-looking strategies have also worked equally well (Stern 1989). Further, in a dynamic setting, both import substitution and export expansion have been necessary, with the former usually preceding the latter and 'laying the foundations for successful export performance (Streeten 1985: p. 58). Indeed, 'outward orientation cannot be considered as a universal recommendation for all conditions and for all types of countries' (Singer and Gray 1988: p. 403). Note that the export bias displayed by the Tiger economies cannot be cited as a model of liberalism. On the contrary, the practice of dumping through market segmentation by making the domestic consumer pay significantly more for the same product than the foreign consumer is more an example of mercantilism than of trade liberalism. The argument that this latter-day strong export bias in some sense may have cancelled the earlier equally strong import substitution bias—thus creating conditions approaching the first-best state of bliss promised by Pareto optimality—is really stretching Vilfredo Pareto's meaning a little too far.[5] The most sensible policy option, therefore, is *not* to choose between these strategies 'because each must be taken to the margin of advantage' (Lewis 1984a: p. 122). The point is that, as noted at different places in this book, development success (for example, in East Asia) has meant administering significant doses of 'efficient' state intervention in order to maximize the gains from foreign trade and investment and ensure faster-than-trend rates of economic growth.

Free Markets, Income Distribution and Equality

Free Markets and Income Distribution

As noted above, the (fictional) regime of competitive efficiency implies a set of shadow (*not* market) prices, which have all the analytical characteristics of profit, wages and rent. If these prices are set equal to each factor's marginal (revenue) product then, by Euler's Theorem, the total output will be exactly apportioned among the factors of production in cases where the production function is linear and homogeneous of degree 'one' (i.e., constant returns to scale obtain). As no (Marxian) surplus output is left over, no exploitation of labour (or capital) is possible—mathematically, that is. Also, as labour markets are eventually fated to clear, there is no possibility of (involuntary) unemployment when the bliss configuration of input and output (shadow) prices prevails.

A related train of thought is as follows. The Fundamental Theorems of Welfare Economics assert not only that every perfectly competitive equilibrium is Pareto optimal, but also that for some distribution of endowments to be determined, every Pareto optimal state is a perfectly competitive equilibrium. The second part of the theorem is important. Does the market ensure that the initial distribution of endowments among the economic agents is equitable? And how does it do so, if at all? The neo-classical answer is that if lump-sum or some other non-distortionary transfers could be made by the gainers to the losers from a change, and if there were still some leftovers, the change in question is unequivocally efficient. Indeed, since no conflict of interests and preferences is recognized, there is no room left here for distributional issues. A faint assurance about the alleged equity of the state of bliss comes from economists like Coase (1960), Buchanan and Stubblebine (1962), and others, who argue that the Pigovian market failure to (re)distribute property rights takes place not because of some inherent defect of the market mechanism, but because such rights are not adequately defined. Hence, it is shown that in a game-theoretic framework, the outcome of a bargaining process about property rights will be Pareto optimal and efficient, and probably equitable as well if property rights are properly defined and freely exchanged. The Pareto optimal situation, according to this line of thinking, will be attained by moving onto a new 'contract curve' through bilateral trading between parties.

Let us examine these arguments. First, as Robinson (1979) points out, the Marxian thesis about the exploitation of labour by the capitalists—that wages and the competitive rate of profits are directly linked with 'surplus value'—is in no way vitiated by the neo-classical fiction about distributing total output according to the marginal productivity theory, which, in turn, does not make a clear distinction between the sources of income and the factors of production. Regarding the Hicksian socially costless lump-sum 'payments' by potential gainers to potential losers from a welfare-raising change, it may be noted that such lump-sum transfers that 'could be made' are never in fact made—following the ascetic tradition of new welfare economics! Indeed, the possibility of such transfers is raised simply as a measuring device to show that an aggregate increase in welfare is possible, even desirable. But this is neither here nor there. If the welfare of those who lose because of the change is to be *actually* increased, then such transfers should actually be made. This is because, on moral grounds, the loss of some cannot be justified by showing that others may have gained more.[6] But such irrational concerns (*because* these are moral) seldom attract the attention of the neo-classical 'liberals'.

Second, it has been shown, for example, by Bowles (1985) that market equilibrium is characterized by (involuntary) unemployment because the wage rate actually paid by the employer exceeds the market clearing wage. This may happen in the rural areas to avoid labour shortages in the peak season (Bardhan 1988) and in the urban areas to economise on on-the-job training costs (Shapiro and Stiglitz 1984). Malinvaud (1984) shows that the most observed unemployment is of the involuntary (disequilibrium) variety, mainly because of the non-existence in the real world of a market-clearing wage rate. He, therefore, concludes that in general, 'permanent market clearing is an untenable hypothesis'. Also, in the Harris–Todaro model, the equality of (expected) wages fails to clear the (urban) labour market, so that equilibrium in a segmented labour market coexists with urban unemployment, which, in turn, is fed by continuing rural-urban migration (Khan 1987a).

Third, for market efficiency to lead to an equitable redistribution of the existing *legally sanctioned* private property rights, the transaction costs are assumed to be zero. But, since bargaining is invariably a costly and time-consuming affair, this assumption will seldom be met, if at all. With positive transaction costs—especially those incurred to keep the free-riders out—the familiar externality scenario will arise, which the market is unable to cure (Furubotn and Pejovich 1972). A more fundamental point is, in the Coase–Buchanan type solution, it is essential that to choose the 'optimum' each individual makes available information about his/her initial endowments to provide a basis for choice among various Pareto optimum states. But such information is hardly ever voluntarily revealed truthfully by economic agents without violating the ground rules of a decentralized regime of free markets. One of these ground rules is that the individual utility functions are not known to each other and that there is no mechanism available to the market to make an individual reveal the information about his/her utility (production) functions to another individual. That being the case, Arrow (1979) shows that 'a procedure which would achieve a Pareto efficient allocation if each agent knew the other's utility function will have a positive probability of falling short of efficiency if this knowledge is absent.' And since such knowledge is absent, it follows that a Pareto optimal solution secured through the bargaining process will neither be efficient nor improvable! Thus, it is not true that a departure from the Pareto optimal state must reduce the aggregate utility (Sen 1987).

This last result is also relevant for examining the question of private property rights—whether the market process, by itself, will lead, à la Coase, to an equitable distribution of (initial) property rights.[7] Arrow (1979) shows that such an outcome depends crucially on the (unstated) assumption that the players in a cooperative game know every other player's payoff—utility, profit, whatever—as a function of the strategies played. But, as shown above, the exist-ence of such knowledge is contrary to the rules of the competitive markets. And even if the initial distribution of resources is unequal, the Pareto optimal solution attained can be one marked with an equality of resources if secured through the bargaining process. *Given the identity of consumer's tastes*, such a solution will be envy-free and equitable (Varian 1974). But the consumer's tastes are hardly ever identical. There is an even more fundamental point, made by Arrow (1972)—the definition of private property rights based on the price system points to the essential non-universality of both. Thus, to the extent that the price system is incomplete and non-universal it needs to be supplemented by some kind of implicit or explicit social contract. Such a contract, however, can only be enforced by the government, perhaps partly by propagating the virtues of voluntary behaviour.

Free Markets and Equality

A central value judgement must, therefore, be made in the poor countries to guide them towards greater equality of distribution of income and wealth between different classes of the society, espe-cially between the vocal rich and the voiceless poor, in order to form supportive coalitions of diverse interest groups holding different views on social, economic and moral questions. Such prob-lems routinely arise in real-life societies by 'giving equal weight to the equal interest of all parties' (Hare 1982) and by always assign-ing the same weight to all individual interests (Harsanyi 1982). An explicit commitment to some such ideal is essential, so that both the costs and the benefits of social change are equitably shared and are seen so by all classes of society. But free markets are insensitive to the heterogeneous claims of diverse social groups, who do not even aim at anything resembling economic equality. Indeed, within the neo-classical scheme of things, such an ideal cannot be pur-sued because the efficient working of the free markets requires dis-tributional insensitivity of Pareto optimality and remaining loyal to the age-old consensus about the illegitimacy of interpersonal comparisons of the utilities of different people in the society. But the promotion of equality as an explicit objective of policy entails a conception of social good, which involves non-minimalist state intervention and the making of interpersonal comparisons of individual utilities (welfares). In particular, it takes changing the basic structure of the society, as defined by the pre-existing configuration of private property rights, which, as noted above, is a job beyond the reach of the Invisible Hand. (This issue is pursued at length in Chapter 7.)

Notes

1. According to these arguments, the development experience of the last four decades—especially of the 'Gang of Four', namely, South Korea, Singapore, Taiwan and Hong Kong—is seen as supporting the liberalist vision. Citing the contrast between free markets and centrally-planned economies, and the recent disavowal of the socialist economic philosophy by Eastern Europe, Haberler concludes: 'I still maintain my early belief in the validity of classical or neo-classical theory and in the superiority of relying largely on competitive markets and private enterprise' (Haberler 1988). In the same vein, *The Economist* (London) declares: 'After three decades the experience of these countries [shows that] history chooses the invisible hand' (Crook 1989). Thus, it is alleged that development economics, born with an interventionist birth mark, is a discredited discipline. But, as shown in the text, such empirical 'truths' lie only in the eyes of the neo-classical beholder!

2. See, also Jones and Sakong (1980), and Pack and Westphal (1986) in addition to the references in text.

3. In Pakistan, the structure of protection has given birth to all kinds of freak cases—industries in which the value added is negative or close to zero, those that are inefficient and yet protected, and efficient ones that are negatively protected (Naqvi and Kemal 1991). Also see Naqvi (1964, 1966), and Bhagwati and Desai (1970) on the adverse effects of quota restrictions (import licensing) on the economies of Pakistan and India respectively.

4. One rather complicated statistical method is to use 'geographical factors as a proxy for identifying the effects of trade on income'. Using this method, 'the relation between the geographic component of trade and income suggests that a rise of one percentage point in the ratio of the GDP increases income per person by at least one half per cent' (Frankel and Romer 1999). However, the method used, though ingenious, would not unambiguously decide the issue raised in the text because there are many other ways, in addition to the geographic factors identified in this study, through which trade affects income and vice versa.

5. Findlay (1988) calls such appeals 'Pareto optimality by inadvertence'.

6. Graaff (1989) makes the same point: 'What does it help to say that, although several men will starve, the cost to the society is low, because they *could* be given sufficient food to prevent their starving?' (p. 254).

7. This result, due to Coase, is often referred to as the Say's Law of Welfare Economics (Calabresi 1968).

Part III

Morality and Development

6

A Moral Perspective on the Market Success and Government Failure Debate

Chapters 4 and 5 provide a fairly complete analysis of the mixed-economy foundations of development economics, emphasizing the fallibility of the Invisible Hand and the inevitability of some government intervention to keep the process of economic development on course. To this end, we have evaluated the free-market gospel according to Friedman (1968), Lucas (1972) and Becker (1983), and their criticism of the neo-Keynesian position on macroeconomic management. The task in this chapter and the next is to highlight, in the same vein, the ethical character of our discipline. We begin this analysis by examining the 'normative' arguments of the uncompromising liberalists, rather the libertarians—for example, Buchanan (1986), Hayek (1960) and Nozick (1973)—who prejudge generalized government failure because it, by definition, compromises economic and political individual liberties. It will be shown that while their unrestrained free-market advocacy does not offer a plausible approach to development problems, it has one positive lesson for development economics: it focuses attention on the importance of selecting an appropriate social-choice rule—one that seeks to relate social (collective) decisions to individual views and choices in a *non*-dictatorial fashion. This is important because social good in a democratic set-up is not taken as independent of the preferences of its individual members. This has been accepted from the beginning of development economics. Thus, the success of development policy has been seen as dependent on the formation of effective development-oriented coalitions to bring about the right kind structural change.

However, it will be argued in this chapter that the public choice theory does *not* necessarily provide a 'normative' argument against the government—certainly not against a mixed-economy set-up. To this end, we first pinpoint the limitations of an essentially positivist Pareto optimality principle, which guarantees market success *and* government failure. This analysis is followed by an examination of the relevance to development economics of other collective choice rules—the justice-as-fairness criterion of Rawls (1971) and Sen's (1992) capability calculus—which emphasize the need for a consequentialist non-utilitarian moral perspective *and* a non-minimalist government to address difficult development problems like enhancing the quality of social justice, and reducing poverty and economic deprivation *because* amoral free-market solutions do not provide a correct approach to these problems.

Government Failure and Universal Market Success

Rather familiar is the *failure* of free markets to work optimally in the presence of 'externalities' in production or consumption—on the tacit assumption that the government will succeed in doing what the markets cannot do. But the liberalists—led by such luminaries as Friedman, Hayek, Lucas, Becker, Nozick and Buchanan—turn this argument on its head to assert, instead, the government failure (and market success) in optimizing social welfare. Such arguments are evaluated in this and the next sections.

Chapter 4 examines at length the positivist, liberalist, anti-government argument that government intervention is fated to be harmful *even* in cases where the markets are generally expected to fail. Hence, according to them, a one-way shift from government control to free market is the only safe route to achieve both economic growth and equity, for the simple reason that government intervention is itself responsible for the less-than-full realization of these policy objectives. It imposes a deadweight 'efficiency loss' on the economy arising from policy-induced distortions in resource allocation. Further, responding to the lobbyists, it seldom works to maximize social welfare. The reference point of these arguments is invariably the Pareto optimality of the competitive solutions, which alone are held to be efficient.

Pareto Optimality as Collective Choice Rule

The oft-cited collective choice rule to prove market success is the Pareto optimality principle. It is, therefore, not surprising that a non-satisfaction of this rule is considered as a sufficient, argument against government and some liberal (and liberated) development economists prefer the allocational principles based on the principle of Pareto optimality to development economics. The observance of this rule is held to be desirable on the ground that it alone is efficient, fair and liberal—efficient, because it is unimprovable; fair, because it insists on reflecting unanimity about the preferences held in a society in any scheme of social judgement; and liberal, because it preserves liberty, which is the basic value to be cherished by all civilized societies, regardless of what other objectives are valued by them. In this dispensation the government is strictly given the task of removing the institutional and attitudinal impediments to the free flowering of competitive equilibrium. Thus, the passion for Pareto optimality is not only held to be rational, but it is also regarded as the only civilized option for all societies, rich or poor.

The Efficiency of Pareto Optimality

This principle lays down that while comparing two states of the economy, if the utility of everyone increases in the event of a change (or, at the minimum, the utility of at least one individual rises) without a reduction in the utility of any other member of the society, this state will be efficient.[1] The anti-*dirigiste* 'temper' of the rule follows from the First and Second Fundamental Theorems of Welfare Economics, which establish a two-way link between competitive equilibrium and the Pareto optimum (for more details, see Chapter 7). Thus, if efficiency is the only objective of public policy, government intervention is redundant because an economy in competitive equilibrium is Pareto optimal and, by definition, unimprovable.

But the story is too good to be true in its entirety. The fact is, if Pareto optimality should become the ultimate social objective to be aimed at (and much of modern welfare economics is based on such a weird premise), that particular woebegone society will have in store for its members, especially the poorer ones, a very parsimonious feast. The reason, as noted above, is that Pareto optimality is held to signify unanimity, which comes about through a voluntary agreement among individuals with diverse interests and aspirations. This principle, according to Buchanan and Tullock (1962), and Buchanan (1986), plays a central role both in political decision making and also in economics. While this makes Pareto optimality a reasonable proposition, it in fact does not work as expected because such outcomes may as well be the socially unjust ones and can also be seen as signifying unanimity *against* changing an unjust state of the economy. But in this case what is preferred may not be the desired outcome demanded—at least not voluntarily—by the actual or potential voters. More importantly, even a voluntary, but passive acceptance of the Pareto optimality rule does not guarantee that it would be endorsed if other, more acceptable options were available.

The rule is deficient in respect of efficiency because it does not work in the presence of externalities, the ubiquity of which in the developing countries (as also in the developed countries) has been widely noted. A typical case is that of public good when the free rider cannot be excluded from its consumption through the market mechanism. Since, in this case, it is in everybody's interest to understate the benefits one expects from the consumption of such a good, a public project producing it will be defeated in an open election even though it is advertised as maximizing social welfare. Since the provision of public goods is a crucial element of the investment programmes in the developing countries, Pareto optimality will typically lead to lower growth as well as equity. The rule also fails to deliver efficient solutions in the absence of a complete set of contingent markets, when the non-existence of strategic behaviour on the part of economic agents cannot be reasonably assumed, or if markets in possession of only incomplete information do not adequately perform their signalling duties—all instances of market failure which are the rule rather than exceptions in the real world. And, in the absence of well-developed capital markets with inadequate risk sharing and pooling, which is almost always the case in developing countries, no significant entrepreneurial activity such as Schumpeter (1934) envisaged will take place.

The 'Fairness' of Pareto Optimality

There are many in-built characteristics which deny Pareto optimality the 'fairness' attribute.[2]

1. The Pareto optimality rule is distributionally neutral partly because it does not recognize any conflict of interest among members of the society, and partly because in its 'eyes' the equal and extremely unequal outcomes are equally preferable! It should be obvious that, with this definition of neutrality, one cannot meaningfully make judgements about the crucial development problems of income distribution. Thus an economy at a Pareto optimum could carry on with a good conscience if those who are deprived of the basic necessities of life, such as food, cannot be made better off without depriving, even modestly, the rich of their not-so-hard-earned wealth (or income). Another property of such an elitist state of bliss is that the society is indifferent to the multiplicity of Pareto optimum points along a given contract curve. Can such a state of bliss be regarded as one in which the poor will also get their due? The answer is that we do not know because Pareto optimality points are neutral with respect to any reasonable distributional considerations, including those relating to poverty.[3]

2. To the Pareto optimality rule, the rich and poor look the same! This follows from Benthamite utilitarianism, which regards social welfare as an increasing function of personal utility levels alone. It denies admission rights once and for all to any type of *non*-utility information and holds that individual utilities are non-comparable. But these very characteristics incapacitate the Pareto rule—which accepts the utilitarian calculus—to *differentiate the rich from the poor* even in broad daylight for the simple reason that to be able to do so one will need to do some interpersonal comparisons of welfare and use non-utility information as well.[4]

Pareto Optimality and Individual Liberty

Does Pareto optimality preserve individual liberty? The answer is firmly in the negative because it is impossible for a Paretian liberal to be really his/her own self in any substantive sense! This follows from Sen's (1970a) 'Impossibility of the Paretian Liberal', which demonstrates the incompatibility of the Pareto principle—both in its strong and weak forms—with even a minimum demand for individual liberty. Assuming an 'unrestricted domain' (U), Pareto optimality (P), and 'Liberalism' (L), Sen demonstrates that 'there is no social decision function that can simultaneously satisfy U, P, and L'. Here liberalism—or more accurately, libertarianism—is defined in a very elementary sense of recognizing the attendant individual's privilege to have a minimum of, what Hayek (1960) calls, every individual's 'protected sphere'. Thus, for instance, each individual should have the freedom and the opportunity to make 'at least one social choice, for example, having his own walls painted pink rather than white, other things remaining the same for him and the rest of the society.'[5] The implication of Sen's Impossibility Theorem, which modifies Arrow's celebrated Impossibility Theorem, is quite disturbing. It shows, that given the assumption U—that is, every logically possible set of individual ordering is included in the domain of the collective choice rule—Pareto optimality cannot be combined with even a minimal dose of liberalism. Indeed, if Pareto optimality is followed to its logical (bitter) end, then 'society cannot let more than one individual be free to read what they like, sleep the way the prefer, dress as they care to, etc., irrespective of the preferences of others in the community.'[6] It may seem, therefore, that even to be able to breathe freely one may have no option but to free oneself from the smothering embrace of Pareto optimality! The only other option left to avoid this impossibility is to go for dictatorship, but that does not even recognize the (marginal) utility of free breathing!

It follows from the preceding analysis that the Pareto rule precludes economists paying any attention whatsoever to the problems of liberty, income equality and poverty. Consequently, they may specialize completely on efficiency, which too becomes an elusive objective to achieve when informational asymmetries and imperfections are common sights, as is almost invariably the case in the developing countries (see Chapter 7). Also, Pareto optimality does not generally permit a conjunction of individual and collective rationality, especially in conditions of uncertainty (Hausman and McPherson 1993). This simply illustrates the point that the Pareto rule is not a universally true principle of collective choice, which retains its validity irrespective of the nature of the society and the basic objectives that it cherishes. But, for these very reasons, it will be suicidal for development economists to follow this rule in undertaking the difficult task of mobilizing diverse pressure groups and coalitions to implement a reformist development policy.

A Minimalist State?

We have already noted that the debate about the relative roles of government and the market is even more central to development economics than it is to Keynesian macroeconomics. It should be interesting to look at the normative arguments on this issue. Adam Smith (1976 [1776]) pleaded for minimum government because the selfish, uncoordinated actions of individuals will do the job of maximizing social welfare better than the government can. However, he was fully aware of the dangers of leaving it *all* to self-interested egotistic behaviour, if not duly constrained by moral and ethical concerns for the interests of the society. Such concerns are, however, not shared by some of his ardent followers. Thus, Buchanan (1986) advocates a research programme which is aimed to 'preserve a social order based on individual liberty' (p. 9), and insists that it can only be based on the Smithian utilitarian philosophy. Focusing on 'catallactics', the science of exchange, Buchanan pleads a return to Adam Smith because this is the only way to have in full view the 'principle of spontaneous order, or spontaneous co-ordination, which is, as I have often suggested, perhaps the only real 'principle' in economic theory as such' (p. 20). For that reason, 'economics should concentrate more attention on market arrangements.' One naturally asks: Is it possible that such an overwhelming concern with market arrangements be extraordinarily conservative? Buchanan does not think so, for the reason that 'choices in the market are not arbitrary, that there are narrow limits on the potential for exploitation of man by man, that markets tend to maximize freedom of persons from political control, (and) that liberty, which (is the) basic value, is best preserved in a regime that allows markets a major role' (p. 5). Within the Buchanan–Smith catallactic framework, economic power becomes meaningless when markets are perfect and competitive. Buchanan, therefore, posits a normative judgement that 'voluntary exchange among persons is valued positively, while coercion is valued negatively', from which arises 'the implication that the substitution of the former for the latter is desired...' (p. 22). From this normative judgement, it is a short step to assert the 'failure' of the government, which appears to him to be exercising power to force a non-voluntary agreement among economic agents and which, for that reason, should be confined to making 'constitutional choices' made by self-interested behaviour.[7] He, however, does not address the question as to how effective—even meaningful—the voluntary exchange would be when, for a variety of reasons discussed below, the relevant markets are missing or non-universal, or when they collapse completely.

Nozick's (1974) moral argument for a minimal (or shall we say Lilliputian) state is, however, based on the principle of the priority of individual rights and autonomy. In this deontological view, rights violation is absolutely forbidden: 'Individuals have rights, and there are things no person or group may do to them (without violating their rights)' (p. ix). He declares that 'the state may not use its coercive apparatus for the purpose of getting some citizens to aid others, or in order to prohibit activities to people for their own good or protection' (p. ix). From this follows Nozick's main assertion that 'moral values involve side constraints on action rather than merely being goal-directed' (p. xi). State action is justified *only* if it is confined to the prevention of the violation of the individual's rights. However, it is morally wrong for the state to do anything *positive* to stop rights violations. By the same token, unfettered markets represent the best social and economic arrangements because they avoid interfering with the individual's moral rights. Here we have what is perhaps the strongest case for the market and against the government on moral grounds. Nozick extends Locke's justification for a system of free markets based on the principle of mutual advantage, which allows free exchange and promotes division of labour, and is for that reason alone the 'best alternative' to a hypothetical state of nature characterized by non-cooperation. He goes further and maintains that, by virtue of its inherent quality of non-interference with the individual's rights, a market system is superior to any other system of cooperation even if the latter can be shown to be the most advantageous.

Taken literally, these arguments do not add up to much. Surprisingly, they rest on no systematic proof—heuristic or formal—in support of their advocacy of the unfettered rights of private property, the justification for which rests solely on procedures and rules framed by the state to regulate the processes of the acquisition and transfer of holdings that secure individual autonomy. But, as Allen Buchanan (1985) notes, they ignore the fact that the individual's voluntary exchanges in the market, though they be morally unexceptionable in isolation, may nevertheless be cumulatively de-equalizing. Justice would, therefore, demand that some limitations be placed on the inequalities created as a result of the cumulative effects of individual exchanges. Furthermore, the existence of these rights does not indicate that it would be appropriate to exercise them through self-interest behaviour (Sen 1987).

Nozick also maintains that any state action to alleviate absolute or relative poverty, such as by subsidizing the consumption of the poor and taxing the income and wealth of the rich, is illegitimate because it conflicts with the individual's (procedural) moral rights. This is stretching the logic too far for its own sake. Also, it is scarcely desirable that the state create a given pattern of distribution of holdings by elaborate rules and procedures—which, according to Nozick, must be considered sacrosanct by all individuals and groups and by the state—and yet forswear the right to change this distribution pattern, even if the consequences turn out to be socially abominable. To maintain that the state can create an unfettered Frankenstein's monster through some legitimate procedure, and further, that it cannot be destroyed even when this creature spells destruction for the entire society, would be to confer an incredible degree of sanctity on rules and procedures per se. Both common sense and universally held mores and social norms contradict the view that individual moral rights against coercion are virtually unlimited. At any rate, 'taking liberty to be the fundamental value does not automatically commit one to a rights-based view of morality or to the view that rights rarely obligate others to give positive assistance' (Hausman and McPherson 1993: p. 703). For this absolute lack of trade-off of rights against all other social values, Nozick's theory has been criticized for being 'libertarianism without foundations'—a criticism with which it is difficult to disagree.

Yet another anti-dirigiste argument—which, though essentially positivist, also has normative overtones—is that government probably could help achieve the social optimum, but will not do so because governments represent and serve vested interests (Becker 1983). This may be too narrow and cynical a view of government.

Notwithstanding their penchant for underhand politicking, governments do have a 'conception of national interest' (Miliband 1983). Further, especially in a democratic framework, there are potent pressures from the public (with no regular vested interests) to make the government act in the national interest. Indeed, if this were not the case—and if democratic governments did *nothing* but legislate and implement vested interests—the link between democracy and economic progress would be broken. Furthermore, such cynical views of the state do not explain how, over time, different interventionist states become development states in some cases, though not in others. The explanation seems to lie in the ability of the development states to insulate economic management from wasteful rent-seeking activities. Even in cases where such insulation is not achieved, it would be naive to suggest that leaving the process to the market would solve all problems. As Bardhan (1988) notes, 'the very reasons why insulation is infeasible are often also the ones which will make first-best policies inoperative, and in the absence of lump-sum redistribution, a policy of relative inaction may be distributionally unacceptable' (p. 66).

The 'Invisible Foot'

A new set of arguments about the innate tendency of the government to fail are used by the development economists of the new-fangled Neo-classical Political Economy school. Using strictly positivistic reasoning, they assert that the all-pervading government intervention in the economic process has led to the creation of the rent-seeking activity (Krueger 1974) and to directly unproductive profit-seeking (DUP) activities (Bhagwati 1982), which entail a wastage of real resources when measured against the efficient Pareto optimal state. Brock and Magee (1984) have used the metaphor of an (inefficient) 'Invisible Foot', which tramples all over the (efficient) 'Invisible Hand'. This odd vision is but another name for the government, which is seen as preventing the forces of free competition from maximizing social welfare through the (unproductive) activities of rent-seekers. Thus, a shift from the market to the government imposes an avoidable deadweight loss on the economy.

This line of thought is not convincing because it assumes market processes to be without cost in terms of providing the necessary information for making production decisions. This position is hard to defend, especially because the information provided by the market is typically incomplete, misleading and costly. Also, as North (1984) points out, 'there is no meaningful standard of Pareto efficiency possible, since one cannot specify a least-cost structure of government for any given level of output.' Even more damning for this line of thinking is that since competitive equilibrium will seldom be Pareto optimal (i.e. efficient), the size of the loss imposed by rent-seeking activity will, at best, be indeterminate.

Market Failure and Government Success

Pigou (1932) clearly spelt out the circumstances in which the market 'fails' to optimize social welfare and the implications this failure has for the government's behaviour. Briefly, external economies (and diseconomies) and public goods drive a wedge between marginal social and private benefits (and costs) and prevent the market from sending the right price signals to economic agents. Because of this lack of 'information', a regime of perfect competition fails to optimize social output i.e., to achieve the first-best constellation of production and consumption. Under these circumstances, the government must, therefore, intervene in order to remedy this informational deficiency of the market. A more modern reformulation of the Pigovian position links market failure to a situation when market-clearing occurs 'without all mutually advantageous bargains having been struck' (Graaff 1989). This proviso is always satisfied in the presence of strategic behaviour, when transaction costs, that is, the costs of getting all parties involved in a negotiated settlement, are positive and high.

Scitovsky (1954) has discussed at length the phenomenon in the context of technological externalities, which provide a strong argument for fostering industrialization and allocating saving among alternative investment opportunities in developing countries.[8] He notes that, to the 'general rule' that the private profitability of investment is a reliable indicator of its social profitability, 'the exceptions are too great and obvious to be ignored, especially in underdeveloped countries....' He then concludes that 'the proper coordination of investment decisions would, therefore, require a signaling device to transmit information about present plans and future conditions as they are determined by present plans, and the pricing mechanism fails to provide this' (p. 306 in Agrawala and Singh (1963). The case of public goods—discussed in the preceding section, illustrates the problem of market failure even more clearly. Public goods—for example, the operation of military establishments, the administration of justice, the provision of free education—have been defined by Musgrave (1959) as 'goods and services, whose inherent quality is such that they cannot be left to private enterprise.' According to Samuelson (1966), the central feature of a public good, characterized by non-rivalrous consumption, is that 'each individual's consumption leads to no subtraction from any other individual's consumption of that good.'[9] But, because of this inherent plasticity of public good, it is in each individual's interest that all contribute to the production of such good. Further, each individual would also be better off if only he did not pay for its consumption. Here we have the problem of the 'free-rider' getting away with his anti-social antics because of the impossibility of excluding a non-paying person from the consumption of the (public) good through the market mechanism. This property makes it difficult to devise (voluntary) co-operative strategies to make the free rider pay for his 'lunch'. But, as Olson (1965) shows, when communities are large, voluntary co-operative agreements among individuals will not solve this problem, and the phenomenon of free riding will lead to the under-production of the public good. In extreme cases, the intensity of free-riding may break the horse's back! Government intervention is clearly indicated in all such cases, which, however, does not necessarily prejudge the form and the mechanics of state intervention.

Alternative Social Choice Rules

Let us now turn to a consideration of alternative social choice rules which share the main concerns of development economics and are more adequate to meet the needs of developing countries—that is, their emphasis on the element of morality in an individual's behaviour, doing social good, creating the right kind of institutions to let the individual's native genius flower and according priority to help the underclass in the society. There are many such rules, which are discussed at length in Mueller (1979) and Sen (1970, 1992), but only three of them are presented here. These rules register cases of systematic departures from the self-interest principle in the pursuit of altruistic *and* not so altruistic objectives, and also provide normative arguments for a non-minimalist government. There are important differences regarding the exact form that such intervention should take, and its frequency and intensity—whether it should be confined to the making of fair rules within which individuals should pursue their interests as they see it (the Rawlsian position), or whether it should be doing a more substantial job of maximizing the good of the individual and the society (Sen's position). But all these rules share a distrust of the unregulated markets maximizing social welfare *all by* themselves.

Harsanyi's Social Welfare Function

Within the utilitarian framework that underlies the Pareto principle, Harsanyi (1977a, b) admits the possibility of making interpersonal comparisons of welfare, which is not allowed by neo-classical economics, and treats these as factual propositions. The motivation of Harsanyi's research is to provide an insight into how collective decision *ought* to be made, while preserving impartiality. To this end, Harsanyi postulates that the individual's preferences are divisible into personal preferences and moral or social preferences. In making known his/her moral preferences, an individual is supposed to reflect the preferences of every other individual by putting himself/herself in the position of the other. This is made possible by postulating that an individual (or, more accurately, the 'impartial spectator') has an equal opportunity of being any other individual. The high point of Harsanyi's utilitarian model is his success in deriving a social-welfare function as a weighted average of the individual utilities. The remarkable aspect of Harsanyi's proof is that, unlike the Pareto principle, it explicitly achieves the result on normative grounds. The additive form of the welfare function denotes the highly individualistic motivation of the model, namely, that *every* individual's welfare matters.[10]

Two points should be noted here. First, the Harsanyi individuals are not the exclusively egotistic individuals with Paretian idiosyncrasies. Instead, they are individuals with moral sensibilities as well who wish to make their decisions in an impartial fashion. Second, if the world is such that the Harsanyi individual's decisions carry a significant weight, as opposed to those of the Paretian individuals, it would be very different from the one that the liberalists prefer. It would be a world where the Invisible Hand of the market is not the only reliable purveyor of the good things of life—or, strictly speaking, of a specific (weighted) sum of the *utilities* of such goods—and where the ubiquity of the moral objectives that a civilized society must aim to achieve is neither a sign of incurable irrationality nor paves the 'road to serfdom'.

Rawlsian Collective Choice Rule

Unlike the Pareto rule, Rawls rejects utilitarian philosophy and the social welfare function approach based on this philosophy.[11] Thus, if the Harsanyi individual, in his passage from his initial self-interested state to another moral state, does *not* carry over any of his characteristics in the initial state (as Harsanyi requires) then what can it mean to say that a self-interested individual *becomes* a moral individual? In general, we cannot 'evaluate another person's total circumstances, his objective situation plus his character and system of ends without reference to the details of our own conception of what is good' (Rawls 1971: p. 174). The most distinguishing feature of the Rawlsian analysis, which makes it especially attractive to development economics, is its insistence on the creation and establishment of just (and progressive) institutions where the extant 'basic structure of the society' is an obstacle in achieving justice with fairness. Within the framework of such institutions, collective decision-making will ensure a just 'assignment of fundamental rights and duties', and a morally right 'division of advantages from social co-operation'. Unlike the Paretian approach, which condones actual welfare losses of some if these can be (notionally) compensated by the potential gains of others, the Rawlsian theory does not allow for such tradeoffs as socially meaningful or desirable: 'Justice denies that the loss of freedom for some is made right by a greater good shared by others' (p. 4).

In the Rawlsian view, central importance is attached to maximizing the welfare of the least privileged classes of the society. This view is consistent with the priority he ascribes to liberty as a society progresses to higher stages of economic development. In addition to his two basic principles of justice noted below, Rawls makes the following important point: 'Now the basis for the priority of liberty is roughly as follows: as the conditions of civilization improve, the marginal significance for our good of further economic and social advantages diminishes relative to the interest of liberty…' (p. 542). In this perception, as Mueller (1979) points out, Rawls sees 'liberty essentially as a luxury good in each individual's preference function' (p. 232). The implication of such an approach is that individual liberty is a reward for a progressive restructuring of the basic institutions of society to facilitate economic progress, with the proviso that the needs of the least privileged are met first. In other words, individual liberty is defined as incorporating a system of rights in such a manner that it is preserved, indeed maximized, if in turn, as a result of the working of social and political institutions, the needs of the least privileged are met—no matter what else is met—in all states of the economy (also see Chapter 7).

The Rawlsian framework is based on the fundamental notions of 'Justice-as-Fairness' and the 'Difference Principle'. The former requires that individuals choose just rules from a hypothetical 'original position' of complete equality. Analytically speaking, this 'original position' is reached by stepping through a 'veil of ignorance' that hides from the individuals in the original position all the advantages that may accrue to them from their own decisions. This analytical procedure highlights the basic importance of impartiality in ensuring that the rules of justice so chosen are 'fair'. The acceptance of the Justice-as-Fairness principle entails that:

1.   'Each person is to have an equal right to most extensive basic liberty compatible with a similar liberty for others'; and

2.   Inequalities are arbitrary unless they 'are both (a) reasonably expected to be to everyone's advantage, and (b) attached to positions and offices open to all'[12] (Rawls 1971: p. 62).

Given these principles, the Difference Principle is used to select just institutions and distinguish them from unjust ones in such a manner as to maximize, in a lexicographic fashion, the welfare of the worst-off individuals in the society.

The operational part of the theory is the concept of the 'primary social goods' that all individuals demand no matter what else they do—that is, 'liberty, opportunity, income and wealth, and bases of self-respect'—which are used as indices of human well-being. The 'Justice-as-Fairness' principle demands that these goods be distributed equally 'unless an unequal distribution of any, or all of (them)... is to every one's advantage', and the Difference Principle requires that the 'least-disadvantaged draw the greatest benefit' from holding these goods[13] (Rawls 1971: p. 303).

Sen's 'Functionings' and 'Capability'

The definition of an individual and his/her social well-being, and the evaluation of well-being in terms of a greatly widened informational base are Sen's central contributions to development (*and* mainstream) economic thinking. He weans us away from achievements *per se* of commodities, utilities, 'primary goods', or 'resources' to focus on the constitutive elements of living—that is, on 'functionings' and 'capability'. This taxonomy rests on the 'assessment of well-being *and* the freedom to pursue well-being'.[14] The functioning is a point in the space to which it belongs and it consists of elements that constitute persons' well-being—for example, being healthy, being educated, being able to walk among one's fellow men/women without a sense of shame—so that its evaluation proceeds in terms of its many constituent elements. Related to these is the 'capability' to function, that is, to achieve different *feasible* combinations of functionings. Formally, it represents a set of feasible vectors, which for a person is his/her capability set. Thus, capabilities are valuable because they enable people some sort of a functioning. However, capabilities may also be desired for their own sake, especially for giving individuals the freedom to choose from the available alternatives.

The point of this approach is to focus 'on substantive freedoms that people have rather than on particular outcomes with which they end up' (Sen 1992). However, while both the concepts are integral parts of Sen's analytical scheme, one can for all practical purposes proceed in terms of the capability to function once the desired functionings have been explicitly stated.[15] There are two reasons for this.

1.   The freedom to choose, which is such a vital element of Sen's theory, is *not* a functioning; it is rather related to the capability set. Thus, the capability set may be relevant 'for the *level of well-being achieved* and not only for the freedom to achieve well-being' (p. 49).[16]

2. Achieved well-being (a functioning) is itself dependent on the capability to function because the act of choosing may itself be a part of living!

The significance of the capability calculus from the theoretical as well as the practical points of view can be made clear by the following considerations. First, Sen's analytical apparatus has significantly greater cutting power in analyzing the poverty problem than say an income-based analysis (which sees it in terms of the lowness of income alone) because 'poverty cannot be dissociated from the misery caused by it'. Further, deprivation is 'ultimately a lack of opportunity to lead a minimally acceptable life', which is influenced by a number of considerations other than income, and which is not adequately (and sometimes not at all) registered in a utility measure of what would be accepted as good life. In other words, it is 'important to go beyond income information in poverty analysis, in particular, to see poverty as capability deprivation' (Sen 1999: p. 361), and to move out of the shadows of the utilitarian calculus—especially to deal with cases of 'entrenched deprivation' which may not at all show up in the utility barometer—even though a person may be 'quite unable to be adequately nourished, decently clothed, minimally educated, and properly sheltered' (Sen 1992: p. 55).

Second, at a more general level, the capability calculus brings to notice the important relationship between the ends and the means of development, so that the success in the achievement of means (say, an increase in per capita income) is evaluated in terms of what it does to increasing the level of well-being of the people (making them healthier, more literate, etc.).[17] Also, we now know that there exists an essential interpersonal variability in the connection between income and well-being.[18] By the same token, a satisfactory answer can be given to the all-important question as to why poverty should be regarded as a social evil irrespective of the prevailing inter- and intra-country disparities between income and expenditure patterns, especially between the poor (say, Bangladesh) and the rich nations (say, the United States). The insight here is to translate relative deprivation into absolute deprivation by moving from the income space to the capability space (Sugden 1993).

Thirdly, as noted in the beginning of this section, the capability analysis greatly enlarges the informational bases of the analysis relating to the development problems; it also explicitly recognizes the essential *plurality* of our concerns and objectives. Thus, unlike the utilitarian calculus, which converts all kinds of economic deprivations (gains) into the loss (or gain) of utility (which too is confined to the inevitably vague mental-state experiences), the capability approach aims to bring out the inner sense of deprivation that the utility measure muffles and hides, by seeking information about the many interpersonal diversities of circumstances which separate means from the ends. This is because the 'indigent peasant who manages to build some cheer in his life should not be taken as non-poor on grounds of his mental accomplishment' (Sen 1999: p. 362).

A few more aspects of the capability thesis are discussed in subsequent chapters, but here let us note a couple of problems with this thesis, which somewhat restrict its reach and salience. First, in this competition between the means and ends of development, which Sen's analysis has intensified—especially, that between the income-related variables and those indicating a person's capability (and his/her freedom to do so) to convert income into specific functionings mentioned above—the means are likely to get somewhat overshadowed by the ends. This is a dangerous trend at a time when the developing countries are increasingly falling behind in their bid to catch up with the developed because of the former's weaker performance with respect to growth[20] as well as on the capability scale. Thus, de-emphasizing the centrality of achieving high rates of economic growth—which incidentally, is the primary mover of the wider development process—is also unwise in view of the adverse European experience with low growth and the associated high rates of unemployment which have led to a wave of crime, morbidity, suicides, political turmoil, etc., even though these countries still rank the highest on the capability scale. This shows that the means to some extent have a dynamics of their own, and these should not be neglected. This is because the income-related improvement in capabilities does not always get reflected (at least not adequately) in the 'hard-core' capability indicators like education and health (Anand and Sen 2000). Also, in specific situations of extreme starvation and famine, income deprivation caused by a drastic fall in the real wages of specific classes of workers who suffer prolonged and severe unemployment may become much more important than capability deprivation (Dreze and Sen 1989).[21] It should be obvious, then, that *economic development is related to both the means and the ends, but it does not necessarily coincide with either.*

Second, there are three important problems with 'operationalizing' the capability calculus: (a) There is the problem of 'weighting' different capabilities and functionings, which are vectors with many elements. This raises a complex index-number problem, which requires settling on the weights to be attached to each of the diverse elements of these vectors (Hausman and McPherson 1993). (b) Yet another important practical issue relates to evaluating the authenticity of the individual reports about their personal *incapabilities,* which prevent them from efficiently converting income into the metric of the desired level of well-being. The informational limitation here is very significant and so is the cost of collecting such information. Needless to point out, some of these seemingly authentic *incapability* reports may form an unsuitable basis for public policy.[22] (c) At least so far, there is no operational metric for the capability approach like the one that exists for the real-income framework (that is, the metric of exchange value), and 'for the Marshallian consumer theory, combined with the Kaldor–Hick compensation test' (that is, the metric of cost-benefit analysis) (Sugden 1993). To this, Sen would reply that it is fallacious, even counterproductive, to accord unifocal priority to just one operational metric: 'the domain of social valuation cannot be taken over by some kind of an allegedly value-neutral engineering solution' (Sen 2000).

A part of the reason for these ambiguities may be the absence so far of a systematic capability theory.[23] This, in turn, points to the need for undertaking this research programme on the vastly expanded informational base that Sen's way of thinking has encouraged (for example, in the form of the UNDP's *Human Development Reports*); that will probably happen in good time.

To conclude, the public choice perspective presented in this chapter shows that the debates now rocking development economics— about freeing it from the clutches of a sterile government that invariably fails to deliver, about making it more 'scientific' by letting it metamorphose into neo-classical economics (which slavishly obeys Pareto optimality like it would a Divine Law), and about emptying it of any remnants of ethical and moral concerns for the sake of achieving scientific rectitude—are really non-debates. These are not even 'scientific' because they fail to recognize the central importance of a widely accepted system of moral values for making scientific statements. They are also myopic because they stick to only one decision-making rule—namely, Pareto optimality, which is unrepentantly neutral with respect to various states of the distribution of income and wealth—which disqualifies it from becoming a basis (much less the sole basis) of a sensible development policy. However, it is also important to explicitly recognize that *there is no such thing as an ideal or sure-fire system of collective choice rules that works equally well at all times, in all societies and for every possible configuration of individual preferences.* On the other hand, a plurality of collective choice rules is required for translating individual preferences into social preferences. Such rules are deeply coloured by the ethical and moral norms widely shared by the society. Hence, an intelligent evaluation of these rules is only possible through an understanding of their relativity to the nature of the society. This matter is explored in some more detail in Chapter 7.

Notes

1. If there are states of economy *a* and *b*, and there is at least one person who prefers *a* to *b* while everyone else is indifferent to both *a* and *b*, then *a* is Pareto-wise superior to *b*. Pareto optimality is satisfied if in set A there is no alternative which is Pareto-wise better than *a*. On this definition, used in the text, everyone in the society is indifferent to both *a* and *b*. (Sen 1970b).

2. However, the Pareto optimality rule takes on a relatively more 'benign' look when interpreted as a 'core' or a 'value', in that these formulations stipulate a perfect redistribution of property rights (Khan 1991). But the equity credentials of the rule become suspect once equity is defined in a more natural sense—à la Rawls—of the redistribution of property rights and income in accordance with the needs of the least privileged in society.

3. Let us understand the meaning of 'neutrality'. Following Sen (1985), suppose there are two states *x* and *y*. The neutrality property demands that if (*x*, *y*) is replaced by (*a*, *b*) in everyone's preference ordering, then we must do the same in social ordering as well. In other words, for making a social choice it does not matter what the nature of *x*, *y*, *a* and *b* is—all that matters is the existence of individual preferences over these states. The problem is posed in the following manner: suppose *x* = equal division of cake, and *y* = nothing for person 1 and equal division for persons 2 and 3. According to the neutrality property, it does not matter if *x*, *y* are replaced by *a*, *b*. Let *a* = nothing for 2 and 3 and all for 1, and *b* = equal division. Neutrality demands that *x* is socially preferred to *y*, if and only if *a* is socially preferred to *b*.

4. To clarify the remarks in the text, it would be best to quote from Sen (1979): 'Can we identify the rich from the poor through the observation that they have more utility than the poor? Not in the Arrow framework, since interpersonal

comparisons are not admitted. Perhaps as those with a lower marginal utility of income? No, of course not, since that will go against *both* non-comparability and ordinalism. Can we then distinguish the rich as those who happen to have more income, or more consumer goods (nothing about utility need be said), and bring this recognition to bear in social judgements? No, not that either, since this will go against welfarism (and against strict ranking-welfarism), since this discrimination has to be based on non-utility information.'

5. Sen (1999) distinguishes between the 'opportunity aspect' of liberty (the one discussed in the text) and the 'process aspect' of liberty. The former is essentially concerned with the effective realization of liberty in one's personal life, and with highlighting the possible conflict between Pareto opimality and the opportunity to enjoy liberty in one's personal life. In contrast, the 'process aspect' may leave us 'incharge of choices over private domain, no matter what we may or may not believe (as a person).' This latter aspect is also important, but it fails to take into account 'the effectiveness of the realization of liberty' (p. 364).

6. Sen (1970a) warns: 'If someone takes the Pareto principle seriously, as neo-classical economists seem to do, then he has to face the problem of consistency in cherishing liberal values, even very mild ones.'

7. Buchanan's work has led to much work on the consequences of alternative constitutional regimes, on the assumption that individuals are guided by self-interest in both economics and politics.

8. A technological externality may be defined as 'the indirect effect of consumption activity or a production activity on the consumption set of a consumer, the utility function of a consumer, or the production function of a producer' (Laffont 1991: p. 112). A related concept is that of pecuniary externality, one that works through the price system. However, the relevant definition used in the text is the one that relates to a technological externality, which defines a market failure.

9. An important example of public good is the acquisition, development and provisioning of improved seed varieties (due to green-revolution technologies) (World Bank 1999).

10. A multiplicative form would not achieve this result because it would give a life-and-death power to an individual who wishes to wipe out the preferences of all the other individuals in the society by simply assigning a zero value to a specific social outcome.

11. Rawls's work is perhaps the most complete modern exposition of the contractarian philosophy of Rousseau, Kant and many others.

12. The conditions listed in the text have been modified somewhat in Rawls's later writings. Thus, in 1982, his first principle has been weakened somewhat by substituting 'a fully adequate scheme' for the 'most extensive total system' demanded in the text. Also, 'under conditions of fair equality of opportunity' is emphasized in the first element of the difference principle.

13. Rawlsian primary goods are divided into 'natural' primary goods and the 'social' primary goods (cited in the text). The former goods (for example, health, intelligence) are the property of the individual (though the *income* from them is not).

14. It should be noted that unlike Nozick who is restricted to guarding 'negative freedoms *from*...', Sen's emphasis is on securing 'positive freedoms *to*.... The

classification of freedom (liberty) into positive and negative is due to Berlin (1969).

15. Of course, Sen advises against disrupting 'the neat structure' of (a) *functionings* achieved being related to the achievement of well-being, and (b) the capability to function being related to the *freedom* to achieve well-being'. (Sen 1992: p. 50)

16. However in an earlier exposition (Sen 1988), freedom is also considered a functioning.

17. A supporting insight into this means-ends relationship is provided by a mathematical result due to John Roemer (1986) that 'equality of resources implies equality of welfare'. In other words, it says that the worth of *resources* be evaluated in terms of what it *yields*.

18. This interpersonal variability may exist due to one or more of the following reasons: (a) It may arise from interpersonal diversities. For example, an ill and handicapped person would need more income, primary goods and resources than a healthy person to convert them into the same metric of well-being. (b) There may be environmental and climatic diversities to affect such conversion of income into capabilities between nation and within nations (c) there may be diversities related to the customary patterns of consumption in specific societies, both rich and poor.

19. An important fallout of this widening of the information base is to make possible interpersonal comparisons of welfare as an important evaluating technique to judge the change in the well-being of the people due to specific measures—something that Robbins (1932), and following him the entire neo-classical profession, would not allow. For details of the aspect see Sen (1999).

20. Baumol (1991) underscores the centrality of the efforts to catch up with the richer countries for *both* the developing and the developed countries: 'we have also seen the importance of the subject even for the industrialized economies when their performance is surpassed by that of the other nations' (p. 7). Incidentally, Baumol notes that mainstream economics is, at present, ill-equipped to handle such growth-related problems!

21. It may be noted that employment has been duly recognized as the channel through which GDP growth impacts on human development (and, in return, capability improvement and human development impact on GDP growth) (UNDP 1996). The experience of Sri Lanka, which has been cited as a shining example of attaining some vital functioning (high literacy and longevity), also shows the same. A very high rate of unemployment (of about 15 per cent or so) has greatly compromised its success in the achieved functionings and led to such problems as morbidity. Yet another star performer on the capability scale (that is, the Indian state of Kerala) has done poorly in terms of providing adequate levels of housing and nourishment, and a relief from morbidity, all because of the lowness of income.

22. A gruesome example of such seemingly authentic incapability reports is the near-universal practice, in the South Asian region at least, of the beggars inflicting near-fatal injuries on themselves to attract private and public charity.

23. Or, perhaps such an effort to construct a systematic theoretical foundation may not be forthcoming any time too soon. Sen (2000) thinks that the very lack of a general theory allows an openness in this kind of work—for example, in the preparation of the *HDRs*.

7

When Morals Matter

It should by now have become apparent that the literature on neo-classical economics as well as that on development economics, which claims to be truly positivistic and 'value-free' is, without doubt, barking up the wrong tree. This is because positivistic (factual) statements become objectively invalid if they are based on a wrong value perspective of the society (Harsanyi 1991). Even the so-called 'objective' statements made on the strength of Paretian philosophy, which is assumed to reflect the principle of unanimity, do involve a moral judgement.[1] Thus, it should be explicitly recognized that ethical and moral norms and values are needed *even* to achieve purely positivist goals—something that the self-interest principle cannot achieve. Thus morality can be fruitfully seen as a resource-saving way of keeping the free riders in check in the provision of public goods of all kind (Srinivasan 1988: p. 6). Furthermore, scientific rectitude, according to Hume's Law, requires that a community evolve widely-held concepts of right and wrong in order to be able to make propositions about what ought to be done, and to derive any prescriptive conclusions from empirical findings.

This chapter builds on the thesis presented in the preceding chapter—which is one of the central themes of this book—and argues that development economics in its next growth cycle must seek a creative symbiosis of ethics and economics, which can avoid both the Scylla of stony positivism and the Charybdis of unrepentant, non-consequentialist libertarianism. To achieve such delicate steering development economics must, however, be illumined by a meaningful and consequentialist moral-economic philosophy. In this context, it would be fruitful for development economics to view the justness of the basic institutions—social, economic and political—as linked both to the maximization of the welfare of the least-privileged individuals in society and to a net reduction in their numbers. Such a development philosophy has a clear political dimension: it should help create, in the words of Rawls (1985), an 'overlapping consensus' about the aims and direction of the development process. To this end, it would seem natural for development economics to break out of its self-imposed anti-ethical shell and live normally—without losing its soul or scientific content—in a world where 'rationality' cannot meaningfully be taken as a synonym for self-interest, and where a moral concern for others would be seen as reflective of normal human attitude, not as a sure sign of irrationality. It would also be normal for development economics to be sensitive to the economic and moral consequences of the exercise of specific individual rights. This is because the central problems that afflict developing countries—attaining high rates of growth, aiming at greater equality, reducing poverty, raising human development—require promoting a just distribution of income and wealth, including that of the extant private property rights, among others.

Thus development economics should pay attention to the capacious public choice theory in order to secure its existence as a paradigm in its own right and enhance its theoretical rigour and practical relevance. This theory tells us that there are not one but several rules which seek to relate 'the individual to a collectivity' (Arrow 1977), the 'contents' of which are essentially shaped by the nature of the society. To set the stage for subsequent discussion, the next two sections are devoted to a consideration of the reasons for relating economic thinking to the universally accepted ethical mores in a society. Some of these issues have been raised in Chapter 6 in the context of the market-government debate, but here the motivation is to examine the moral foundations of development economics. In this context, we also note later in this chapter the irrelevance from the point of view of development economics of the strand of thinking which recognizes as sacrosanct the right of the privileged few to perpetuate the *status quo* with respect to an unjust state of the economy on the ground that doing anything positive about it would breach individual liberty.

The Morality of Development Economics

It is widely alleged that the amorality of economics was preached by Adam Smith, who laid down the maxim: 'It is not from the benevolence of the butcher, the brewer, or the baker, that we expect our dinner, but from their regard to their own interests' (Smith 1975 [1776]: pp. 26–27). Adam Smith, who also wrote the *Theory of Moral Sentiments*, has probably been misunderstood as issuing a call against relying on moral principles to explain the mysteries of the economic process.[2] On the contrary, he believed that 'inbuilt constraints derived from morals, religion, custom and education' are central to the working of the free-enterprise system (Coats 1971: p. 9). The 'credit' for putting economics into a positivist box goes to Robbins (1932), whose cult of ascetic positivism seems to have conquered the minds of neo-classical economics, depriving them of their heart![3] As intended, such scientific puritanism has made economics immune to ethical clamouring—but with the unintended consequence of making it immune to common sense as well. According to this line of thought, rational behaviour is taken as a synonym for self-interest maximization, so that any activity other than maximizing self-interest is considered to be irrational. Fortunately, however, such thinking is going out of fashion.[4] This trend should be noted by development economists, who need not be defensive at all about their 'natural' susceptibilities to moral concerns for fear of being treated as unscientific because 'the morality of economic agents influences their behaviour and hence influences economic outcomes'—a fact which should make even neo-classical economists interested in morality (Hausman and McPherson 1993: p. 673).

Selfishness and the Status Quo

As discussed at length in Chapter 6, the strongest status quo-preserving social choice rule is the efficiency-oriented Pareto optimality principle, which is also held by some as a moral ideal because it possesses the 'minimum-benevolence' property. Any existing state will, for instance, be unabashedly Pareto optimal if the conditions of the poor cannot be made better without worsening the living standards of the rich! The anti-reform property of the rule springs from its insistence on neutrality with respect to the distribution of income and wealth, with a view to preserving 'unanimity'. But the mere fact that a given state—for example, of 'entrenched deprivation'—is accepted sullenly by the poor, partly because the 'socially cultivated sense of contentment and serenity may even affect the perception of [deprivation]' (Sen 1999: p. 363), does not necessarily mean that it is also endorsed by them. On the other hand, political and social forces that sustain such a state will not, generally, have their active support. Further, the seeming endurance of an undesirable state of affairs will vanish with the appearance on the horizon of the first rays of hope of change in their uneventful survival.

The inherent conservatism of Pareto optimality, which admits of no externalities and public goods, and never falls prey to information lapses and asymmetries, is also highlighted by the First and Second Fundamental Theorems of Welfare Economics. The First Theorem is generally invoked to support unalloyed fealty to free-market solutions, because these alone are deemed unimprovable and efficient. However, development economics cannot afford unbending loyalty to such abstract ideals, because competitive equilibrium can coexist with glaring social inequities and extreme poverty (Sen 1987; Feldman 1991), and even with inefficiency (Stiglitz 1991). The Second Theorem appears to be more progressive, but here, as elsewhere, appearances can be deceptive. What it says is that under assumptions even more strict than those required for the First Theorem to hold—that is, quasi-concavity of utility functions and the convexity of production possibility sets—the Pareto optimal state will also approximate a competitive equilibrium, indicating a correction of the sub-optimal initial endowment patterns. However, such a happy confluence will follow only if people voluntarily furnish information about their initial endowments—a condition that is seldom, if ever, satisfied. Also, the Second Theorem seeks to do the implausible—that is, it judges alternative distributions while remaining neutral on distributive issues! This neutrality property, however, means that it cannot deal with problems of distributive justice and poverty. Its insistence on non-distortionary lump-sum transfers which need never be made, robs the rule of even its 'minimum benevolence' and renders it of little value for development issues, which require making large transfer of resources from the rich to the poor.[5] The rule does not fare any better even when extended (by Arrow and Debreu) to situations marked by uncertainty and inter-temporal resource allocation. This is because it requires that: (a) all economic agents be identically uncertain, (b) a complete set of contingent markets exists, (c) transaction costs be zero and (d) strategic behaviour be absent. True, with these assumptions, the Pareto optimality principle may become dynamically valid, but it amounts to little else because it is still incapable of handling even a little bit of 'reality' in the developed or developing countries. Thus, for example, many key contingent markets (for risk-sharing) may not exist, and the information available to economic agents is likely to be asymmetric, imperfect and costly. Further, instances of externalities may be too frequent to ignore and *public* goods may be badly needed even to be able to enjoy consuming *private* goods![6]

Altruism and Economic Change

Fortunately, the progeny of Adam Smith has not been too completely lacking in imagination to see that 'rational' behaviour need not be—indeed, is never—antiseptically self-centered, even though positive economics demands it and some development economists of neo-classical persuasion tend to accept it without question. Aristotle's advice—'we should behave towards our friends as we would wish our friends to behave towards us'—has not been entirely lost on economists. The central thrust of such arguments and proposed rules of behaviour is that selfish behaviour alone is not an adequate description of real life, and that moral considerations do influence human behaviour—and, if only for that reason, such rules are relevant to the conduct of *both* positive and normative economics. Also, the rule of law, based on equity and justice, is essential to prevent the economic agents, which do not always produce efficient outcomes because they are quite often fed by asymmetric and misleading information, from working against the interests of a civilized society.[7] The same qualification would apply to the somewhat starry-eyed view that altruism alone makes the world go round, because that would amount to trivializing the problem of social justice. In general, it is always a creative symbiosis of selfish and selfless behaviours which has accounted for success in the real world.[8] Such a symbiosis will serve development economists well by making available to them a larger canvas to work on.

Sidgwick's (1874) principle of 'equity' requires that 'whatever action any of us judges to be right for himself, he implicitly judges right for all similar persons in similar circumstances.' Harsanyi's (1977a) 'equiprobability model for moral value judgement', described in the previous chapter, also requires that the individual possesses not only personal preferences but also *moral* preferences. These moral preferences 'guide his thinking in those—possibly very rare—moments when he forces a special impersonal and impartial attitude, that is, a moral attitude, upon himself.' Hare (1963) equates equity with the property of universality of personal preferences, emphasizing that the individual's rational behaviour should not be any different when acting in 'similar circumstances'. The key insights of these models are that individuals are motivated to act both for personal and moral reasons, and that every individual's welfare matters. While personal preferences may be guided by the self-interest maximization rule, moral preferences reflect the Harsanyi individual's capacity to make an impartial moral value judgement by putting himself into another individual's position. This would satisfy the impartiality criterion for evaluating value judgements that he/she is not 'unduly influenced by (his/her) personal interests and personal preferences'.

Unlike the Harsanyi and the Hare rules, the Rawlsian choice rule rejects the monocentric focus of ethical philosophy on Benthamite utilitarianism, which measures well-being by the metric of (total) utility regardless of its distributional implications. Instead, it argues for a wider informational base to measure human happiness. The central concepts here, as described in Chapter 6, are: 'Justice-as-Fairness' and the Difference Principle. The point of these concepts is that free and equal citizens of a society should 'not view the social order as a fixed natural order, or as an institutional hierarchy justified by religious or aristocratic values' (Rawls 1985). Therefore, if the existing social order does not accord with the universally accepted notion of justice in a society, it must be changed by a system of voluntary cooperation between free and equal persons.

An important aspect of the Rawlsian conception, which should make it especially attractive to development economics, is that it is not a metaphysical but a 'moral conception worked out for...

political, economic and social institutions' (Rawls 1985: p. 224). This politically oriented conception seeks to create an 'overlapping consensus', which includes 'all the opposing philosophical and religious doctrines likely to persist in a democratic society', to guarantee social unity and secure 'the allegiance of citizens to their common institutions'—based on the 'public acceptance of a political conception of justice to regulate the basic structure of the society.' While there may be formidable implementational problems with operationalizing such a delicately balanced reformist agenda, its emphasis on maximizing the welfare of the 'worst-off' individuals—with a view to achieving a just distribution of the *benefits and burdens of cooperation,* while preserving individual freedom—should secure an 'overlapping consensus' about its basic objectives.

Sen's contribution to the social choice theory, also reviewed in Chapter 6, builds on the Rawlsian analysis in four different, though related, ways.

1. Like Rawls, Sen rejects the utilitarian unifocal concentration on the maximization of total utility metric as a measure of social welfare, irrespective of how it is distributed among diverse social groups and different individuals in the society. To this end, the informational base is widened by admitting non-utility information as well, to offer a fuller account of the social good than utilitarianism can and to evaluate social well-being in terms of the *plurarity* of its irreducible components. Also, like Rawls, he is sensitive to distributional and moral issues in restructuring the basic social institutions to secure greater social justice, especially for the underclass.

2. However, unlike Rawls, who focuses on the evaluation of rules using procedural values, Sen seems to develop a substantive account of the good of the individuals and of the society. Also, unlike Rawls, whose basic ideas (i.e., 'justice' and 'fairness') emphasize evolving a 'system of fair rules within which individuals with different ends can cooperate with mutual advantage', Sen's overarching concern is to emphasize the normative relevance of the considerations of social good (Sugden 1993). In this respect, Rawls echoes the contractarian–libertarian moral philosophy wherein 'priority is assigned to rights, rather than good' (Rawls 1985). On the other hand, Sen's analysis belongs to the welfarist (including the utilitarian)

tradition, which aims to maximize social welfare—that is, to do overall good to the society, while recognizing the individual's freedom to choose.

3.   Both Rawls and Sen emphasize the centrality of giving freedom to individuals to make choices and pursue their diverse objective in any account of individual and social well-being. However, Rawls equates well-being with the *means* to freedom by an equitable distribution of the 'primary social goods'—'rights, liberties, and opportunities, income and wealth and the social bases of self-respect, which every one wants irrespective of whatever else he/she wants'. By contrast, Sen moves away from the commodity space to the capability space, to what a person can in fact do or be. Accordingly, he is focused on the *extent* of freedom (and presumably also on how it is distributed among different individuals in the society). This is because there are significant inter-personal differences in the individual's ability to convert Rawlsian 'primary goods' into the individual's freedom of choice (see note 18, Chapter 6). Further, freedom is an *end* in itself, an intrinsically (and *not* only instrumentally) valuable element of human well-being. (A good society is a society of freedom.) Thus, the capability to pursue human well-being is itself a measure of social good. The point of this exercise is to shift analytical attention from mere 'achievements to the freedom to achieve'.

4.   In Sen's analysis the *externally given* Rawlsian 'primary goods'—or Dworkin's (1981) 'resources'—need to be converted into a (pluralistic) metric of human welfare *internal* to the individual. Such a conversion, by its very nature, is *not* identical for all individuals. Rather, it differs with interpersonal and inter-group variations of person-specific characteristics. This distinction is no linguistic hair-splitting because if we are interested in the freedom of individual choice then we have to look at the *choices* that the individuals do in fact have, given their external and internal circumstances.

With the Rawlsian conception of justice and Sen's capability calculus on its side, development economics will be released from the neo-classical confines of Benthamite utilitarianism, and the Paretian exclusive insistence on efficient states and individual selfishness which even some development economists have approved of in their unguarded moments. Development models should instead feature 'free and equal individuals', who think not only of their selfish interests and projects but also about the welfare of other persons, especially of the worst-off individuals in society. In them too, welfare will be measured by the availability of primary goods that are useful to everyone regardless of what his/her exact objectives are and by the capability of the individual to convert these goods into personal well-being. The aim of looking at the economic universe from the moral perspective is to restructure the basic social, political and economic institutions, which have a direct bearing on the individual's well-being and social welfare. Such a laudable aim need not be utility-maximizing at all, because radical structural change is likely to cause greater disutility to those adversely affected by such change than it would add to the utility of the underclass whose pleasure-sensing faculties may have been impaired by 'entrenched deprivation'.

On the Immorality of Moral 'Rights'

As noted several times in this book, an important purpose of introducing ethics into development economics is to put at our disposal the philosophical analyses which accord priority to moral 'rights' and freedoms. However, what is *not* needed are those theories (for example, that of Nozick), which insist that certain individual rights must be jealously guarded so that it is possible to exercise them irrespective of their (utilitarian) consequences. A moment's reflection should show that an unregulated exercise of certain rights—for example, the rights of private property—has a profound adverse effect on the basic structure of society. Thus, insensitive non-consequentialism can turn 'moral' rights into crass immorality. While rights do have intrinsic value, they cannot be treated (which is what the libertarians do) as an alternative to the notion of well-being.

Nozickian Theory of Entitlement

Nozick (1974), nicknamed by some as the rich man's Rawls, offers a theory of entitlement and 'historical justice'. As noted briefly in

Chapter 6, there is no conception here of promoting the good of the individual and the society by doing something positive to stop (even discourage) the violators, but only an uncompromising insistence on *preventing* an encroachment on individual's moral rights. Once the state enforces rules to safeguard negative freedoms, it has done its duty—the rest has to be done (or not done) by the individuals acting in their own interest. The theory is strictly, even heartlessly, deontological (that is, non-consequentialist) and procedural in that unlike the welfarists, it is *not* concerned at all with maximizing social good. While the holdings acquired through illegitimate means such as theft are not just, Nozick sanctifies with the attribute of justice any existing distribution of holdings that is based on legitimate procedures regarding the structure of property rights:

> *The general outlines of the theory of justice in holdings are that the holdings of a person are just if he is entitled to them by the principles of justice in acquisition and transfer, or by the principle of rectification of justice (as specified by the first two principles). If each person's holdings are just, then the total set (distribution) of holdings is just (p. 153).*

Nozick explicitly recognizes that 'past injustices' may shape 'present holdings in various ways', and also (though only in a footnote) that

> *if the principle of rectification of violations of the first two principles (the principle of justice in acquisition and transfer) yields more than one description of holdings, then some choice must be made as to which of these is to be realized. Perhaps the sort of considerations about distributive justice and equity that I argue against play a legitimate role in this subsidiary choice (p. 153).*

Having made this important observation, Nozick does not pursue the all-important question of the rectification of past injustices in acquisition, perhaps because he considers it as 'subsidiary choice'. Instead, he specifically rules out any 'patterning' of the existing structure of property rights, such as would be induced by deliberate government action, since doing so would constitute a violation of the individual's rights: 'From the point of view of an entitlement theory, redistribution is a serious matter indeed, involving as it does the violation of people's rights' (p. 168). That may very well be so, as in extreme cases redistributive polices may become arbitrary and oppressive. Thus, not every corrective action can be justified on egalitarian grounds, because 'past circumstances or actions of people can create differential entitlements or differential deserts to things' and are therefore morally justified. But if this position is taken literally, such a procedural view of distributive justice would, for instance, rule out any corrective action against the feudal structures of landholdings found in many developing countries today, just because the ownership titles were transferred legally, even though—as in India, Pakistan and Bangladesh—many such transfers were made by a colonial government to their local collaborators as a reward for their 'unsocial' services.

But such a view should not be acceptable. If, according to Nozick's principle, it does not matter how happiness comes about, what the sources of a given state of happiness are and how that happiness is shared—whether grabbed by a few or distributed more widely—surely, something is very wrong with our social vision. A dramatic illustration of the immorality and inefficiency of strict non-consequentialism is provided by the incidence of famines, which, in certain case, are a direct result of a legitimate exercise of legal property rights, and of the defence by the state of such rights.[9]

The Priority of Liberty

A common concern of the moral right arguments is their uncompromising insistence on liberty and an absolute lack of trade-off between it and other social (especially egalitarian) objectives. Thus, for instance, 'the right to life is the right not to be killed, it is not the right to be given sustenance' (Hausman and McPherson 1993: p. 703). Indeed, capitalism is the preferred arrangement because the separation of economic and political power ensures individual liberty as no other system does, and not so much because it delivers the goods (Friedman 1962).

Hayek (1960) advocates that individual liberty is assigned priority over all else. As to the problem of ensuring a modicum of distributive justice, he 'solves' it by denying even the need for doing anything positive about it. This is because, according to him, 'even the poorest today owe their relative well-being to the results of past inequality' (pp. 40–46) State intervention in such matters is morally undesirable because it paves the way for totalitarianism. Nozick views freedom as strictly negative; it takes the form of constraints on individual action only. Nozick rules out the possibility of an individual (or the state on his behalf) taking positive action to be able to correct the adverse consequences of other individuals indulging their rights. This is because 'individuals have rights and there are things that no individual or group of individuals may do to them.'

Buchanan (1986) shows that minimum government and unfettered markets follow from the moral argument that liberty has priority over all other values, presumably at all stages of economic development. Since only free markets, run by atomistic, profit-maximizing economic agents preserve individual liberty, such arrangements are superior to any involuntary arrangements reached through the government (see Chapters 5 and 6 for details). In this contractarian view, which is really more a method of arriving at a moral judgement than a substantive moral theory, the free markets are preferable because they basically represent a system of cooperation between individuals, which they can (voluntarily) use to their mutual advantage. The job of the government is only to organize an infrastructure of rules within which a liberty preserving system operates without any further hindrance.

All these arguments are designed to reinforce the libertarian *faith* in the price system, which is seen by them as offering 'the best possible avenue for the generation of support for free institutions'. It follows that individual liberty is to be accorded priority over all other social and economic imperatives, like ensuring a high rate of economic growth, equality in income and wealth, and providing basic amenities of life to the least privileged in the society. (As noted above, a similar view is also implicit in the Paretian principle.) However, this line of argument suffers from a fatal flaw, which is that it defines specific economic arrangements as voluntary or involuntary according to whether they are made through the market or by the government. It then proceeds to derive from this definition the conclusion that market arrangements are superior to those made by the government. However, this is not a logical result at all, but a restatement of a definition.

Moral Contents of Development Policy

Numerous examples are given below to illustrate the need for a clear (consequentialist) ethical vision to comprehend and solve the central development problems. Thus, what Robbins (1932) calls 'valuation and obligations' intermingle with 'ascertainable facts' to produce acceptable solutions for such issues. In other words, pure selfishness should be combined with 'benevolence' to make an adequate model of human motivation and conduct and to analyse key development issues meaningfully. A purely 'selfish approach' will dehumanize the perennial human problems of want, poverty and economic deprivation, and jeopardize their resolution for lack of a strong moral concern for the lot of the underclass. The rising incidence of world poverty and increasing inequalities between nations and within nations are proofs of the failure of amoral market solutions. Such solutions are expected to offer nothing more, and nothing less, than a catalogue of ineffective remedies, the only merit of which is that these are guided solely by the self-interest principle!

The Poverty Issue

Let us first consider the problem of poverty, the full magnitude and complexity of which is now being realized at the national and global levels. The 1995 World Summit for Social Development emphasized the need for planned action to address the multifaceted character of the problem on economic *and* moral grounds. It felt that the problem was too difficult to be left to the self-interest antics of the free markets, which gave little room to altruism, and that the tools of neo-classical economics were completely inadequate to analyse the poverty problem. With respect to the latter, Koopmans (1957) points out that neo-classical economics assumes 'each consumer can, if necessary, survive on the basis of the resources he holds and the direct use of labour, without engaging in exchange, and still have something to spare of some type of labour which is sure to meet with a positive price in any equilibrium.' Sen (1984) shows that the efficiency-oriented analyses of poverty (and famine), which focus only on the metric of *food availability* to model the 'survival' requirement, may be seriously inadequate in resolving the problem. The fact of the matter is that famines have occurred in (efficient and affluent) situations where food availability was not the problem. The villain of the piece in most cases has been the widespread 'entitlement' failure of the poor caused by a radical decline in the real incomes of the rural poor—due, for example, to the inflation of food prices—which, in turn, entails the denial of an elementary freedom to them. Thus, an adequate development model must feature the dynamics of income earning and purchasing power in addition to those relating to the supply of foodgrain.

To complicate matters, the poverty problem has a moral dimension as well. Thus, it cannot be comprehended, let alone be solved, if it is held—as Emperor Haile Selassie did during the Ethiopian famines of 1973—that '...wealth has to be gained through hard work... (so that) those who don't work starve' (cited in Sen 1992: p. 77). A religious attachment to this apparently innocuous principle meant that little state relief effort was forthcoming. This observation also illustrates the general point that an adequate resolution of the poverty problem is incompatible with the non-consequentalist moral rights theories (for example, that of Nozick) and that solving it will also take a compelling sense of moral commitment, beyond the reach of the self-interest calculus. Also required is a re-examination of the moral basis of property rights, which is related to the prevalence of the feudal structures of landholding—the title to which is acquired and transferred by the owners legally. But, as noted above, the very existence of such legal structures may, in some cases, be the root cause of extreme poverty, even of famine, in developing countries.

Reducing Inequality

Next to poverty, the problem of inequality—the yawning chasm between the economic or social position of some individuals in relation to that of the others in the society—is one of the most basic issues that development economics is concerned with. It makes poverty starker and harder to bear. Indeed, the two are related to each other. Thus, in the above-mentioned case of extreme social deprivation (that is, famine), the poverty problem can be seen as one of drastic inequalities in the capabilities of the famine victims in relation to those of the better off in the society, and also, in this case, of the great inequalities in the holdings of 'primary social goods' This relationship holds generally: 'other things being the same, poverty reduction is more difficult to achieve in unequal societies than in egalitarian ones' (*WDR* 2001).[10] It is, thus, appropriate that the 'quality' of poverty reduction programs is judged by reference to its inequality-reducing effects. This is because widening inequalities are unacceptable even when associated with some improvement in the lot of the poor, partly due to the 'envy' factor. The basic aim of an egalitarian order is, therefore *'raising the average level of welfare* and *reducing the differences'* (Tinbergen 1985: p. 175).

The Pearson Commission (1969) noted: 'the widening gap between the developed and the developing countries has become the central problem of our time.' The intensity of the problem has greatly increased since then in the wake of, and due to, globalization and privatization, which have led to a great concentration of wealth in the hands of only a few mega-multinationals. While the richest 20 per cent claim 86 per cent of world GDP, 82 per cent of world exports and 68 per cent of total foreign investment, the share of the poorest 20 per cent is just 1 per cent in all these respects. Worse still, a freer flow of goods and capital (but *not* of labour), which globalization of world markets has promoted, has only exacerbated the inequality problem worldwide (UNDP 1999).

Yet both the efficiency-oriented economic analyses and the non-consequentialist moral right theories make light of the problem. This apathy to rising inequalities within and between countries is largely caused by an insufficient understanding of the moral dimension of the inequality problem. To help see the ethical dimension of the problem clearly, let us note at the outset the inadequacy of some of the moral-right theories reviewed in this book. Thus, for instance, even the Rawlsian (maximin) principle of 'justice-as-fairness' is not an adequate principle of equality—even though the two are related in spirit if not in words. Thus, in recommending an improvement in the welfare of the worst-off individual(s) in all states of the economy, the Rawlsian principle does not put limits on the extent of the simultaneous endeavour by the best-off in the society to improve their lot. Hence, this criterion of justness may be consistent with a situation in which relatively small efforts to improve the welfare of the worst-off individual(s) are accompanied by immense favours towards the best-off, thereby widening the gap between the two! This result may follow even if the allowable inequalities in the Rawlsian system do work out to everyone's advantage. Hence, as Tullock (1986) points out 'the maximin principle of justice [as fairness] is *not* a plausible principle of *equality*, for whether or not such an alteration (in the basic social structure) would make that more *just*, it would certainly not make it better with respect to inequality.' He also dismisses the Rawlsian principle as a principle of redistribution 'because the Rawlsian method surely would not lead to less income redistribution than we now have.' However, this criticism is only partly valid because the Difference Principle imposes an egalitarian requirement on the distribution of the primary social goods, which include income. Yet there is a case for enhancing the distributive content of the Rawlsian maximin principle of justice, which should be made consistent with a reasonable degree of equality. One line of thought is to convert the ownership of Rawlsian primary goods, which everyone wants no matter what else he/she wants, into the (poor) individual's 'capability' to live well. Another approach is to link the degree of inequality in different states of the economy to the position of the worst-off individual(s) in those states with respect to inequality and further, to stipulate that for one state of the economy to be worse than the other, the welfare of the worst-off individual(s) must be worse within that state. However, the stipulation just mentioned becomes relevant only if the level of welfare of the worst-off groups is the same in alternative states of the economy. The intuitive meaning of this somewhat complex formulation is, however, quite clear: 'the maximin principle of equality would first have us maximize the relative position of the worst-off group, and then minimize the number of people in that group, as long as we were not thereby increasing the complaint of the remaining members of the worst-off group' (Temkin 1986).

Once the problem is defined in this way—relating inequality to the maximization of the lot of the worst-off individuals *and* to the minimization of the number of persons so situated, and/or to the incapability of different individuals to live well—it dispels much of the confusion surrounding the 'reasons for redistribution', which Tullock (1986) decries as 'chaotic'. He does so partly because he thinks that 'most people in discussing income distribution are extremely charitable. It is the amount they actually give away which is modest,' (p. 29); and partly because 'most of the (income) transfers in most societies, democratic or dictatorial, do not go to the poor. They go to people who for one reason or another are politically well-organized' (p. 30). There is some weight in Tullock's argument that it is mostly the politically vocal middle class and not so much the voiceless poor who get the most from income transfers caused by the state-sponsored social security programmes. However, this is not necessarily an argument for dismissing the issue, as Tullock does, but to rest the rationale for redistribution on sounder (consequentialist) moral grounds. Also, the 'fact' that charity is inadequate, or that it does not reach the poor, cannot be used to argue against increasing the volume of charity or ensuring that it does reach the target group. Nor does it prove that the value-neutral market solutions will accomplish these objectives better.

Competition, Cooperative Action and Distributive Justice

A direct outcome of the anti-moralist, efficiency-oriented analyses has been their exclusive emphasis on competition, and the price system—which essentially draws inspiration from the (now obsolete) Darwinan evolutionary process—as the only form of economic activity through which both private gain and social good are brought into consonance and maximized.[11] The importance of cooperative action is recognized in certain game-theoretic situations, but seldom as a star performer.[12] The non-consequentialist moral-right theories also eulogize the competitive solution on the ground that it preserves individual freedom. Not only that, in the Nozickian analysis this solution is considered superior to any other solution, including the one based on a cooperative strategy. Yet competitive behaviour may not lead to optimal social outcomes as: (a) due to asymmetry of information and it being incomplete and costly, a competitive solution will *not* even be Pareto optimal, and (b) by the Heisenburg principle, such behaviour may change the objective reality accordingly, which would make the task of structural reforms more difficult.[13]

The importance of cooperative action comes out more clearly in relation to the issues of distributive justice. Thus, Arrow (1972) while arguing against a reckless use of the scarce resources of altruisim, does recognize the non-universality and incompleteness of the price system, which for that reason must be supplemented by an explicit or implicit social contract. The Rawlsian concept of 'justice-as-fairness' rests on the overarching idea of 'society as a fair system of cooperation among free and equal persons' (Rawls 1985).

In such a social context, economic agents are concerned about the welfare of the other members of the society. It is through the cooperative action of such concerned individuals that 'just' social, economic and political structures can be created. This is particularly true of developing countries where structural change calls for cooperative action to resolve these problems in a satisfactory fashion, because 'if we jointly prefer a cooperative to a competitive one we have the ability to modify our society for the good of all' (Valen 2000).

On Equality

Another relevant issue on which both neo-classical economics and the non-consequentialist moral theories are evasive though it is high on the catalogue of development priorities is that of equality, which is the obverse of the inequality issue discussed above. Typically, the emphasis is on such (implicit) values as 'opportunity', 'rights' and 'liberty', but nothing significant, even relevant, is mentioned about equality, even though without it social cohesion and a universal (voluntary) participation in the development process can be threatened by poverty, and political and social stability. To clarify the fundamental issue of equality, which has been pursued since the days of Jeremy Bentham, it will be helpful to understand its centrality in any viable agenda for social reform.[14] It may be noted at the outset that equality between the rich and the poor does not mean *complete* equality. Indeed, no one, including Karl Marx, has ever suggested this. All that equality is meant to imply is that economic processes are directed to minimize, though not eliminate, the inter-class distributional differences as far as is economically and socially permissible. Perhaps, the most used (and misused) is the utilitarian concept of equality. However, it is inadequate because of its insistence on using the utility information only as an index of individual and social welfare, and because it is interested only in the maximization of *total* utility irrespective of how it is distributed between different individuals. This exclusive insistence on utility information, marginal and total, can lead to a situation in which more income is given to the less needy, simply because he is the hard-to-please type, and the poor person who is easily satisfied even with small mercies gets lesser income! But equally interesting information about a person's welfare is of the non-utility type—for

example, the possession of certain types of goods, or the possession of certain capabilities to do some basic things essential for
human survival. Thus, for instance, keeping in view some realistic
limits on information, one can settle for resourcist egalitarianism.
Accordingly, briefly recapitulated below are two such types of equality measures, which explicitly use the relevant non-utility information: (1) *Rawlsian equality* and (2) *Sen's basic capability equality*. Both
views are 'resourcist', in that the former takes the form of the possession of social primary goods, while the latter emphasizes outcomes and the freedom to achieve these, rather than the resources
themselves, as indices of human well-being. But both insist on an
objective notion of well-being rather than on a subjective one (for
example, the Benthmite pleasure-pain calculus).

1. *Rawlsian Equality:* As explained in Chapter 6, the central thrust
of the Rawlsian conception of equality is its focus on bringing about
institutional changes, such as to 'make the worst-off best-off'—
that is, such action would raise the welfare level of the worst-off
individual in the society as far as it is possible to do so (Rawls
1971). This is the so-called Difference Principle. Rejecting utility
as the basis of individual welfare, Rawls defines welfare in terms of
a bundle of 'primary goods', which are defined as 'rights, liberties
and opportunities, income and wealth, and the social bases of self-
respect'. Institutional arrangements, which guarantee the access
of the worst-off individuals to these primary goods, should be both
efficient and equal. The Difference Principle is held to be 'just'
because it is chosen 'fairly' in the 'original position' to ensure
impartial decisions about the structure of the society. Unlike the
utilitarian principle, Rawls allows interpersonal comparisons to
judge the fairness of the distribution of primary goods among
individuals because such comparisons are no longer confined to
the intangible and highly limiting mental-state comparisons in
the utilitarian calculus. Instead, he proceeds on a wider and more
tangible informational base.

2. *Basic Capability Equality:* There are many problems with the
Rawlsian principle of equality also because the needs (for primary
goods) of a disadvantaged person—say, a cripple or a sick person—
do not get registered at all in his calculus. The recognition of this
shortcoming leads one to go a step beyond the Rawlsian emphasis

on equality with respect to primary goods towards 'what goods do to human beings'. The focus here is on basic capabilities, rather than on the resources and primary goods which are merely means to the individual's freedom to achieve well-being (and not just happiness) and to secure equality and justice. Equality is insisted on with respect to such capabilities, which essentially represent the individual's opportunities to achieve valuable 'functionings' (Sen 1988). This notion is important because an equal command over resources may convert into unequal capabilities thanks to extensive human diversities, which show up most dramatically in the case of 'entrenched deprivation' (Sen 1992). As explained at length in Chapter 6, shifting attention from goods to capabilities has the advantage of explicitly making interpersonal comparisons of people's capabilities to convert the acquisition of primary goods into the metric of good life—something that the concept of equality fails to do. Making such interpersonal comparisons is vital because without them 'we cannot even understand the force of public concern about poverty, hunger, inequality, or tyranny...' (Sen 1999: p. 365).

Human Development

The insight that increasing material plenitude need not always translate into human happiness—certainly not to the same extent—seems to underly the UNDP's 'human development' conjecture, which insists that 'enriching the lives and freedoms of the ordinary people is fundamental' (UNDP 2000). It essentially seeks to eschew 'commodity fetishism' (a là Marx) and puts human beings 'at the center of the development process' in order to enable them to lead a minimally acceptable life (Streeten *et al.* 1981a). Further, it denotes an increase in the *quality* of life actually achieved and not just the *processes* through which it is achieved (Sen 1988; UNDP 1990). To this end, the search for happiness does not stop when per capita income has risen adequately. As noted in Chapter 6, these increments in income need to be converted into 'capabilities', which essentially signify the freedom to choose from a set of alternatives. Achieving such a comprehensive development success will involve, among other things, changing the structure of property rights into just forms, and making adequate provisions for greater education, health care and public goods of various kinds (for example, food security). All of these enhance human 'happiness and/or reduce human deprivations', and contribute to social and political stability. We will come to these issues in Chapters 8 and 9 but it suffices to note here that sustained human development is *inconsistent* with adherence to the following principles:

1.   *The Pareto optimality rule,* which is content with a state of economy where further Pareto improvements are not possible; which is distributionally neutral and inconsistent with individual liberty; which can live happily with extremes of riches and poverty; which is strictly market oriented and positivist in that such improvements stop when the economy achieves the 'first-best' state of competitive equilibrium; which insists that state action, if at all, need not go beyond making (notional, *not* actual) lump-sum, 'distortion-free income transfer to compensate the 'losers' from a change and, finally, which precludes reformist action to change the unjust structure of property rights that markets tend to perpetuate, and, to some extent, promote.

2.   *Benthamite utilitarianism,* which restricts human happiness to the (mentally experienced) metric of utility; which does not go beyond maximizing total utility, irrespective of its distribution among, say, the rich and the poor; which cannot distinguish the rich from the poor and which does not give admission rights to non-utility information in forming judgements about human happiness.

3.   *The Nozickian moral-rights philosophy,* which restricts the role of the state to ensuring 'negative freedoms' enjoyed by individuals; which considers distribution of income and wealth as an infringement on human freedom; and which advocates minimal government and free markets to maximize individual liberty that must be accorded priority over all else.

4.   *The strictly competitive market strategies,* which leave little room for cooperative action.

The above-mentioned perceptions of reality are inconsistent with the full flowering of human development because (with the exception of [2]) they require a minimalist state; and because they either do not have a moral basis (as in [1]), or have one that is inappropriate (as in [2]) or really immoral (as in [3]). The Prisoner's Dilemma case has been used to illustrate the shortcomings of 'strictly dominant' individualistic strategies, which lead each of the prisoners (that is, the economic agents) to follow non-cooperative strategies. Further, repeated simulation studies have shown that cooperative strategies ensure a superior collective outcome to that of the dominant individualist strategies. By contrast, the human development conjecture assumes a consequentialist approach, requires a non-minimalist state to maximize social good by ensuring equitable outcomes (and not just efficient outcomes) as the objective of economic policy, and insists that these be 'people-friendly' and not just 'market-friendly'. In the human-development perspective, non-utility information will be needed as well to be able to make interpersonal comparisons of individual welfare (which are not allowed by positivist analysis) with a view to measuring the differential impact of the acquisition of resources and primary goods (including income) on human capabilities. It would recommend cooperative action because strictly market-oriented, positivist, competitive strategies do not yield socially desirable outcomes.

Notes

1. As Sen (1970b) points out, 'unanimous value judgements may provide the basis of a great deal of welfare economics, but this is not so because these are not value judgements, but because these judgements are acceptable to all.'
2. Sen (1987) shows that, contrary to the popular view, Adam Smith was not an unrepentant votary of self-interest. 'The fact that Smith noted that mutually advantageous trades are very common does not indicate at all that he thought self-love alone, or indeed prudence broadly construed, could be adequate for a good society' (p. 23). For a 'balanced' evaluation of Adam Smith's economic and philosophical viewpoints, see Skinner (1989).
3. Robbins laid down that 'it does not seem logically possible to associate the two studies (ethics and economics) in any form but mere juxtaposition. Economics deals with ascertainable facts; ethics with valuation and obligations' (Robbins 1932: p. 148). To see how completely Robbins captured the minds of mainstream economics, one just has to read the following ode to selfishness by the Nobel Laureate, Stigler: 'Let me predict the outcome of the systematic and comprehensive testing of behaviour in situations where self-interest and ethical values with wide verbal allegiance are in conflict. Much of the time, most of the time in fact, the self-interest theory (as I interpreted on Smithian lines) will win! (1981: p. 176). It is quite another matter that no such empirical study has been done so far to show the triumphal march of unalloyed selfishness in a real-life economy!

4. Harsanyi (1991) pointedly remarks: 'there was a time when many economists wanted to ensure the objectivity of economic analysis by excluding value judgements, and even the study of value judgements from economics'. (A very influential advocate of this position has been Robbins, 1932.) Luckily, they have not succeeded; and we now know that economics would have been that much poorer if they had' (p. 704).

5. The very limited size of the resource transfers required by the Second Theorem seems to be adequate only to meet the requirements of a 'well-ordered society' assumed by neo-classical economics, which suggests that it is unfair to blame the Theorem for not doing what it is not designed to do. However, the development economists who demand the Theorem to do a development-related job must be blamed for sheer irresponsibility.

6. Recently, the Second Theorem of Welfare Economics has been extended to acknowledge the existence of public goods as well (for example, Laffont 1979). However, as Sen (1987) remarks, the informational requirements regarding the initial distributions of endowments of this extended result may be as daunting as that of the static version of the Theorem.

7. Thus, Keynes emphasized the need to save capitalism from itself by restricting private property rights by taxation (which incidentally, has already been done in Western democracies), and by allowing for appropriate state intervention (see Chapter 4). On the eventual beneficence of self-interest Keynes has this to say: 'It is *not* a correct deduction from economics that enlightened self-interest always operates in the public interest. Nor is it true that self-interest generally *is* enlightened...' (Robinson 1973: p. 81).

8. Empirical studies show that in the case of Japan—the most illustrious example of economic success based on a free-enterprise system—qualities like group loyalty, goodwill, sympathy and respect for others have played as much a decisive role as pure self-interest maximization behaviour (Sen 1987).

9. Sen (1984) cites such a case: '...in guarding ownership rights against the demands of the hungry, the legal forces uphold entitlements, e.g., in the Bengal famine of 1943 the people who died in front of well-stocked food shops protected by the state were denied food because of lack of legal entitlement and not because of their entitlements being violated' (p. 458).

10. Rising inequalities also make the task of poverty reduction much more difficult. Thus, a recent ODI (Overseas Development Institute) study shows that 'high inequality countries need over twice as much growth as the low-inequality countries to reach the target of cutting poverty by half by the year 2015 (Hanmer *et al.* 2000).

11. The great 'virtue' of the so-called 'red-in-tooth-and-claw' world capitalism, practiced by the MNC, is that it is characterized by cut-throat competition.

12. However, see the recent work by Kreps (1990), who does assign a starring role to cooperative action.

13. An interesting, though somewhat disconcerting observation is that learning economics may make people more selfish (Hausman and McPherson 1993)!

14. The analysis in the text draws largely on Sen (1983b).

Part IV

A Futuristic Perspective

8

Development Economics as a Paradigm

This chapter draws together the threads of the main arguments presented so far in this book to highlight both the strengths and the weaknesses of development economics in relation to the major issues of economic development, for example, growth, distribution, employment generation, poverty reduction and enhancing human happiness. The next chapter then evaluates its (net) worth to meet the new challenges of the 21st century, once some of its early shortcomings are remedied. Even at the risk of some repetition, I begin by looking at the founding father's intellectual legacy bequeathed to posterity.

The Intellectual Legacy

The lineage of development economics has been variously described. Sen (1988) considers William Petty to be 'certainly' the 'founder of development economics' because of his earthshaking observation that 'the French grow too fast' and his concern with measuring economic progress in a broad enough sense to include 'each Man's particular happiness' (p. 10). Lewis finds the subject buried in the 18th century writings of Hume, Cantillon, Smith and Wallace, among others. 'The theory of economic development established itself in Britain in the century and a half running from

1650 to Adam Smith's *The Wealth of Nations* (1776)' (Lewis 1988: p. 18). Further, he points out that many of the concepts of modern development economics were already in currency in those days.[1] For example, Adam Smith emphasized that economic growth (referred to as 'the Natural Progress of Opulence') is the defining characteristic of the development process. Much later, Marshall (1920) spoke about the 'high theme of economic progress' (p. 461). These observations suggest strong links between the classical economics of the days of yore and modern development economics, which spells out the broader principles of economic development. Further, it suggests that neo-classical economics, by sidelining the growth-related issues, has deviated from the central concern of economics—that is, to explain the reality and to change it for the betterment of humankind.

However, highlighting the continuity of development economics should not be misconstrued as doing 'normal science'; nor should it be seen as old wine in new bottles, though ripened with age. The fact is that development economics, as we understand the term today, was formally inaugurated between Rosenstein-Rodan's 'big-push' conjecture (1943); the Singer–Prebisch hypothesis (1950) about the asymmetrical working of international trade, which highlights the dangers of a no-holds barred, export-led growth and Lewis's celebrated two-sector model (1954), whereby growth flows from an unlimited supply of labour in the rural sector, which is drawn to the capitalist urban sector at an unchanged wage rate. Then there were such early lights as Gerschenkron's 'pioneers–latecomers' syndrome (1952); Nurkse's 'balanced-growth' hypothesis (1953); and Mahalanobis's heavy-industry advocacy (1953). A little later in the day came Scitovsky's (1954) dynamic external-economies conjecture, which was followed by Hirschman's (1958) and Streeten's (1959) 'unbalanced-growth' hypotheses. In these contributions we have the first glimpses of a genuine 'paradigm change'—of a change in focus from the off-and-on neo-classical dabbling in the steady-state behaviour of general-equilibrium economic systems, to the full-time occupation of development economics with the central issues of economic development. To this end, the new development paradigm highlighted the growth of the key inputs (labour and capital) over time, and the forces that convert these into a sustained increase in wealth of (poor) nations. It aimed to accelerate the growth process, distribute the fruits of economic progress more equitably and reduce poverty on a durable basis in as short a time as possible.

In this new scientific research programme, the process of economic development appears complex, mysterious and like a many-splendoured thing. Unlike the neo-classical paradigm, its central propositions cannot be straightforwardly deduced from a few simple axioms. It is initiated, and then sustained, by continual economy-wide, inter-sectoral shifts that help capital (saving) accumulation in the capitalist (i.e, manufacturing) sector, where the sun of economic prosperity first rises before lighting up the surrounding environment. These shifting input-output configurations move not into the shadows of a 'stationary state', but towards a more dynamic production structure, helped by a perfectly elastic (or unlimited) supply of labour in the rural sector (resembling the Marxian reserve army of labour), inter-industry linkages, economies of scale, externalities and complementarities. At the center of this process of structural transformation, the rate of growth is determined by the profit rate in the manufacturing activity multiplied by the capitalist's saving, which keeps on rising to finance capital formation and economic growth, while wage income does no better than finance the current consumption of its recipients.

This central tendency of the manufacturing activity racing to the top of the development ladder is by no means inconsistent with agriculture growing at the maximal rate, a point *not* clearly reflected in the development policies of many developing countries. This tendency has been understood as being associated with an initial worsening of the distribution of income between capital and labour, which is expected, however, to work out eventually to everybody's advantage by accelerating capital formation and economic growth. Such a growth would be a 'balanced' one in case of the elastic supplies of the key industrial inputs making maximum use of the horizontal and vertical interdependencies between agriculture and manufacturing sectors. However, it would be an 'unbalanced' one if investment resources were assumed to be fixed with the explicit aim of eventually attaining some kind of a dynamic inter-sectoral balance by exploiting dynamic external economies.[2] The state may have to intervene as a *facilitator* of the development process and also as a *caveat emptor* which conveys correctly the relevant information to consumers and producers efficiently. All of this is of vital importance because factor prices do not reflect opportunity costs when sizeable external economies exist, or when large complementarities bring strange bed-fellows together. The less the opportunities of mutually profitable international trade and investment, the more important will the developmental role of the state be in propelling the development process in more productive directions, especially where free markets fear to tread.

Relationship with Neighbours

Development theory and, to some extent, development policy has drawn freely on alternative development paradigms, namely, Keynesian economics and its immediate successor, the Harrod–Domar model, and the Marxian, structuralist and institiutionalist explanations of economic reality. From the former, development economics has inherited the courage to declare independence— or, more accurately, autonomy—from mainstream neo-classical economics and to deny the latter's ubiquitous reach and relevance. Indeed, some of the discipline's intellectual armoury consists of concepts which have been directly inspired by Keynesian economics. Examples of such concepts are that of 'rural underemployment'— a 'first cousin' of the Keynesian unemployment equilibrium—and the vision of a mixed economy in which the state plays a dominant role to correct the strategic macroeconomic imbalances that the market cannot do much about. However, the cross-fertilization of ideas was the most intense with the Harrod–Domar model and Solow's neo-classical growth model from where development economics has derived some of its key insights—those concerning the centrality of the national savings rate (s), the capital–output ratio (v), the growth of the labour force (n), and technological change (A) as the key determinants of the warranted growth rate (w). But it is not enamoured of their neo-classical concerns about the attainability and/or sustainability of the (mythical) steady-state growth paths, which are not amenable to policy manipulations (because these cannot move in a positive direction unless associated with the growth of n). Making light of the highly restrictive assumptions on which the Harrod–Domar and Solow models are based, development economics has been more interested in the models' predictions,[3] namely, those relating to the role played by the growth of labour supply as well as its efficiency, which set the upper limit on the sustainable (warranted) growth rate of output; and to the basic result that, given a technological fixed capital–output ratio and growth rate of employment, the economy can be made to grow twice as fast only if the savings rate is twice as high. (Note that 'capital' here mainly denotes physical capital; but with some stretching of the model's labour-efficiency term it can also be interpreted as including human capital.) Also helpful has been Solow's extension of the Harrod–Domar model that a changing capital/output ratio can be an efficient means of achieving the steady-state growth for a while, though not permanently because of the tendency of the diminishing returns to capital, unless arrested or reversed by appropriate technological change (or, more accurately, by an improvement in total factor productivity). This conveyed a message of hope that there is tendency for the low-income economies with a higher rate of return on capital to converge to the high-income economies, where this rate tends to decline with a growing surfeit of capital.

Yet another source of inspiration for development economics has been the Marxist/structuralist analysis, which has informed the former with a sense of history, a sensitivity to the institutional constraints ('fetters') on growth and development, an awareness of the importance of class power and class alliances in the production-distribution nexus, and an attitude of healthy skepticism towards the neo-classical faith in the mutual-benefit claim, which states that notwithstanding the manifold asymmetries in the distribution of political and economic power between competing trading parties, domestic and international exchanges work out to everyone's advantage. Given below are a few examples of such propositions of the Marxist/structuralist origin which are now standard stuff (in duly modified forms) in development economics.

1.   An efficient allocation of resources and the fullest development of the production potential (i.e., 'the forces of production') are not independent of the specific configuration of the relationships of ownership and control (i.e., 'the relations of production').

2.   The feudal structures—interpreted as 'a type of socioeconomic organization of the society as a whole, a mode of production and of the reproduction of social classes' (Brenner 1990: p. 170)—tend to obstruct the flow of incentives to the direct cultivators, and minimize the 'trickle-down' effects of growth.

3. The adoption in the initial period of certain profitable technologies (i.e., those promising increasing returns to scale) by the vested interests, so that 'the more [these are] adopted the more it is attractive or convenient for others to join the bandwagon', tends to 'lock-in' the future path of economic development (i.e., makes it 'path-dependent') (Bardhan 1988: p. 50).

4. Perhaps the most internalized of the Marxian/institutionalist insights relates to the inevitability of 'unequal exchange' between unequals—between the 'center' and the 'periphery'—which then disqualifies excessive export orientation and an over-reliance on (private) foreign investment as reliable engines of growth, much less development. More generally, within the context of such 'closed loop' unequal relationships, the initial level of social capability casts a long shadow on the subsequent configurations of development trajectories (Abramovitz 1986) and also reinforces the path-dependence of the development process noted in 3.

5. A lasting imprint of the Marxian thought on development theory and policy is the understanding that the development process needs to be guided (though not in as much micro detail as centralized economies attempt to do) in the socially desired directions—that is, in directions where the faint-hearted market forces would never dare to flow.

However, in inducting ideas from competing development paradigms, development economics has sought to leaven them with moderation and, in some cases, even transform their character; but in every case it has stamped them with a mark of its originality. This is especially the case with borrowings from Marxist/structuralist and institutionalist sources. Thus, for instance, historical determinism and the inevitability of class conflict—though not denying such possibilities in cases where a regular venting of popular ire is not allowed—do not appear in its vision of economic development, which, in turn, leaves ample room for individual freedom and rationality (though not necessarily in the narrow neo-classical sense). Thus, even when the 'path dependence' of the development process is emphasized, it is to highlight that its future course can be peaceably altered most effectively by corrective policy interventions in the initial conditions, which are then sustained subsequently (Maddison 1991; Adelman and Morris 1993). A more striking example of such creative adaptation relates to the prescription of the best way out of the Marxian 'contradictions of capitalism'—namely, the inherent incompatibility of the growth of the capitalist system beyond a certain stage, which then acts as a 'fetter' on the fullest development of the forces of production. The Marxian way out is by engineering a social revolution (Baran 1957); but development economics would recommend that the way to save capitalism from itself is by a maximal development of the capitalist modes of production in tandem with far-reaching egalitarian reforms, especially those focusing on the redistribution of assets. This is how its mixed-economy prescription—namely, 'a mixture of free enterprise or market elements with an often considerable element of public intervention in favour of low-income group in the population' (Tinbergen 1985: p. 174) works. Yet another Marxian notion which has been peaceably accommodated in development economics is 'commodity fetishism', which conveys the sense of the historical evolution of social relations within the matrix of commodity exchange. The important Marxian insight here is that the terms and character of commodity exchange are not independent of the mechanism through which the actions of individual economic agents are coordinated (through the market or by conscious planning). This notion carries over into development economics as a criticism of the tendency to over-emphasize 'commodities' at the expense of 'capabilities' and *economic* rather than *human* development—topics which have been discussed at length in Chapters 6 and 7 of this book.

Building up the Heritage

Before proceeding any further, it is useful to highlight some of the areas where the 'traditional' development paradigm is improvable. First, it is important to clear up the fog of confusion which is traceable to the centrality it assigns to the savings rate (s) per se to raise the growth rate of output (g)—an aspect of the Harrod–Domar model that development economists have accepted uncritically. The correct proposition that a higher rate of growth of savings is a *necessary* condition for the economy to grow at a higher-than-trend growth rate *for some time* was at times confused with the wrong statement that a higher growth of savings is sufficient per se to achieve a sustainable long-run increase in the rate of output.[4] The latter statement is *wrong* because structural transformation (the rising share of the manufacturing activity in GDP) would raise the capital–output (v) ratio as well, which is incompatible with the saving to capital–output ratio (s/v) remaining equal to the growth rate of labour force (n) in steady-state equilibrium (for details see Hahn and Matthews 1965). Also, a lot of saving can go waste due to a rise in the capital–output ratio in case of an inappropriate choice of investment projects, or because inefficient investment may not get translated into a corresponding increase in the (warranted) growth rate. The experience of a number of developing countries, which have attained high rates of saving (i.e., in excess of 20 per cent of the GDP), but not the corresponding high rates of investment and growth (for e.g., India), illustrate such perverse tendencies.

Second, following the Harrod–Domar–Solow models, the centrality of 'endogenizing' population growth in the process of economic development—that is, of the two-way interaction between the economic and demographic variables—was ignored by development economics, which regarded population growth as *exogenous* to the development process. The importance of this neglect can be seen from the fact that development success (failure) in the last 50 years has been due as much to an increase (decline) in the GDP as to a reduction (increase) in the growth rate of population. Thus, the splendid success of East Asia and the modest success (even failure) elsewhere have come about because, unlike the latter, the former could forge a tighter link between the growth rate of output and a decline in the fertility rate flowing from the voluntary decisions of the household. This fact has highlighted the need to achieve Demographic Transition in the shortest period of time—a point explicitly noted by the classical economists, and shown later on by Coale and Hoover (1958) as a precondition of a sustainable growth rate of per capita income.

Third, the critical role of technological process, spurred on by the creation of new ideas—which, because of their non-rivalrous nature, share some aspects of public goods—was highlighted by Schumpeter (1934), in generating a sufficiently high (*ex ante*) rate of investment to raise output on a permanent, rather than on a transitory, basis. However, it was generally not given a central place in his scheme of things. On the other hand, this aspect, though basic to classical growth theories, was not clearly reflected in development *policy*, even when development *theory* recognized it in isolated cases. Looking back, this appears to be a rather surprising omission because Harrod's emphasis on 'technical progress as a built-in propensity in an industrial economy' marked a turning point in the neo-classical doctrine, which treated it as exogenous to the system, 'shocking' it to move on to a higher growth path (Robinson 1967: p. 98). Part of the reason for this neglect may be that most expositions of the Harrod–Domar model have regarded techno-logical progress as exogenous to the model. Further, Solow's model is seen as concerned with rescuing the Harrod–Domar model from its knifge-edge predicament by letting the capital–output ratio vary due to technological change (for e.g., Hahn and Mathews 1965: pp. 5–15). However, a more important aspect of the Solow model (1957), which asserts that because of the diminishing returns to capital, the growth rate of output can only be sustained by appro-priate doses of technological change, was not given much promi-nence in development economics. Yet another neglected implication of his model is the possibility of 'convergence', namely, the possi-bility of the developing countries closing the gap between their per capita incomes and those of the developed countries. This possi-bility was seldom seriously discussed in the development literature until the East Asian experience (and earlier that of Japan) demon-strated its realism.[5]

Fourth, *human* capital, especially education was assigned only a secondary importance, next to physical capital, in development models—and then too, it was not always explicitly stated. This omission is strange because Solow showed clearly that about seven-tenths of the increase in gross output per hour of work in the US between 1909 and 1945 was due to 'technological progress in the broadest sense', which is now understood as improvements in total factor productivity. What it means is that the contributions of physical capital and labour are considerably less important than development economists would normally have thought—to the cha-grin of Lewis and Marx! Later, Denison (1967, 1985) showed in his growth-accounting framework that a full 30 per cent of the per capita growth of output between 1929 and 1982 was accounted for by education per worker, while 64 per cent of it was explained by the advances in knowledge. Thus, the fastest growing countries have been those where the enrolment levels were the highest in the initial period—for e.g., South Korea and Taiwan (IMF 2000a). However, a few caveats may be introduced at this point to explain, though not justify, why development models may not have taken account of human capital:

1. It looked rather odd that the growth phenomenon should almost entirely be explained by factors exogenous to the model, as is the case with the Solow model.

2. It appears that human capital may be a *superior* good, the demand for which increases as higher level of development is reached.

Thus, in sharp contrast to the European experience used by Denison, empirical studies done for developing countries show that 60–70 per cent of the growth in per capita income can be explained by *physical* capital formation caused by inter-sectoral shift of resources, 10–20 per cent is accounted for by education and human capital, with the remaining 20–30 per cent being contributed by the residual (i.e., by improvement in total factor productivity) (Bosworth and Collins 1996: IMF 2000a). In the same vein, it has been shown that faster growth in education and human capital is a necessary, but *not* sufficient, condition for enabling developing countries to catch up with the developed countries (Nelson and Phelps 1996; Barro 1997). It follows that developing countries should not underemphasize physical capital formation until a fairly advanced level of development is reached and the demand for highly skilled labour sharply increases. In this context, a relevant finding is that the return to education is significantly reduced once it is related to educational *performance* (output) rather than to the increase in inputs to education (for e.g., schools built, etc.), which suggests that the return on educational output may have been over-stated to some extent (Sirageldin 2001).

Fifth, even though Lewis was careful to emphasize the vital importance of a dynamic agriculture to sustain structural transformation of the economy, his two-sector model led to an *extractive* view of agriculture, which tended to grossly underestimate the growth potentialities of the agricultural sector.[6]

Sixth, the original development paradigm has also been criticized for its alleged 'bloody-mindedness' with respect to the distributional aspects of growth.[7] In Lewis's two-sector model with unlimited supplies of labour, economic growth is a function solely of the profit rate: 'the central fact of economic development is that the distribution of income is altered in favour of the saving class' (Lewis 1954), cited in Agarwala and Singh (1963: p. 417). Thus, in this model, the distribution path is completely determined by the growth of capitalist income, with the wage-earners losing out to the capitalists because a rise, for whatever reasons, in the real wage rate signals a weakening of the growth impulse. In the Fei-Ranis model (1963), a less fatalistic scenario is presented—once all surplus labour has migrated and the urban wage starts to rise, the wage-earners will find their lots improved. Thus, in the growth process, no one income group loses out *absolutely*. In this respect, however, one should think that development economists were marching with the spirit of the times. For instance, in the classical savings function, routinely used even by the neo-Keynesians, the rate of growth of income is simply a function of the savings of the profit-earners multiplied by the profit rate. Following them, Lewis (1954), Galenson and Leibenstein (1955), and Kaldor (1955) feature the classical saving function, whereby all saving is done by the capitalist. The empirical studies done by Kuznets (1955) lent respectability to this view by reference to the forces of history, according to which income inequity tends to increase in the initial stages as income rises—following an inverted 'U' pattern—and to be higher in the poor countries than in the rich countries. That may be so, but the fact that growth was accompanied by income inequality should not have been taken to mean that no steps can, or ought to be, taken to remedy this. At any rate, extensive recent research casts doubt on this line of thinking and emphasizes the direct contribution made by low income inequality to economic development. It also points out that growth combined with a more equitable distribution is superior to growth combined with a less equitable distribution (for e.g., Aghion *et al.* 1999; World Bank 2001).

Finally, once again moving with the spirit of the times when logical purity demanded the reduction of a plurarity of causes to *one* original cause—for e.g., individual and social welfare measured with respect to the Benthamite metric of utility; of utility *alone* to the exclusion of all else—there has also been a monocentric emphasis in development literature on raising per capita income as the measure of economic progress, while issues like improving the distribution of income, and more generally equity and social justice, may have been sidelined somewhat. Two other reasons for the neglect of the latter set of issues have been: (a) the acceptance by development economics of the finality of the divorce between ethics and economics pronounced by Robbins (1932), which downplayed the distributional and moral aspects of the development process, and (b) the (implicit) acceptance by at least some development economists of the efficiency-oriented Pareto optimality public choice rule, which has banished ethical issues from consideration.

Elements of the Development Paradigm

The preceding analysis points out some of the defects of our intellectual heritage with respect to our understanding of the development process. But a somewhat defective heritage is better than no heritage at all, and at any rate, it does not mean that we do away with it altogether and opt for an irrelevant (neo-classical) framework of thought. Indeed, with the lively ongoing intellectual debate, such 'defects' have led to a more adequate development paradigm. Contrary to Hirschman's (1981c) assertion that development economics is a 'done thing' because it has not responded creatively to the many challenges it faced both from the Left and the Right, a spate of sympathetic review articles and full length books have appeared at regular intervals to add complexity, rigour vigour and relevance to the original development paradigm.[8] There are also regular fora—the World Bank, the Asian Development Bank (both pillars of world capitalism)—where development economics is regularly discussed, though mostly with a view to converting it to the neo-classical (market-friendly) point of view! Finally, the UNDP's human development conjecture has led to the inclusion of new ideas and hard data in its annual *Human Development Reports,* which has meant a significant broadening of the conventional development paradigm. With such credentials and vitality, development economics can hardly be faulted for intellectual moribundity. In fact, its response to the changing realities of life in the developing countries and to the new theoretical advances made in mainstream economics has been both positive and creative. We shall pursue these matters in the remaining part of the present chapter. The analysis presented in this book is put in a somewhat holistic framework in order to highlight the distinctive features of development economics and ensure that it does not wilt under the stress of exogenous shocks (for e.g., globalization) due to any lack of self-confidence.

Growth and Distribution

The analysis presented so far stresses the need for an integrated approach to economic development, in which some of the trade-offs between the crucial aspects of the development process are reconsidered and resolved to the extent that it is feasible to do so. Thus, for instance, it is vital to secure both the growth of the GDP *and* its better distribution. This is especially the case when assets, rather than just income, are more equitably distributed (Ferreira 1999). This is important because both are required to enhance people's capabilities, expand their freedom to make choices and raise the economic well-being of the people (and/or to reduce their deprivations). This view of economic development is, however, more comprehensive than that of the founding fathers, who in their enthusiasm to run the engine of growth ever faster, and not seeing the *two-way* positive links between growth and equity clearly enough, did not adequately emphasize the question of an equitable redistribution of income and wealth, though not ignoring it altogether. Their basic idea was not only to do one thing at a time and do it well, but also to reduce the development process to a single causative factor (namely, economic growth), and then let the 'trickle-down effects' take care of income distribution. This faith in the trickle-down effect can be attributed to the alleged success of the Industrial Revolution in raising the share of labour in total output by a secular rise in real wages.[9] But the belief in the trickle-down effect was soon questioned by Singer (1950), Prebisch (1950), Baran (1952) and Myrdal (1956a), among others, who highlighted the forces that limit the size of the trickle-down effect, or the 'spread effect', within countries and between countries.

There is a consensus now that economic growth is likely to be higher with less inequality. Thus, the feudal societies will experience lesser growth than the more industrialized ones where the intra-sectoral linkages are stronger, but this realization has sunk very slowly into development thinking. Kuznet's hypothesis, which on the basis of somewhat skimpy empirical foundations predicts rising inequalities in the early stage of growth, sparked off a series of cross-country studies—for example, those by Adelman and Morris

(1973), Papanek and Kyn (1986), and Ahluwalia (1976)—to test the U-shaped relationship between growth and distribution. Kuznet's hypothesis was initially supported, but with the caveat that the relationship may be the accident of history (U-shaped) or the outcome of specific policies (J-shaped). However, more recent evidence is mixed: there is no systematic positive relationship between inequality and a particular stage of economic development (Galor and Zeira 1993; Deininger and Squire 1998; World Bank 2001). Further, the evidence suggests that there is a negative correlation between the average growth rate of income and any known measure of income distribution (Benabou 1996), that when capital markets are imperfect, which is a common occurrence in developing countries, there is *no* absolute trade-off between efficiency and equity, and that there is considerable 'scope for redistributive policies which are also growth-promoting' (Aghion *et al.* 1999). In other words, growth and distribution form an irreducible set of objectives of development policy (Alesina and Rodrik 1994) and these two can together form a mutually reinforcing virtuous circle if proper development policies are implemented (Naqvi 1995).

Not only has the distributional problem been investigated thoroughly, but research has also been done on the ways and means of correcting the de-equalizing biases of growth. One approach has been to reorient the production structure in a labour-intensive manner so that employment can grow faster and raise real wages, especially that of unskilled labour. Leontief (1983) conjectures that such a sequence explains the relatively more equitable industrial growth in Europe in the 19th century. In our own times, Japan and South Korea are the principal examples of such a growth strategy, which seeks to minimize the trade-off between growth and equity (Chow and Papanek's study [1981] on Hong Kong is in the same vein; see also World Bank [1999, 2000]). Another route to enhance the distributional content of growth is to devote an increasing proportion of the increments in national income to the provision of basic needs (Streeten *et al.* 1981), or to the creation of assets owned by the poor (Chenery 1975). In contrast to this 'incrementalist' approach, there are other approaches which focus on the creation of assets for the poor even *before* growth takes place (Adelman 1978). The relationship between growth and inequality is likely to be negative if the initial distribution of income and assets is less, rather than more, unequal (World Bank 2001). An important aspect of the problem is that the people's evaluation of their well-being is essentially a relative matter because they relate their welfare to their location relative to the mean (van Praag *et al.* 1978). Thus, any successful programme of redistribution must ensure that structural reforms aimed at a redistribution of assets are carried out and the rate of increase of income of the poor is kept higher than the rate of increase of income of the rich (Naqvi and Qadir 1985).

The Question of Sectoral Balance

An important, though unfortunate, fallout of the original development model was the development of industry *at the expense of* agriculture. For instance, Lewis's two-sector model was misunderstood as advocating an extractive view of agriculture. In his model, agriculture is seen as home to the 'unlimited supplies of labour', which must be drawn on to serve as an input into industrial production.[10] Not only labour, but also capital would flow to the industrial sector from the agricultural sector to support sustained capital accumulation and accelerated economic growth. The Fei–Ranis model (1963) also popularized the extractive view of agriculture as a self-sacrificing provider of inputs for economic growth. Such a concept of agriculture, emphasizing extraction from it rather than assigning it a positive role with a personality of it own, was mainly responsible in the late 1950s and early 1960s for agricultural stagnation, and increasing rural poverty in the developing countries. As a direct result of underinvestment in agriculture, the productivity of agricultural labour in developing countries has remained significantly lower than that achieved by the developed countries at a similar stage of development on the eve of the Industrial Revolution (Timmer 1988). This view has also been damaging because, as Johnston and Mellor (1961) show, 'economic development is characterized by a substantial increase in the demand for agricultural products, and the failure to expand food supplies in pace with the growth of demand can seriously impede economic growth. The result is likely to be a substantial rise in food prices, leading to political discontent and pressure on wage rates with adverse effects on industrial profits, investment, and economic growth.' Earlier, Kalecki (1971) had echoed the same theme: 'True, the process of development is constrained by the availability of capital; but investment is determined not only by savings but also by the supply of wage goods, which are typically supplied by the agricultural sector.' There is another reason why the development of agriculture is crucial to the aggregate growth rate. It relates to the possibility of varying the capital/output ratio between agriculture and industry to maximize total output in terms of the required capital inputs—an echo of Solow. Recognizing that 'extremely low capital/labour ratio in the dominant rural sector is at the heart of the development problem,' it would clearly be desirable to 'spread the scarce capital resource between the low capital/labour-ratio agriculture sector and the relatively higher capital/labour-ratio industrial sector in order to lower the capital intensity of growth' (Mellor and Johnston 1984).

A vast body of literature has emphasized the dynamic linkages between sectors, especially between the agricultural sector and the manufacturing sector. The central point of these and other contributions to this area is to emphasize the *contributory* role of agriculture to economic development, and the factors which lead to the modernization and growth of the agricultural sector itself.[11] Among such factors, technological change figures prominently because, as Schultz (1964) pointed out, continuing investments in traditional technologies are quickly thwarted by diminishing (marginal) returns. Hence, an 'endogenous' technological change should help agricultural growth, especially food output, which, by the same token, also enlarges the size of the market for urban output. This enlargement of the market takes place by increasing the real income of the rural poor, generating rural employment and lowering food prices through technological change.[12]

Labour Markets

Another unfortunate consequence of the original development model has been the rather simplistic view of the labour markets in developing countries, that labour commands very low, or even zero, wage in the agricultural sector because of an unlimited supply. Thus, in this model, the scattered, non-unionized labour migrate unidirectionally from the rural backwaters to the urban 'growth poles', where they expect to be fully employed. Indeed, this aspect of development economics, which stresses that the marginal product of labour is zero in agriculture, was used (mistakenly) by Schultz

(1964) to deny the very existence of development economics.[13] (See also, Chapter 9, notes 16 and 17.)

This has provoked a large body of literature examining the peculiarities of the labour market in developing countries, in general, and of the rural market in particular.[14] The research in this area has been helped by the advances made by microeconomic theory about the information and risk problems, by the availability of better and larger data on the labour markets in developing countries, and by learning from the objective reality in these countries. Kalecki (1971) and Mellor (1986) show that a rising real wage in agriculture (caused mainly by a secular decline in the price of foodgrain) plays a critical role in expanding the size of the market for industrial goods and reducing rural poverty. An important theoretical contribution in this area is the Harris–Todaro model (1970) (generalized by Khan [1980]), which explains urban unemployment, and analyses the consequences of government policies to reduce it. In the model, the rural wage is determined competitively but the urban wage is set institutionally. Further, it is typically higher than the rural wage, which starts (and sustains) Lewis's process of rural-urban migration in the *hope* (measured by the relevant probability) of finding (full) employment in the urban sector. Is this hope fulfilled? Lewis said 'yes'; but Harris and Todaro say 'no' because of the labour-market distortion caused by an institutionally set urban wage, which is typically too high. Does it help, then, to provide a wage subsidy to cure the urban unemployment problem? It probably does not, because it only increases the number of the urban unemployed by attracting rural labour in the *expectation* of finding more employment there. It is interesting to note that the Harris–Todaro model, rooted in the realities of the developing countries, not only corrects a defect in the neo-classical model—which conjures up the myth of permanent market-clearing in the labour market—but, as shown by Malinvaud (1984), is also an untenable hypothesis even in the developed countries. Incidentally, this is one of those many instances where development economics has something to give to neo-classical economics.

The Market versus the Government

The development paradigm discussed in the preceding chapters assigns a complementary, rather than an adversary, role to the market and the government. However, writing when the development process was just beginning to unfold its wings, the founding fathers—Rosenstein-Rodan (1943), Singer (1950), Prebisch (1950), Nurkse (1953), Scitovsky (1954), Hirschman (1958) and Streeten (1959)—may have emphasized government intervention more than would be warranted in today's environment to take care of the then near-ubiquity of cases of market failure, of markets which are far from perfect or too thin, or which simply do not exist. However, an even more fundamental motivation at the time must have been to wean economists away from an uncritical acceptance of classical (and neo-classical) metaphysical *belief*—such as that held by Haberler (1950) and Viner (1952), among others—in universal market clearing as a panacea for all economic problems including those relating to economic development. In particular, due to the perverse working of the terms-of-trade transmission mechanism which undermined the role of trade as an engine of growth, a series of steps *had* to be taken by the government to encourage import-substituting industrialization. This was done with a view to laying a firm foundation for latter-day export expansion and maximizing total output by taking advantage of inter-industry and intra-sector complementarities—an insight that subsequent empirical research has not proved to be mistaken (Bruton 1998). In these situations, investment decisions are required to be taken simultaneously to secure a structure of outputs corresponding to the structure of income elasticities of demand (Nurkse's 'balanced growth' doctrine); or when, due to the shortage of investible resources, investment must be undertaken sequentially to achieve a balanced production structure only gradually (Hirschman's and Streeten's 'unbalanced growth' doctrine). In both these cases, the profit-maximizing private producers could not be relied upon to optimize output without the active support of the government. This is because of the presence of externalities—that is, as output expands for one firm, its output-raising consequences for other firms cannot be (fully) internalized, which, in turn, would prevent market prices from summarizing the necessary information required by the profit-maximizing private investor. Of course, if individual firms could have secured information *costlessly* about the strategic responses of the other firms, then profit-seeking behaviour could do the job; but the point is that such information is seldom, if ever, complete, symmetric and costless. In the latter case, the basic propositions of neo-classical economics cease to hold. In particular, 'market equilibrium may not exist…; when equilibrium exists, it is, in general, not Pareto efficient; it may not be possible to decentralize efficient resource allocations…; market equilibrium may be characterized by an excess demand for credit or an excess supply of labour (that is, the law of supply and demand no longer holds)' (Stiglitz 1988: p. 156).

The intensity of state intervention and its form, however, remains an open issue even though the times have changed greatly. The fact is that, with the tragic exception of Africa (especially, sub-Saharan Africa), a large of number of countries have made significant economic progress, some growing spectacularly (East Asia, China) while others only modestly (South-East Asia, Latin America). Furthermore, information has become much more cheap, spreads at a phenomenal speed and is far too decentralized now than was the case in the past (see Chapter 9). Thus, while it may not be feasible or desirable to centralize information (because that would be too costly), some kind of planning activity is still required, if only to provide a directional focus to economic growth at a time when international inequities of income and wealth are rising rapidly. However, it may have to be only of the indicative type where the markets for such information do not exist, where it is too costly or fragmentary, or where comparative advantage unfolds itself only slowly with the passage of time (Scitovsky 1987). But it may have to be more comprehensive where the strategy of investment emphasizes giving priority to capital goods-producing heavy industries. Such a strategy aims to facilitate the development of downstream industries, expand the industrial base in areas where the country is perceived to have a dynamic comparative advantage and generate 'forced saving'. These industries are also human-resource intensive, with significant spillover effects on the rest of the economy (Bradford *et al.* 1991).

The relevance of the central ideas of development economics in the context of the new realities, now and in the future, is discussed at some length in the next chapter. However, the point to note here is that contrary to the popular notion, there is no evidence of development economics ever going for an all-out *etatisme*. For instance, as noted in Chapter 3, the founding fathers in Pakistan and India explicitly rejected both the (unalloyed) capitalist model and the communist model. Instead, a 'mixed-economy' model has been preferred to the communist model. At any rate, in the modern context, the recommended state intervention need only be, to use Lowe's (1977) terminology, of the 'instrumental-inference type' (which involves setting macro goals and action directives derived from an empirical feasible plan), rather than an 'alternative to the market, based on command and fulfillment'. While the government must remain engaged in economic activities to make the Invisible Hand a little more visible to the naked eye, the productive and the complementary role of the private sector should also be duly accepted. And even when the private initiative is not forthcoming to the extent required, due to too much risk or uncertainty, the government should still, as in the past, establish industries with the explicit aim of eventually selling these to private takers, if and when they are ready to invest. In such circumstances, government intervention is more likely to crowd in, rather than crowd out, private investment (Streeten 1993). The Pakistan Industrial Development Corporation (PIDC) performed this role in the 1960s. The same has been the case in India. In fast-growing East Asia and China, where the government has sought through various means (for e.g., directed credits) to pick the 'winning' producers (i.e., those with the greatest potential efficiency, once firmly put on their feet), such a strategy has been crowned with spectacular success. It is necessary to repeat much of what was done in the past to align the market and government in a productive direction, especially because the market-friendly policies in the last 20 years have not produced the desired results.

True, the government does not always succeed where the market fails, but development experience shows that the government *has* succeeded splendidly in raising agricultural productivity by helping technological change through research institutes, and by ensuring adequate prices both to the producers and the consumers of food— a result that could not have been secured by the private sector. Further, governments have managed to create fairly impressive infrastructures and industrial structures in most of the developing countries (World Bank 1991). If the element of success has been greater in one case (for e.g., South Korea) than in the other (say, India or Pakistan), the difference is attributable to the quality of government, the flexibility of its response to external shocks and to the quality of political leadership in these countries—it does not necessarily hinge on the government being less dominant in the former than in the latter. Reynolds (1977) confirms this point by explicitly attributing the differences in the comparative growth experiences of developing countries to the differences in the managing capabilities of various governments. This, however, also underscores the counter-productive nature of dysfunctional state intervention as much as the limits of the market to maximize social welfare.

Keeping these facts in view, the critics of development economics, who still cite the *dirigiste* practices in developing countries as the prime cause of their failure when many have succeeded mainly *because* of them, appear somewhat ridiculous. First, such arguments commit the error of trying to establish the superiority of a nonexistent phenomenon (free markets in South Korea vs pervasive governments elsewhere) by comparing it with yet another nonexistent situation (i.e., Pareto optimality). Second, it is not logically permissible to infer general 'statements'—the unambiguous superiority of the market-based solutions—from singular statements about the successes/failures of specific countries, due to a variety of reasons. The fact is that the scenario of a generalized market success is sheer neo-classical romanticism, which conveniently blithes over the fact that market success is guaranteed *only* if the most unlikely concatenation of favourable factors occurs—that is, if there are enough markets, if both the consumers and producers behave competitively, and if equilibrium exists. However, the non-satisfaction of *any* of these conditions leads to a withdrawal of the guarantee of market success (Debreu 1959). And, even where the markets do succeed, the outcomes may not be socially desirable. Indeed, the markets may (successfully) 'work by strangulation', to use Joan Robinson phrase, if the initial distribution of income is highly unequal (for e.g., in the presence of a feudal system). Third, it is hard to understand what to make of such proofs in practice. Should one abolish governments altogether and leave everything to the Invisible Hand? The fact of the matter is that if the government must always fail, then there is no guarantee that the market will always succeed, especially where none exist (Arrow 1974). Also, the fact that government rent-seeking may simply be replaced by private rent-seeking, because the 'agents' in the free market often commit 'fraud' on the 'principals' due to information asymmetry, robs the market-friendly philosophy of much of its 'neatness' (Streeten 1993). As Pack and Westphal (1986) point out, 'the factors responsible for a government's inability to intervene effectively may also preclude its following the neo-classical prescription.'

Ethics and Development

There is, however, a more controversial issue which is actually the most fundamental problem, and which has caused considerable 'inner tension' in economics in general, and development economics in particular. It is the failure to synthesize basic economic propositions with a set of universally held ethical norms of behaviour in the society, with a view to healing such tensions.[16] This failure hinders scientific vision because ethical considerations mingle with economic compulsions effortlessly at the level of the economic agents' primary motivation, which then translates into social action. Indeed, in the real world, the *plurality* of *motivations* is the rule rather than the exception, and one would be hard put to prove that either mere self-interest or pure altruism explains a large enough segment of social or individual action.[17] Thus, 'a society of unmitigated egoists would soon knock itself to pieces; a perfectly altruistic individual would soon starve' (Robinson 1973: p. 10). Indeed, it will be highly inefficient to make real-life societies work without generous reinforcement from such moral norms as 'fairness' and 'trust' (Hausman and McPherson 1993). For instance, if each member of the society tries to maximize his/her share of the national cake without regard to what others get, then there may be no democratic way left to remedy the situation, except by rousing people's moral responsibilities to the society. At any rate, even at a purely logical level, the importance of a 'right' moral or value perspective must be clearly recognized due to the fact that objective statements not only become invalid because they are contrary to facts but also because they are based on a wrong value perspective (Harsanyi 1991).

And yet most of development economics has been practised by strictly observing positivism to ensure scientific objectivity—and perhaps also not to annoy the mainstreamers too much by confronting them with two heresies (*etatisme* and ethicalism) rather than just one (*etatisme*). However, it is a case of good intentions paving the way to the hell of total irrelevance: the fact is that by opting to remain positivist, development economics is faced with a motivational vacuum which cannot be filled even by a lot of rudimentary hard-headedness. Thus, if it is true that mainstream economics 'has been greatly impoverished by [its] growing distance' from ethics (Sen 1987: p. 7); then the predicament of development economics will be the more so because of this unnatural separation.

It follows that if the recent attempts to make development economics truly 'positivistic', so that it conforms as closely as possible to the neo-classical prescription of cold-blooded market-oriented efficiency, do succeed, then development economics will become less able to tackle development issues. Indeed it will lose its very identity if it does not yearn for the forbidden apple of morality, because the most fundamental issues of human existence that development economics must explicitly tackle have a clear moral dimension. Such attempts are especially counter-productive now that globalization is crowding out the remaining elements of altruism from economics (UNDP 1999). Fortunately, the recent attempts made by the UNDP's *Annual Human Development Reports* since 1990 to expand the development paradigm and make it more responsive to human concerns like health, literacy, human rights, etc., has made it possible to bring ethical issues within the development economist's calculus (see Chapter 9). Yet the hardcore treatments of the subject continue to feign the Olympian certitude of positivism just to acquire the mesmerizing appeal of being one of the neo-classicals!

What influences, then, explain the neglect of ethics in economics, especially in development economics? Perhaps, once again, it is the spirit of the times; indeed, the same spirit that has moved economists since the time of Adam Smith (1775), a professor of moral philosophy, who was misunderstood as pronouncing the separation of economics from ethics, later formalized by Robbins (1932) into a divorce. More recently, Stigler (1981) laid down: 'Economists seldom address ethical questions as they impinge on economic theory or economic behaviour' because man is 'eternally a utility-maximizer, in his home, in his office—be it public or private—in his church, in his scientific work, in short, everywhere' (p. 176).

However, the fact remains that the extant agnosticism towards ethics should now finally end in order to add greater cutting power to development economics (and also to mainstream economics). To rapitulate the highlights of the discussion in Chapters 6 and 7, the following points need to be made. The point of departure for extending the development economists' problematic and making the discipline internally consistent is to de-emphasize—while not discrediting it altogether—the Pareto optimality principle as an operational principle to avoid confusion in the formulation of development policy. The reason is, this positivistic rule is not always efficient, nor is it a preserver of individual liberty. Also it is distributionally neutral, and essentially status quoist by construction. This is because *it cannot even distinguish the rich from the poor,* which is a consequence of the utilitarian and welfarist 'nature' of the principle, and also because it does not allow interpersonal comparisons of utility. As the non-utility indicators of welfare are not admissible in the utilitarian framework, the income levels enjoyed by the rich and the poor can also not provide a basis for setting up a scheme for redistributing income to the poor. But economic development, to make any sense at all, must be concerned with distributional problems, which are inescapably complicated by moral considerations.

Another idea discussed in this book is that development economists must not uncritically accept Nozickian non-consequentialism, with its strictly procedural and negative view of human freedom. From this perspective, state intervention is allowed only to prevent interference with the entitlements of those who pass the test of procedural formalities. However, no intervention is allowed to prevent anyone from the exercise of his her (legal) freedom even if that has extremely adverse consequences for the rest of the society. The state is also not allowed to intervene to redistribute income and wealth, which again is seen as an infringement of individual liberties. It should be obvious that such views cannot be of much use in developing countries, where a non-dictatorial redistribution of income and wealth is the essence of the development process.

What else is there, then, for development economics to draw on from contemporary economics to give it a 'warm heart'? The answer is, there is quite a lot. For instance, as noted at several points in this book, the public choice theory provides an excellent source for thinking about such matters. Thus, for example, especially relevant for development economics is a modified Rawlsian principle (1985) of 'justice-as-fairness', which involves maximizing the welfare of the least privileged in the society, with the explicit proviso that the number of persons so situated is minimized at the same time. However, doing so requires making deep *changes* in the existing social order, which, in general, is neither fair nor just. Another such principle is Sen's capabilities perspective on development issues, which explicitly admits non-utility information to be able to make interpersonal comparisons of individual welfare and relate it to such vital problems as inequity, poverty and human deprivation. These are important issues, which development economics must take cognizance of to repair the damage done to development thinking by unrepentant amorality.

Endogenizing Demography

As noted above, development economics must respond creatively to the old-new demographic challenges. A key element of this response is to endogenize demographic variables, such as, fertility, age-composition and migration. We now know that in the (classical) 'magnificent dynamics', population was treated as an endogenous variable—Malthus treated it as one. An example is the wage-fund theory wherein any attempt to improve the worker's lot by increasing wages is only rewarded by an increase in labour supply, which, in turn, reduces wages; the reverse holds true if wages are held below the subsistence level. By the time of Lewis's work, however, population had come to be regarded as an exogenous variable.[18] It was treated as such in the Harrod–Domar model, which, as we have noted, influenced both development theory and practice. However, Lewis did implicitly endogenize population by according centrality to labour surplus, which is continually fed by population growth (apart from the fact that its supply exceeds the demand at the going wage rate) as the primary initiator of the development process. Moreover, population growth would lower the rate of return per capita on capital formation and would slow down the rate of absorption of labour in the urban sector. Yet the dominant tendency in development economics (and also in neo-classical economics) has been to keep it in an exogenous box. Coale and Hoover (1958), however, explicitly showed that a higher population growth would lower savings and capital formation. Coale (1973) duly emphasized the role played by the economic factors explaining the determinants of fertility—namely, the decision to produce more (less) children is an integral part of household decision-making—and of the couple having a clear understanding of the advantages flowing from having a smaller family. If the parents do not do so, they may desire more children than is socially desirable, and the converse is applicable as well. This is a good example of an externality, that is, of market failure—in the absence of the possibility of making profits, the information regarding contraceptives may not be made available by the market. By the same token, it is a case where government intervention can prove very useful. More explicit on this are the fertility models of Becker (1960) and Mincer (1962) which consider the activities of child-bearing and child-rearing as 'internal' to the optimization of decisions taken by households. Further, attempts have been made to measure the effects on fertility behaviour, of the family income, income distribution, labour force participation and wages (Kelly 1980). Some modelling activity has also gone on—the Bachue model is an instance—to relate the economic and demographic variables.

The point of the above-mentioned response of development economics to real-world issues has been to find ways and means to *reduce* the growth rate of population—a programme which has been crowned with success in nearly all the developing countries. Thus, between 1990 and 1998, the population growth rate has declined from an average of 3.4 per cent to 2.4 per cent in low-income countries, and from 2.8 per cent to 1.5 per cent in middle-income countries (World Bank 2000). Indeed, the former are quickly reaching the replacement level of population (of about 1.8 per cent) and may fall below it before long. But success on this score is not going to be achieved without incurring an opportunity cost. Indeed, Nature has already brought to the fore, in both the developed and the developing countries, the opposite issue of 'population ageing'—as if to ensure that humankind does *not* run out of its stock of nagging problems! This new phenomenon has already severely strained the resources of the developed countries, but its next victims are going to be the developing countries. These are fortunately still passing through a phase of Demographic Transition—that is, a passage from a high-fertility-high-mortality to a low-fertility-low-mortality sequence—where a delayed decline in the fertility rates (much later than the decline in mortality rates) will for a time stretch the size of the working-age cohort. This is referred to as a one-time 'demographic gift' before the phenomenon of population ageing begins to drain this working-age pool of labour. The challenge in the 21st century will be to bring about far-reaching organizational reform to make use of this gratuitous gift of Nature.

To this end, developing countries must make bigger investments *now* to produce a highly trained and skilled population. However, the problem is that while the successful developers (for e.g., China, East Asia) are taking advantage of the 'demographic gift', most others (including India, Pakistan) have not done much in this regard. This neglect is bound to lead to a decline in their competitiveness and a rise in inter-cohort rivalry (Sirageldin 2001).

The Development Economics of Supply and Demand

The (original) development model has been variously described as demand-oriented and supply-oriented. The latter description is supported by the fact that the study of growth '... is about accumulation of physical capital, the progress of skills, ideas, innovations, the growth of population, how factors are used, combined, and managed and so on. It is therefore, principally, about the supply-side" (Stern 1991: p. 123). Lewis (1954) also made the supply-side considerations prominent by viewing the insufficient availability of fixed capital (and inadequate saving) as the main constraint on growth. In view of the (allegedly) low supply elasticities, he did not assign significant role to demand-management policies. Thus, for instance, the Keynesian remedy of increasing effective demand to cure unemployment in a developing country would only be penalized by greater inflation. It was thus contended (for e.g., by Lewis) that instead of leaning on the Keynesians, the development economist should learn at the feet of classical economists (especially Ricardo) because of the latter's emphasis on capital accumulation and a greater supply of savings as crucial factors in the development process. However, as noted by Syrquin (1988), the Harrod–Domar model (Harrod 1939; Domar 1946), the two-sector Lewis model (1954), and the balanced-growth model of Rosenstein-Rodan (1943) and Nurkse (1953) are more appropriate instances of greater emphasis on the demand-side factors.

While physical and human capital accumulation continue to be the constraining factors on growth, the inadequacy of effective demand, especially among the rural poor, also limits the growth of output and employment. An even more compelling illustration of this aspect of the problem is the case of famines, which have been caused not only by the short supply of food but more often by a failure of the 'exchange entitlements' of the poor due to a radical decline in their real incomes for a variety of reasons (Sen 1981a; Alamgir 1980). This argument can also be reversed: the growth-promoting impulses emanating from the demand side will not translate into higher levels of output (and employment) by widening the wage-goods market if the supply elasticities are not high enough (Mellor and Johnston 1984).

However, it would be more fruitful if development economics acquires both blades of the Marshallian scissors, the supply blade as well as the demand blade, to 'enjoy' greater cutting power. In other words, it is more fruitful to think of development economics as an economics both of supply and demand—just as all of economics is. Thus, Klein (1978, 1983) has reformulated the problem as one of linking up the open Keynesian income and product accounts (the demand side), the Leontief input-output framework (the supply side), and the flow-of-funds accounts (the financial side) to get a complete picture of the economic universe, and to devise and implement policies on both the supply and the demand sides of the equation.[19] It is necessary to have such a comprehensive analytical framework to analyse the effects on the economy of an increase in the prices of food and energy, and the costs associated with protecting the environment, controlling population growth and increasing agricultural output. Such information is needed for policy-making both in the developed and the developing countries 'because an adequate explanation of wage income cannot avoid the explicit treatment of physical production involving labour inputs as well as capital inputs' (Klein 1983: p. 2). There is an 'educative' aspect to such an exercise as well, which is also very important. The vast data requirements for building such systems lead to a further strengthening of the database required for development policy. Many developing countries, including Pakistan and India, already have medium-sized macroeconometric models and fairly disaggregated input-output tables, and attempts are also being made to build financial flow-of-funds accounts. Such efforts should continue to enhance the 'empirical content' of the development paradigm.

Notes

1. For example, Lewis (1988) finds in these early writings many of the current development principles—the size of agricultural surplus and the availability

of foreign exchange determining the size of the non-farm population; the concept of gains from trade; the distinction between tradeables and non-tradeables; the determination of net saving out of profit rather than wages; and a significant promotional role for the government.

2. There is a historical context to some of these principles. For instance, the experiences of the 'pioneer' (the European) countries, which, according to Rostow (1956), Ohlin (1959) and Gerschenkron (1962), show that they grew by taking advantage of vertical interdependencies between sectors. The 'latecomers' could grow even faster than the pioneers by learning from the latter's experience and by drawing upon their 'book of blueprints' of technical knowledge *free of cost* (Bell 1987).

3. The evaluation of specific theories by reference to the reliability of their predictions rather than by the realism (unrealism) of their assumptions is a Popperian methodological ploy (Popper 1980), advocated by Friedman (1953), and one that is now widely accepted by the economic profession.

4. As Solow (1988) points out, '... it is an implication of the diminishing returns that the equilibrium rate of growth is not only not proportional to the saving (investment) rate, but is independent of the saving (investment) rate.'

5. According to IMF (2000a), 24 per cent of the developing countries have managed to converge to the developed countries' (mainly, the US) income levels. However, as noted by Barro (1997), convergence needs to be redefined as 'conditional convergence'—measured by the difference between actual income (y) and long-run (potential) steady-state growth (y^*)—to depict a universal growth phenomenon. This redefinition of convergence also explains why a poor country's actual growth may *not* converge *if* its long-run steady-state growth is also low by virtue of a low savings rate, which is true in the case of quite a few developing countries (including Pakistan).

6. Thus, for instance, Hirschman (1958) supported a subservient role for agriculture in the growth process. He wrote: 'Agriculture certainly stands convicted on the count of its lack of direct stimulus to the setting up of few activities through linkage effects—the superiority of manufacture in this respect is crushing'.

7. Lewis, (1955) laid down: 'First, it should be noted that our subject-matter is growth, and not distribution.' However, it should be noted that he was careful enough to point out that inequality of income per se was not enough 'to ensure a high level of saving'. It is 'only the inequality that goes with profits that favours capital formation and not the inequality that goes with rents' (pp. 419–20 in Agrawala and Singh [1963]). It is for this reason that Lewis and others favoured land reforms 'for reasons of equity as well as output (Lewis 1984b: p. 130). At any rate, Singer (1950) and Tinbergen (1959) were explicit about the distributional issues.

8. A two-volume *Handbook of Development Economics* (Chenery and Srinivasan, 1988, 1989) has been published by North Holland, which runs to the impressive length of 1773 pages. It includes comprehensive surveys in as many as thirty-two areas, including such important matters as trade and development, fiscal policy, project evaluation, processes of structural transformation, migration and urbanization, and the economics of health, nutrition and education, to name only a few. An extensive bibliography is appended to each of the surveys.

9. However, the founding fathers were not altogether wrong about the strength of the trickle-down effects. This is because when rates of growth of per capita income exceed 3 per cent per annum, growth does become equalizing. However, the fact is that when growth is slow (say 1.5 per cent per annum) then it need not be equalizing (Naqvi 1995). Thus, based on the 1970 census, Fishlow (1972) found that, in Brazil, income inequalities grew bigger, with the poor losing out even in *absolute* terms, notwithstanding—or, perhaps, as a result of—positive growth rates.

10. Contrary to the popular view, Lewis (1954) strongly argued for a rapid growth of agriculture to accompany, or precede, overall economic growth. He explicitly stated that industrial and agrarian Revolutions always go together, and that 'economies in which agriculture is stagnant do not show industrial development'.

11. Johnston and Mellor (1961) wrote: 'It is our contention that balanced growth is needed in the sense of simultaneous efforts to promote agricultural and industrial development.'

12. Note an important point here: in this view, higher food output leads to *lowering*, instead of a rising, of food prices. This is how it should be because continuously rising food prices would *contract* the size of the market by reducing the real income of the rural poor, who spend an overwhelming proportion of their income on food.

13. This view is mistaken because all that is required for the validity of the Lewis model is that the urban sector attracts rural labour at a *constant* real wage. This constancy may, in turn, be ensured by population growth, greater women participation in the labour force and other such factors (Lewis 1984b; Bell 1987).

14. See, Rozenzweig (1989) for a useful review of the literature on this topic.

15. The unemployment equilibrium condition in this model is denoted by the equality of the rural wage to the expected urban wage.

16. It is interesting to note in this context that the two-volume *Handbook of Development Economics* (Chenery and Srinivasan 1988, 1989) does not include any separate review of the literature on the subject because there is not much understanding of its importance! Only Sen, at the beginning (Chapter 1) and Streeten towards the end (Chapter 22) of the *Handbook*, talk about the subject— the former mostly relating to his 'capability' theory while the latter talking about the role of altruism in cementing international cooperation. The same is true of the most recent survey of literature by Stern (1989). But, of late, the subject is beginning to receive more attention—for e.g., Hausman and McPherson (1993)—even though its impact on the academia is, at best, indeterminate.

17. As Solow (1980) pointed out, without positing some kind of ethical norm of behaviour it is not possible, for example, to explain why some times the labour market should *not* be self-clearing: 'Wouldn't you be surprised if you learned that someone of roughly your status in the profession, but teaching in a less desirable department, had written to your department chairman offering to teach your courses for less money? Normally, the answer would be in the affirmative: yes, I would be damned surprised if someone did this to me or to you. Although it may not be the economically optimal situation, it would be most desirable that someone did *not* undercut me or you.'

18. Looking back, it is somewhat ironical that Lewis, notwithstanding his many intellectual journeys back in time to 'visit' Adam Smith, Malthus, Mill and the rest, did not take notice of this aspect of the classical growth model.

19. Klein is careful to note that the income-and-product accounts include some very important supply-side elements as well.

9

Development Economics and Globalization

The basic aim of development economics, as described in this book, is to *explain* the nature and mechanics of the state of the development process as it has unfolded in the developing countries so far, and to *change* this state for the better by increasing per capita incomes, reducing distributional inequities, lowering the incidence of poverty and improving human 'capabilities' to convert increments in per capita income into some meaningful metric of personal well-being. In this penultimate chapter, we consider the applicability and the relevance of these basic ideas in the context of the manifold challenges of globalization, and the unceasing ways in which it has transformed the economic universe at unimaginable speed. To motivate the discussion, let us first spell out in some detail the nature of this challenge and then set out what the developing countries should be doing in the coming decades to swim mostly *against* the tide of unfavourable events, which are likely to be at least as important as the favourable ones. The main assertion—which, incidentally, reflects a rare consensus of liberalist and developmental thinking—here is that, given the extant OECD protectionism, the developing countries can benefit from globalization (or, at least, minimize the wrenching pain of change) *only* if they succeed in putting together a beneficial strategy that permits them to interact with the developed world from a position of economic strength. However, as opposed to the liberalist contention, there is no presumption here that domestic adjustment is all that is required to bring the developing countries to such a position. On the other hand, development economics would emphasize that successful export orientation (that which avoids immiserizing growth) rests on a knowledge-creating and productivity-raising pattern of industrialization, which comes only from efficient import substitution. Furthermore, it is contended that the external environment needs to be reformed as well to strengthen the developing countries' external balances on the back of high rates of growth of per capita income, sustained over long enough time periods and a significant degree of human development. While there is a clear understanding of the mutually reinforcing linkages between trade, investment and growth, it is also understood that the Uruguay-Round (UR) Agreement is not adequate enough to permit a full flowering of the development process; and that what little it has achieved is being thwarted by the protectionism of the developed countries (UNCTAD 1999).

The Challenge of Globalization

The modern phenomenon of globalization, which represents the gathering strength of a clear trend—the growth of trade outstripping that of the GDP—is integrating, more tightly than ever before, national economies into a 'Global Village'. What distinguishes the new globalization from the older episodes (for e.g., in the 19th century) is a much *freer* and *faster* movement of goods, services, capital, labour and knowledge around the globe than could be imagined even a decade ago—thanks mainly to the revolutionary technological advancements which have extended the reach of the human mind in much the same way as the Industrial Revolution technologies strengthened the hold of the human hands on his/her destiny. Opinions about the inevitability of its beneficial outcome, however, differ. Thus, on the one hand, it is hoped that world production will be maximized, but its distribution between nations is expected to be unequal, even though (with few exceptions) all countries may gain from it in absolute terms. However, on the other hand, the unequal market access and the adverse terms of trade seem to be at the root of the systemic inequities of the new world trading order, which put the developing countries at a permanent disadvantage vis-à-vis the developed countries. In this view, the gloomy Singer–Prebisch (1950) predictions about the development possibilities of the former is revisiting, like the melancholy ghost of Hamlet's father, the turbulent scene of international economic relations and beckoning the developing countries to respond to this all-powerful phenomenon—cautiously, positively and creatively. Hence, while globalization is the defining characteristic of development thinking in the 21st century (World Bank 2000), this is *not* in the sense that it will help transform the slow-growing developing economies into fast-growing economies that eventually catch-up with the developed economies in the foreseeable future, as soon as all restrictions on trade and capital flows are swept aside to let the market forces reign supreme. Unfortunately, this neo-classical vision of mutually beneficial international economic relations has never worked in the past and will not do so now. Instead, as in the past, the relevant vision (which development economics has provided) is that of an asymmetrical working of the network of international flows of goods, capital, labour and ideas in which the powerful (developed) countries rule the roost more than ever before. Let us, therefore, look at this alternative vision to formulate a realistic response to meet the emerging challenges of globalization. But before that, getting a taste of the liberalist medicine should help.

The Bitter Liberalist Medicine

The standard policy recommendation, based on neo-classical orthodoxy, asserts that globalization will work out to every country's advantage by freeing domestic and foreign markets, liberalizing trade and capital flows, setting the international and domestic prices 'right', and minimizing government intervention. The hope is that, if all this is done, the growth and welfare of the (rich and poor) national economies, and of the world economy will be maximized by stimulating the rates of physical and human capital formation and by ensuring a least-cost creation and transmission of knowledge. This unshakeable faith in the beneficial working of the 'free' domestic and international markets—that the economic horizon will brighten up if the government can somehow remove itself from the scene of crime—rests on three basic results of international trade theory: (a) Free trade is superior to no trade (Samuelson 1939), (b) restricted trade is superior to no trade (Kemp 1962) and (c) free trade is generally 'fair' (Stolper and Samuelson 1941; Metzler 1949). Thus, it is asserted that if world trade is organized according to the dictates of the comparative-advantage principle and the Heckscher–Ohlin–Samuelson (HOS) (Heckscher 1933; Ohlin 1939; Samuelson 1949) prescription, the factor rewards of the scarce factor will decline and that of the surplus factor rise everywhere, both relatively and absolutely. Hence, world trade will grow faster and the gains from trade get distributed more fairly when it is completely free than when all-enveloping protectionism prevails. Further, since the distribution of income due to globalization is expected to be the first-best (by definition), there is no room for making even normative judgements about enhancing its egalitarian content because it is assumed to be 'unimprovable' in respect of efficiency and equity. It follows that the most efficient and equitable way to economic prosperity for each country, rich and poor, according to the HOS prescription, is that since each country's exports intensively use its most abundant factor, the exports of developing countries should be labour-intensive and its imports capital-intensive. Such being the rewards of implementing the first-best neo-classical prescription, the 'natural' thing is to reposition each country's production structures according to the HOS prescription and go for a 'big-bang' liberalization of trade and capital flows, even voluntarily— that is, by the developing countries, even if the developed countries do not follow this advice, because it is beneficial for the former. Yet another implication is that an export-led development, mostly financed by large *private* capital flows, offers a superior strategy of economic development, notwithstanding the OECD protectionism, which, it is claimed, barks but does not bite!

These are important claims, which need a closer scrutiny.[1] To this end, the following main questions are addressed in this chapter: (a) What makes globalization work?; (b) Does globalization necessarily mean a regime of 'free markets'? (c) Has globalization accelerated growth and improved the distribution of income worldwide? But before we do that, let it be noted at this juncture that the three basic theorems cited above compare *free* trade with a state of complete autarky in the first case; and *freer* trade and autarky in the second case. It is, therefore, not strictly correct to apply these propositions to real-world situations where the relevant comparison is between more and less international trade. The only valid generalization is that blanket protectionism is welfare-reducing; however, the same stricture does not apply to selective protection measures taken by the developing countries to promote industrialization and/or help their balance of payment by imposing temporary restrictions on destabilizing capital flows.

What Moves Globalization?

There are at least four factors which have spurred globalization on, increasing the size and the speed of global movement of goods, services, capital, and knowledge, which promise to make a decisive impact on production and consumption patterns throughout the world:

1. The first such factor is the recent phenomenon of the 'fragmentation' (also referred to as 'outsourcing') of hitherto monolithic production processes into smaller ones, which transcend national borders (Jones 1993), and which, incidentally, makes it harder for national producers to dodge the Ricardian Law! It is claimed that thanks to these value-sharing arrangements, the various links of a given production chain are distributed efficiently and equitably between countries, which, though not having a comparative advantage in the whole production process, may yet find a place in the production network by producing components, spare parts, etc.[2] It has been estimated that about one-third of total world trade in the mid 1990s took place within such production networks. This trend towards fragmentation is the most obvious in the production of transportation, and machinery, parts and components (World Bank 2000). Three aspects of this phenomenon should be noted:

   (a) These production networks, which criss-cross like a spider's web, have widened the influence of a handful of OECD countries whose vested interests have been decisive in forcing the pace of trade and capital liberalization.

   (b) Production fragmentation is primarily a reflection of the growing importance of the multinationals (MNCs), which actually run these production networks to maximize their own profit in international trade. This 'fact' has obvious implications for the type, quantity, and location of the goods and services these networks produce, and for the direction of their 'spill-over' on the economies of the developing countries. One little piece of evidence is relevant to evaluate the size (and sign) of their potential benefits: three-fourths of the foreign direct investment (the FDI) in the 1990s reflected the mergers and acquisition activities of the MNCs, and added little to the productive capacity in those emerging markets which were fortunate enough to get them. Worse still, a large part of this arbitrage profit-seeking capital has been 'highly unstable' and 'an unreliable source of development finance' (UNCTAD 1999).

(c) These arrangements have had the unintended effect of lowering the demand for, and the real wage of, the *unskilled* labour, as opposed to the skilled labour. The former find themselves cast ashore in a rather unfriendly environment in which they can be 'exchanged' on unfair terms for workers in other countries, which, in turn, threatens their job security (Rodrik 1997).

2. The second factor moving globalization is the emergence of the new internet economy, also referred to as the 'knowledge economy'. It seems to have made the emergence of free, fair, and global markets both inevitable and irreversible, mainly through business-to-business (B2B) exchanges, which could be worth $4.3 trillion in the US alone by the year 2003. It has also eased the constraints of time and geography on the increasing contacts between economic agents around the globe. The internet revolution is likely to slash 'transaction costs' down to the zero level mainly by squeezing the middlemen out of circulation. It is now asserted that domestic and international markets are presumably becoming (almost) perfect because of this invention, which may repair to a great extent the informational deficiency of the economic agents in both the developed and the developing countries—all of which may, incidentally, be cited as a good enough reason for the greater relevance, for development policy, of the liberalist prescription, which has rested its claim to superiority mainly on the *reality* of perfect competition and zero transaction (and transporting) costs. However, such claims fly, literally, in the face of reality! Most recent

studies show that the internet revolution, which seems to have lost some of its steam, has not—at least, *not yet*—succeeded in eliminating 'price dispersion' (i.e., the differential between the highest and the lowest price of the same product). In other words, it does not equalize the product price to marginal cost, which is a sure sign of market imperfection.[3] Yet another alarming aspect of the internet revolution is the heavy concentration (93 per cent) of the internet users among the richest 20 per cent countries, while the poorest 20 per cent countries 'house' only 0.2 per cent of the total users. According to the OECD statistics, 95 per cent of secure internet servers and 97 per cent of websites are concentrated in the OECD area, with the US dominating it. Such an asymmetric ownership pattern—referred to rhetorically as the Digital Divide—is going to increase the differential of the growth rates between the rich and poor nations due to the (very fast) growth of the internet economy (UNDP 1999). This, in turn, would further widen the de-equalizing tendencies of international trade, and greatly erode the 'catching up' potential of the developing countries. Yet another factor which is concentrating the potential benefits of the knowledge economy in a few (rich) hands is the increasing trend towards patenting the creation of even spurious knowledge—for example, 'reverse auctions', 'group buying', etc.—which makes the cost of acquisition and transmission of knowledge rise significantly above the neo-classical zero level.[4] Even worse, the trend to monopolize knowledge creation is expected to hinder its spreading to the developing countries by raising its price to the users, causing a perverse transfer of resources from them to the rich countries, creating the 'wrong' type of knowledge, and obstructing innovation and research.

3. The third factor is that the wheels of international trade are now oiled by a large pool of international finance, which in the last decade of the 20th century increasingly took the shape of Foreign Direct Investment (FDI) by the MNCs. The FDI increased 17-fold between 1973 and 1996, from $21.5 billion to almost $350 billion, which implies an average annual growth of over 12 per cent (WTO 1998). The rising number of financial transactions has created a global 'financial system', which is, however, global only in name because it really acts as a proxy for a handful of financial markets located in the developed countries. In this system sits a multi-trillion pool of investible funds, which is available to the developing

countries as well—though on a much reduced scale after the East Asian crisis of the late 1990s—provided that the 'right' conditions are created to attract them. The creation of these right conditions, however, implies a great restriction on the autonomy of the national governments in the design of domestic and international development policies. This would not be so bad in itself if such restrictions were not arbitrary and served the interests of the host countries as well, which is seldom the case. Yet another obvious outcome of the global financial integration has been that financial instruments with similar risks pay similar return in all the world markets, which looks like a confirmation of the HOS rule noted above. Moreover, this fact may not, in principle, be detrimental to the developing countries. But what *is* detrimental to their interests is that it has created pressure groups, which have been instrumental in forcing developing countries to liberalize capital-account transactions rather too abruptly, and which have added an element of volatility to capital markets. The net effect of such 'big-bang' liberalization of capital flows has been to destabilize the economies of the developing countries by making exchange-rate management a near impossibility; so much so that 'under free capital mobility no regime of exchange rate will guarantee stable and competitive rates; nor will it combine steady growth with financial stability' (UNCTAD 1999: p. 130). The most dramatic (even tragic) illustration of the destabilizing effects of the modern world financial system is the East Asian economic crisis during the period from 1977 to 1999. Yet another detrimental aspect of its 'liberal' nature is that it is almost exclusively focused on the movement of capital, but not on labour, which makes globalization distributionally *de-equalizing*. Further, it is also contrary to the prediction of the HOS rule. Worse still, capital flows have gravitated to the service industry, which accounts for two-thirds of the total FDI, and to 'enclave investment' where its productivity is minimal from the host country's point of view. But it no longer flows in the veins of the manufacturing activity where its revitalizing effect can be the biggest (World Bank 1999). All this has added to the payments difficulties of the recipient countries by increasing their external-resource needs, which are becoming ever more dependent on the vanishing beneficial type of FDI.

4. Finally, the GATT, which metamorphosed into the WTO in 1995, has apparently been bending over backwards to promote a

rule-based free trade in a *multilateral* and non-discriminatory fashion. To this end, it has sought to discipline, though not with much success, the arbitrary use of non-tariff barriers—the unilateral imposition of voluntary export quotas and anti-dumping duties on developing countries—to protect the 'sunset' industries (textile, leather products, etc.) in the developed countries. Also, the WTO's 'democratic' dispute-settlement mechanism—democratic, because the trade disputes are now decided on an unweighted, one-country-one-vote rule—is not of much help because the large expertise costs required to mount litigation against the offending party gives a distinct advantage to the bigger and richer countries over the smaller and the poorer countries (World Bank 1999). Also, the WTO is increasingly preoccupied with the specific concerns of the developed countries (for e.g., environment-related restrictions, the imposition of labour standards, etc.), most of which have adverse implications for the developing countries. These matters are pursued further in the following discussion. It is enough to note here that the WTO, notwithstanding its heroic efforts to secure market success for the developing countries, has not had much success on this score. This shows that the reduction, if any, in the incidence of non-tariff restrictions by the developed countries have been more apparent than real and EC agricultural protectionism remains green as ever (the size of agricultural subsidy has ballooned to $360 billion a year, which is $30 billion more than the total GDP of Africa!). It also indicates the freeing of the movement of capital, while the mobility of unskilled labour remains restricted. All this, and the misuse of the TRIPS Accord by the MNCs (discussed in the next section), has greatly tilted the balance of advantage against the developing countries. The fact is, the earlier expectations about the potential benefits of the Uruguay Round Accord have proved to be a vast exaggeration. Thus, it has been estimated that about $700 billion worth of extra exports from the developing countries could not materialize for lack of access to the OECD countries—an amount equal to 12 per cent of the combined GDPs of the developing countries and four times the total inflow of FDI during the 1990s (UNCTAD 1999: p. 143). The reason for this disappointing performance is that the Uruguay Round (UR) has certainly failed to create a 'level playing field' in the international trading system, which continues to work principally to the advantage of the developed countries.[5]

Does Globalization Mean Free (Freer) World Markets?

The central issue to be decided in order to evaluate the potential benefits of globalization promised by the neo-classical trade theory is, does it necessarily imply free (or freer) markets? This is due to the fact that if the answer to this question is in the negative the expected result, i.e., leading each trading country and the world on to the highest possible welfare peak by directing resources into the most efficient and equitable channels, will *not* follow. Now there are at least four basic reasons why, from the developing countries' point of view, a largely, if not an entirely, negative answer to this question is more likely. First, world trade is regulated by the GATT/WTO system, which is *not* run by the Invisible Hand; and, for all its (tall) claims, the system is not becoming any more multilateral. The principal instrument used by the system to secure export expansion is the reciprocity principle, which is essentially *mercantilist* in nature.[6] This is because the opening up of domestic markets for the exports of the trading partners is a *concession* to be traded for getting a similar access to their exports, and such concessions are seldom 'voluntarily' extended by the trading partners to each other. Indeed, each GATT-sponsored Round since 1947 has sought to achieve a balance between domestic and foreign concessions by trading interests for interests. Also, world trade is increasingly threatened by a proliferation of regional trading blocks, through which more than 80 per cent of world trade now flows. However, it must be conceded that the rapid expansion of world trade, which has grown faster than the growth rate of GDP since 1950, has to a considerable extent been the result of GATT's efforts.[7] In spite of this, it will be even logically false to attribute to free-trade philosophy (and globalization) the expansion of world trade secured by the application of the (mercantilist) reciprocity principle, and that too through non-Vinerian bilateral arrangements!

Second, and this is even more fundamental, world trade and finance is essentially being run by 1000 powerful multinational *monopolies*, of which 85 per cent reside in one of the OECD countries or the other, and which control 87 per cent of world output (*The Economist*, 2000b). Under these circumstances, an exploitation of the weaker side should normally be expected. But I will come to this point a little later. At present, I wish to point out that globalization does *not* represent the working of the free markets, because

the real world has been taken over by the big MNCs whose acquisi-
tive adventures continue with unabated intensity in all sectors of
the economies in the free world. The recent wave of hostile take-
overs, the total value of which in 1999 rose sharply to $3.4 trillion,
signify the stirring up of an unmistakable trend. According to a
sympathetic interpretation, this marks the emergence of a capitalism 'more transparent, more efficient, and yes, redder in tooth and
claw' (*The Economist,* 2000c). But, in fact, according to a KPMG
study, a large number of these mergers have ended up in financial
disasters, destroying a large part of shareholder value and adding
substantially to skilled job losses as a means of achieving elusive
efficiency outcomes.[8] These snowballing conglomerations seem to
possess a comparative advantage in grabbing rather than giving;
worse still, they have obstructed competition and innovation.[9] Nothing illustrates this trend better than the virtual takeover of the knowledge economy by rent-seeking (would be) monopolists, which will
impose an increasingly larger deadweight loss on the developing
countries. As briefly noted above, the trend to patent even trivia
means that the economic space is going to be filled with powerful
monopolies, a full 97 per cent of which would be located in the
industrial countries.[10] What is nothing less than scandalous is that
these monopolies, taken out in any one country (say the US), are
protected all over the world by the World Intellectual Property
Organization's Patents Cooperation Treaty (UNDP 1999).

This brings us to perhaps the worst aspect of globalization under
the Uruguay Round, the so-called TRIPS Accord, which was created to protect intellectual property rights against greedy imitators
but has turned to be a veritable economic octopus. It is now being
misused by the MNCs to make money at the expense of mostly the
developing and the very poor countries. In most cases, these intellectual property rights are really contrived, mostly designed to check
the future flowering of technological know-how in the developing
countries. As a result, a lot of scientific research which should be
benefiting the entire humanity never reaches where the markets
are 'missing'! Thus, for instance, much biological research that is
now being increasingly financed by the MNCs does not spill over
to the poor countries, partly because it is unfit to cure even such
simple diseases as malaria, which kills 1 to 2.5 million people in
impoverished sub-Saharan Africa each year. The reason is simply
that there is no 'market in malaria'. Even more ominously, the MNCs

are misusing the TRIPS Accord 'to own the genetic codes of the very foodstuffs on which the world (and especially the developing world) depends, and even human genome itself' (Sachs 1999). Also, the transmission of Green Revolution technologies, which transformed agriculture around the world in the 1960s and 1970s, as long as these were handled by public-sector agencies, have become difficult and vastly more expensive because the farmers must now pay stiff technology fees to the MNCs producing such seeds (El Feki 2000). Rather than in any way helping the helpless farmers in the poor countries, these MNCs seem to be more interested in applying new biotechnological knowledge to boost the productivity of the farmers of rich countries.[11] This is telling proof of one of the main observations of this book: Free markets seldom work to the benefit of the large majority of humankind because of the highly unequal distribution of economic and political power between the rich and poor countries. Thus, to correct the rising inequities of the world economic system, the MNCs must be saddled with a definite sense of purpose and direction by well-informed global public policy.

Globalization, Growth and Distribution

The basic theorems of international economics given at the beginning of this chapter assure us that free trade will lead the economy, all by itself, to the highest feasible peak, given the highly restrictive assumptions on which it rests.[12] In particular, it predicts that international trade will be growth-promoting once the (relatively inefficient) domestic rate of transformation in production is brought into equality with the (more efficient) foreign rate of transformation in production, at the internationally given ('right') price. It should also be welfare-promoting, as the two rates of transformation are brought into equality with the domestic rate of substitution in consumption (Naqvi 1969). Thus, as trade resumes, factor intensities in export and import activities change in the efficient direction, and factor rewards are also expected to become the first-best—more for the relatively abundant factor and less for the relatively scarce one in each trading country. However, *even at the theoretical level,* such high expectations are not justified. First, the neo-classical assumption that, among other things, perfect competition prevails in all countries is no longer true (that is, if it ever was in the first place)—the snowballing MNCs seem to have programmed the Invisible Hand to act merely as its stalking horse! Second, the promised first-best results will not flow if production functions/consumption patterns between the trading partners are *not* identical. Also, there are problems with defining factor abundance in physical terms or in price terms, and the unique (one-to-one) relationship between product prices and factor prices that the HOS proposition demands cannot be guaranteed if the number of factors and goods exceed two, which is always the case in the real world (Johnson 1965). Little surprise then that the empirical tests of HOS Theorems have not succeeded in establishing its truth (Bhagwati 1965). Third, while capital moves practically unhindered within and between countries, the same is not true of unskilled labour, from which follows that the distribution of income between capital and labour can only worsen in the event of free (or greatly freed) movement of factors. Fourth, international trade is not really free; it is constrained by the WTO-approved (and not-so-approved) tariff and non-tariff restrictions, the latter being more prevalent in the developed countries, blocking off market access to the exports of developing countries. However, capital movement between the developed and the developing countries is now completely free (or nearly so), but this has only added to the balance-of-payments difficulties of the latter (UNCTAD 1999). Finally, as noted above, international trade is run on the mercantilist (reciprocity) principle and not on the free-trade principle, and is essentially confined within regional blocs, which implies that globalization need not yield *any* of the first-best results promised by the neo-classical theory. An implication of this principle for the developing countries is that within the present GATT/WTO system, market access to the exports of developed countries should be granted only as a quid pro quo for similar concessions to the developing countries exports, and it should *not* be given on a voluntary basis. However, the many conditionalities imposed by the multilateral donors force the developing countries to liberalize voluntarily, while the developed countries have not offered any such voluntary concessions (IMF 2000a). All this makes the world trading system inherently inequitable for the developing countries.

Indeed, globalization has worked much worse in practice. Only one example would suffice to show this. The rapid (big-bang) dismantling of restriction on capital controls by the developing countries to allow a free run to the MNCs did provide them some of the needed capital (physical and human), though that too flowed predominantly to the East Asian countries. But, as the events of 1998–99 show, what was given to these countries by one hand over a fairly long period was withdrawn suddenly by the other hand. As a result, these economies, which enjoyed growth rates of 8 to 10 per cent year after year for several decades, kept their 'economic fundamentals' in excellent shape and were eulogized by the donors for good governance, slumped to the abyss of economic distress, and their hard work of decades to achieve high rates of economic (and human) development was undone almost overnight. Further, as if to add insult to injury, this colossal market failure engineered by the MNCs was blamed entirely on the Asian 'crony capitalism', on their weak financial structures and poor governance! Even worse, the international donors sought to cure this market failure by bailing out the Western private creditors at the expense of the prosperity and well-being of the debtor countries, 'which surely served neither the cause of efficiency nor of justice' (UNCTAD 1998: p. 11). Incidentally, the countries that did *not* open up their capital markets so much (for e.g., India, Pakistan) were spared the trauma!

The East Asian crisis has brought to the fore the fragility of the international trading and financial systems and also their essentially de-equalizing (even, dehumanizing) character. We now know that the mighty forces of globalization are impervious to the clamourings of the developing countries for a better deal and are being misused to serve the (narrow) interests of the MNCs. Also, they have not brought *any* net benefits to the developing countries—at least, not so far. As noted above, the great onrush of private capital during the 1990s—cited as one of the great gifts of globalization to the (developing) world—has been mostly the result of MNC mergers, which accounted for well over half the total FDI inflow during 1992–97. Further, much of this was in the service sectors, and has the potential to add to payment difficulties of the developing countries (UNCTAD 1999). The East Asian crisis has also underscored the need to rein in globalization by restricting capital flows, especially of the 'hot-money' type: 'in the absence of a global mechanism for stabilizing capital flows, capital control will remain an indispensable part of the developing countries' armoury of measures for the purposes of protection against international financial stabilizing' (UNCTAD 1998: p. xi)—an echo of the Keynesian (and neo-Keynesian) prescriptions for creating a stable world economic system.

Partly as a result of these sins of omission and commission by the developed countries and the inherent defects of the GATT/WTO system, which perversely grants redress to mostly the rich through its expensive and skill-intensive dispute settlement mechanism, the global distribution of income and wealth has worsened. While the share of developed countries increased from 67.3 per cent in 1960 to 78.7 per cent in 1994, that of the developing countries (excluding the former Soviet Union and Eastern Europe) declined from 19.8 per cent to 18.0 per cent during the same period (Streeten 1998). Since 1994, the situation on the ground has only worsened. Thus, 'the income gap between the fifth of the world's people living in the richest countries and the fifth in the poorest countries was 74 to 1 in 1997 up from 60 to 1 in 1990 and 30 to 1 in 1960' (*HDR* 1999: p. 38).

The Nature of Response I

The discussion in the preceding section should be a sufficient refutation of the neo-classical assertion that international trade is an adequate substitute for domestic efforts to stimulate economic growth. Indeed there is a real danger that if developing countries leave themselves at the mercy of the vagaries of international market, they may experience what Bhagwati (1958) christened 'immiserizing growth' (i.e., the loss of welfare caused by an adverse movement of the terms of trade). To reinforce these fears, there has been a steady deterioration in the purchasing power of the developing countries' exports: 'Income losses were greater in 1990s than in the 1980s not only because of larger terms-of-trade losses, but also because of the increased share of trade in GDP' (UNCTAD 1999: p. 85). The hardest hit on this score is sub-Saharan Africa, which is having to pay a very high price for getting integrated into the world economy *without prior preparation* (*HDR* 1999). The prices of its exports have, on an average, been falling (by 25 per cent in 1997–1999) while barriers on its exports are being imposed mainly by Japan, Northern America and Europe. It has been estimated that its exports could rise by 14 per cent, that is, by about $2.5 billion if these restrictions are removed (*The Economist* 2001: p. 17). Thus, efforts should be made to reform the WTO so that it becomes consistent with the growth requirements of the developing countries. To this end, global efforts should be made to undo OECD protectionism and renegotiate the UR Agreement with a view to broadening the scope for infant-industry protection, clearly recognizing the endemic balance-of-payments problems of the developing countries.[13]

Assuming that such efforts are being made, there is an urgent need, especially in the economically blighted Africa, to recharge and energize the traditional engines of growth through the balanced/unbalanced development prescription. The main aim should be to grow fast enough—say, increase per capita income at a rate of over 3 per cent per annum—in order to participate fully in the globalization process. Indeed, the former is a necessary condition for achieving success in the latter. This has been the experience of all countries that have been successful developers (mainly East Asia and now China)—those which have grown fast enough to double per capita income in a period of 6 to 10 years, converge with the developed countries, reconcile the trade-off between growth and equity, achieve substantial gains in poverty reduction, and ensure sustainable macroeconomic stability.[14] This could be termed as the modern version of Leibenstein's critical minimal effort (Leibenstin 1957) in order to achieve the Rostowian take-off into self-sustained growth (Rostow 1956). The most commonly cited contributory factors required for this scenario to materialize are the ones traditionally identified by development economics: high rates of physical and human capital formation and domestic saving, and agrarian and structural transformation—the latter denoting a rising share of the manufacturing sector in the GDP. My contention is that this time-tested strategy of development continues to be the best guide of development policy in the 21st century as well.

The Economics of Structural Transformation

The single-most important set of ideas, on which successful development policy must rest, relate to those which revolve round Lewis-type models of economic development. As noted in the preceding chapters, such models see the process of growth as the progressive absorption of surplus labour (and capital), displaced from the less productive agriculture sector to the more advanced manufacturing sector, as the center of gravity gradually shifts from the former to the latter. The saving and investment rates continuously rise as the share of profits in total GDP increases with a corresponding rise in that the manufacturing sector. This is referred to as the process of 'structural transformation', which can be regarded as the Fundamental Law of Economic Development.[15] These development models predict that as long as the agricultural wage lags behind its marginal product and there is a gap between the agricultural and urban wage, the growth-promoting inter-sectoral reallocation of labour and capital will continue.[16] The heart of the development problem is, therefore, the ability of the agricultural sector to yield sufficiently large agricultural surpluses and make available a large enough part of such surpluses within agriculture and for productive investment in non-agricultural sectors.[17] Simultaneously, the non-agricultural sector, financed by this agricultural surplus and the reinvestment of industrial profits, must grow fast enough to absorb the labour force being reallocated (Ranis 1988). The structural transformation process comes to an end once the dualistic character of the economy—that is, the labour-surplus condition, when the supply of labour exceeds the demand for it at the going wage—is eliminated.

The reason why development policy should rest on Lewis-type models of economic development and not on the prescriptions of neo-classical economics, is the former's focus on the essential inter-sectoral *production asymmetry* between an initially large agricultural sector and a much smaller manufacturing sector so that the accumulation of capital (which is assumed to be done exclusively by the capitalists, while labour is only a consumer) plays a double role: 'not only does it increase the level of national output, but it moves the composition of national output in the direction of the efficient outcome' (Kanbur and McIntosh 1990: p. 116). In this framework, surplus labour migrates to manufacturing at a rate faster than the increase in agricultural production so that agricultural productivity also rises.[18] Also, in this process, the required increase in the saving rate is generated to finance the additional capital accumulation necessary for sustaining a rapid structural transformation of the economy.

Empirical studies confirm structural transformation to be the most widely (even vividly) noted universal 'stylized fact' (or 'regularity') of the development process (for e.g., Kuznets 1955; Chenery *et al.* 1986; Syrquin 1988)—one that holds for the developed *and* the developing countries. Thus, during the 1965–1995 period, the growth rate of GDP was strongly linked with the growth rate of manufacturing: a 3 per cent growth rate of GDP has been associated with an even higher growth rate of manufacturing, a less than 3 per cent growth accompanies an even lower manufacturing growth, and a zero growth of GDP is always a combined result of negative growth in manufacturing and positive growth in other sectors (UNIDO 1996). Cross-country regressions for 1960–1973 and 1973–1985 show that inter-sectoral labour reallocation does make a significant contribution to GDP growth, even more in the rich and middle-income countries than in the poorer countries, and that industrial development is at the heart of the development process (Dorwick and Gemmel 1991: p. 273). Also, the regressions done on a sample of 40 developing countries show that during 1970–90 the rate of investment and the share of manufacturing in the GDP are among the most significant factors explaining the growth rate of per capita income, and the size of the coefficients and their significance (measured by the t-statistics) rise steadily as the growth of per capita income increases. The values of the coefficients are the lowest for countries scoring growth rates of less than 1.5 per cent per annum and are the highest for those which have grown in excess of 3 per cent (Naqvi 1995). Furthermore, the growth rate of per capita income has been strongly correlated with the increase in the share of 'heavy' industries—an echo of (Mahalanobis 1953)—which are generally more intensive in human capital, where R&D expenditure is the heaviest and where the spill-over effects are expected to be the largest in size (Bradford *et al.* 1991; Grossman & Helpman 1994).

Rostow (1956) echoed the same theme: he explicitly stipulated that economic progress requires a doubling in the rate of capital accumulation. However, we know now that to make real progress the 'right' ratio is 30 to 35 per cent of GDP, as the experiences of East Asian countries and that of China amply illustrate. Further, to achieve a high growth rate of GDP, the efficiency of investment must be raised (i.e., the capital/output ratio lowered) to prevent capital inefficiency from eroding the (warranted) growth rate corresponding to a high saving rate—which is, incidentally, Solow's (1957) contribution to our understanding of the growth process. To this end, labour-saving techniques of production have been widely recommended to maximize the growth rate of employment in agriculture and manufacturing (Ranis 1988). Also, as noted in Chapter 8, there is a need to keep a dynamic balance between the growth rate of the agricultural and manufacturing sectors (Johnston and Mellor 1961).

The 'Orderly Transformation' Scenario

Yet another extension of the ideas presented above is the concept of 'orderly transformation' (Naqvi 1995), which states that a high rate of economic growth, *if properly managed,* can be essentially 'orderly' with respect to the basic relationships among the principal variables, especially those relating to the changes in per capita income, distribution of income, poverty reduction and macro-economic stability. Put more positively:

> *a high rate of growth, macroeconomic stability, and distributive justice have moved together—signifying orderly transformation of low-income countries into middle-income (and even high-income) economies. Indeed, a stronger statement is possible: the developing countries suffering from low growth of per capita income are generally worse-off with respect to macroeconomic stability and distributive justice as compared with those enjoying medium growth and high growth (p. 549).*

The contribution here is to integrate growth, equity and macroeconomic stability into a single, overarching conception of growth; to reaffirm some of the basic insights of Lewis and other founding fathers of development economics, especially those relating to the centrality of the structural transformation process for achieving broadbased economic development; to amend their insights where their prognostications have not been proved correct; and to 'complete' the list of stylized facts by emphasizing the importance of keeping the key macro-variables (for e.g., the budgetary deficit, the trade deficit, the exchange rate depreciation, etc.) within 'safe' limits as the growth process gathers momentum.

An important aspect of the orderly transformation scenario is that contrary to the seemingly 'bloody' development scenario sketched in Lewis's model—in which profits rise while rural (real) wages lag behind significantly—the distribution of income and poverty do *not* necessarily worsen as high rates of growth are achieved; indeed, growth tends to be equalizing. Thus, when due attention is paid to setting the initial conditions right (for e.g., by implementing wide-ranging land reforms), the fast-growing countries have, with few exceptions, enjoyed lesser income inequality (a lower unemployment rate and a higher share of wages in the GDP), a lower incidence of poverty, and a higher level of 'human development' (i.e., lower infant mortality rate, higher adult literacy and a higher percentage of population having access to basic health services). Finally, the high-growth countries tend to be macroeconomically more stable. Thus, the average inflation rate declines steadily as one moves from the low-growth to medium-growth and high-growth countries; due to a lower rate of inflation, export activity is strong and, given a comfortable position of exchange reserves, the incidence of currency depreciation is the least in the fast-growing countries compared to the medium and slow growers.

These findings emphasize the centrality of achieving a high enough growth rate of per capita income *in the shortest period of time* to make the growth process broadbased and attain a modicum of convergence. This policy should now (and in the future) be even more acceptable than it was in the 1950s, because Lewis's growth fundamentalism has not turned out to be as 'bloody' as it might have looked initially. We know now that no country has succeeded in reducing poverty significantly on a sustained basis in the absence of a fast enough growth of mean income; that success in poverty reduction is most plausible when the growth rate has been high (the per capita income rising at over 3 per cent per annum for several decades) than if it is low and that if the growth rate is less than 1.5 per cent, then all the nagging trade-offs, which make the job of economic management difficult, will have to be faced. Yet another aspect of this concept is to reaffirm one of the most basic lessons of development economics—namely, that the 'orderliness' property of economic development can be realized *only* by efficient economic management and the job cannot be left to the magic of the markets (Naqvi 2000).

Neo-classical Explanations of Economic Growth

To see the originality of the Lewis-type formulation and its relevance to the problems of developing countries, let us compare it with the neo-classical explanations of economic growth. The question we ask is, does the latter also focus on the crucial aspects of economic development? The answer is flatly in the negative! To prove this contention, let us first compare Lewis's model with the neo-classical *two-sector* growth models (for e.g., Uzawa 1961, 1963). Stripped down to its essentials, this latter class of models assume a two-sector economy, in which one sector produces capital good and the other consumption good; but the capital good is assumed to be 'malleable' so that it can be combined with any amount of labour to either reproduce itself or produce a consumer good.[19] Also assumed are constant returns to scale, capital being infinitely 'long-lived', no technological progress taking place and 'well-behaved' production functions. In this formulation, both sectors use capital and labour (even though the production functions in the two sectors are different). A classical saving function is assumed, but, by the logic of the model, the profit rate (and the wage/rental ratio) in the two sectors must also be the *same* in the neo-classical models, while it is *different* in the Lewis model. This implies that in the neo-classical models the rate of increase in the outputs of the two sectors must be the same and that the production structure does not undergo any structural transformation, which is fundamental to the Lewis's model.[20] This, in effect, proves our contention.

Let us now compare Lewis's model with the neo-classical endogenous growth theory, which claims to have made development economics redundant because it too, like the latter, recognizes the importance of exploiting the economies of scale in the development process to raise per capita income over time (Romer 1986; Lucas 1988). In this conceptualization, which marks a definite improvement on the earlier neo-classical growth models (for e.g., the Solow model), technological change is *not* exogenously given, but is endogenous to the development process. Yet another highlight of this model is that a low initial level of *human* capital and knowledge is recognized as the primary obstacle to sustained development. The policy recommendation flowing from this theory is, therefore, to raise productivity by encouraging investment in human capital and knowledge, and innovation—which, according to this model, is the *only* thing that the government needs to do, if at all, to propel the process of economic development. Government intervention is required here because technological change is an externality not seen by private firms. All these are very valuable points, though, to some extent, these are in the nature of reinventing the wheel.[21] However, growth in this model does *not* require inter-sectoral asymmetries in production. Indeed, as if to reaffirm its neo-classical birth mark, the endogenous growth theory assumes a *one-sector economy*, or one where all sectors are symmetric in nature (Krugman 1992), which prevents it from highlighting the growth-promoting inter-sectoral transfer of the surplus factors of production. This feature alone makes this theory unsuitable to handle the central productivity-increasing and growth-promoting structural transformation aspects of economic development. As if to make the new theory totally irrelevant for development policy, it assumes constant returns to capital, thus ruling out the possibilities of both increasing and diminishing returns to the same (Solow 1994). It also assumes that aggregate saving arises from a single consumer (with an infinite time horizon) optimizing his/her inter-temporal consumption plan (Stern 1989). It follows that the endogenous growth theory, for all its invaluable insights into the development process, fails to provide 'a powerful organizing framework for thinking about actual growth phenomenon' of economic development (Pack 1994: p. 55). The reason is, it too does not focus at all on inter-sectoral asymmetries in the production process. To summarize, the modern neo-classical growth theory does *not* constitute a theory of economic development. Presumably, it has left the job undone so that development economics does it again in the 21st century!

The Nature of Response II
Human Development

The next step is to protect human development from the undesirable consequences of globalization and improve upon it. Fortunately, the set of policies most relevant in this context have long been identified in the development literature. The focus has been on devising more comprehensive and pluralistic indicators of social welfare than per capita GNP, which could form the basis of public policy. Buchanan and Ellis (1995) sought to include life expectancy at birth, infant morality, general health indicators, food, energy intakes, etc., in an index of the quality of life—as an end-product of the efforts to improve economic performance. To this end, they constructed a second index correlated with the first one. Then,

Lewis (1955), often accused of spreading 'growth fundamentalism', explicitly stated: 'The advantage of economic growth is not that wealth increases the human choice—the case of economic growth is that it increases his freedom...' (p. 420). Morris (1979) suggested a Physical Quality of Life Index (PQLI), including life expectancy, infant mortality and literacy as components. The problem here is that life expectancy and infant mortality are significantly correlated. The basic needs approach, which enjoyed the blessings of the World Bank, strongly argued for going beyond what Marx dubbed as 'commodity fetishism'. Even though somewhat 'open-ended' with respect to its theoretical underpinnings, this approach did correctly highlight the need for making a greater provision for the social sectors, with a view to providing 'all human beings with an *opportunity* for a full life' (Streeten *et al.* 1981). Building upon these earlier insights is the view that the development process is essentially a matter of expanding people's 'entitlements' and 'capabilities'—ultimately, of enlarging people's choices—and of concentrating on the ends (such as longevity, literacy, freedom) rather than on the means (namely, growth) (Sen 1992). At a deeper philosophical level, the aim of this research has also been to move away from a 'mono-concentration' on GNP to a pluralistic conception of economic progress—inspired by a rejection, for the same reason, of the Benthamite focus on the metric of utility alone by moral philosophers like John Rawls (see Chapters 6 and 7). What is essentially involved here is 'informational broadening' with a view to making valid statements about comparative deprivations (Sen 1999).

Similarly motivated is the concept of 'human development', spelled out at length in the UNDP's invaluable *Annual Human Development Reports,* which have regularly appeared since 1990. It encompasses 'the production and distribution of commodities and the expansion and use of human capabilities', and 'the process of widening people's choices and the level of their achieved well-being'. It 'focuses on human choices rather than on the provision of goods and services that deprived groups need' (UNDP 1990: p. 9). An HDI (Human Development Index), taking account of longevity, knowledge and basic income, replaces the growth rate of GNP as an indicator of human development, even though care is taken to emphasize that the former is a necessary, not sufficient, condition to achieve the latter (Haq 1995). The first two elements of this index measure the formation of human capabilities, while the third one serves as a proxy measure for the choices people have (and make) in putting these capabilities to use. There are some obvious problems with this approach, as there are with the way the HDI is constructed. First, it uses the *level* rather than the *changes* in the components of the HDI index (Aturupane *et al.* 1994); the database of the index is to some extent arbitrary, even misleading in some respects (data on life expectancy are available only for a few countries) and non-comparable in other respects (i.e., adult literacy). As a result 'HDI is conceptually weak and empirically unsound, involving serious problems of non-comparability over time and space, measurement errors and biases' (Srinivasan 1994). Second, focusing on the ends *rather than* the means of development may lead to an over-emphasis on education and health to the detriment of the income factor in HDI.[22] This would, of course, be committing a grave mistake because the role of the income component is to serve as a proxy for some important aspects of the quality of life that are missed out in the exclusive concentration on life expectancy and basic education (Anand and Sen 2000). Also, there is a danger of going from one extreme to another—from a mono-concentration on GNP to one on education and health.[23] In my opinion, the latter, if pushed too far, may derail the development process by not giving the GNP (devil) its due. Third, it must be noted that a lot of criticism of GNP per capita can be taken care of by choosing the 'right' strategy of income *generation,* which reduces poverty and enhances employment to a greater extent than alternative strategies do (for e.g., in some respects, a labour-intensive strategy may be superior to a capital-intensive strategy on this count) (Ranis and Stewart 2000), and by emphasizing that additional income so generated is *used* to promote more education and better health. Fourth, it should also be kept in view that whatever may have been the situation in the 'outliers', high rates of growth of per capita income (especially when in excess of 3 per cent per annum) on a sustained basis have, on the average, been negatively correlated with poverty and employment (Roemer and Gugerty 1997).[24] It is, therefore, important that the baby is not thrown away with the bath water. Fifth, the suggestion that the GDP be adjusted by the relevant Gini Coefficient to yield a more welfare-oriented (cross-country) ranking by correcting the HDI for inequalities in income distribution is certainly well-taken, but it is problematic when the

Lorenz Curves intersect over the relevant range. However, even when they do not intersect, the welfare ranking is not invariant with respect to the type of the inequality measure used.[25]

The following points of the research on human development may be noted in the context of framing an effective response to globalization.

1. Here we find a broad support for a mixed-economy approach to economic development and its high moral content, with a clear role for the state to maximize social good. Thus, for instance, central development issues like poverty, inequality, intolerable tyranny and violations of liberty need *both* a normative and a positivistic focus, and they invite state intervention to take care of the externalities— all of which challenge the liberalist *belief* that competitive markets offer a long term solution to the perennial problems of human existence.

2. The human development perspective contrasts sharply with the contractarian–libertarian approaches, which would keep state intervention on the periphery of economic endeavour and let it do only such (admittedly important) things as devising a framework of 'fair rules and procedures which safeguard some vital individual rights (a là Nozick), while leaving the rest to self-interested individuals in the hope that they do what is best for them. These approaches assign priority to rights, while the human development perspective (and that of development economics) would emphasize maximizing the social good, which is defined as including the protection of vital individual rights and liberties as well.

3. The UNDP's analysis has certainly broadened the scope of development economics with its emphasis on the need to *directly* address the central developmental problem of raising the level of economic well-being of the people by linking development success to the extent of improvement in the individual's capability to convert income into well-being, and by showing that because this link is by no means automatic, it should be managed by a non-minimalist (democratic) state. It may be noted that as a step in this direction there is now a widespread consensus on the need to use the higher incomes generated by (high rates of) economic growth to raise the 'quality' of life by greater social spending and by

reducing the inequalities of income and wealth (for e.g., *WDR* 2000). This is a valuable consensus designed to link economic development more tightly to human happiness and well-being, which needs to be further strengthened in the 21st century, whatever conceptual ambiguities there may be in the human development perspective.

4. It may be noted that the UNDP research explicitly points to that aspect of the development process where privatization, liberalization and globalization have been totally unhelpful for human development—even more than for economic development—where to achieve the socially desirable outcome, domestic and global governance mechanisms are required to regulate the non-universal, incomplete, or missing markets, and where having a correct moral perspective is as important as the quest for efficiency—in short, where the neo-classical vision of economic progress is singularly inadequate.

Also helpful for an effective human development policy is the fact that while human development enlarges people's capabilities to choose freely from a large menu, such freedom is neither *absolute* nor simply *negative*. Instead, it is *relative* to the extent that the fruits of economic growth cannot be monopolized only by a privileged few (i.e., the notorious 'free riders') to the exclusion of the majority of the population. As noted in Chapter 7, economic and human development would also negate the Nozickian entitlement principle (1974). Instead, individual freedom should more properly be seen as *positive* in the sense that it is not just a matter of respecting some legal *procedures*, it also entails a duty (on the part of the individuals and the state) to prevent the undesirable social consequences of an unfettered exercise of individual freedom, especially by the rich. The process of human development is much wider in scope. It involves more than protecting individual liberty as an *absolute* value, regardless of what such an exercise means for the fulfilment of other worthwhile social objectives. The point of emphasis here is that the economic freedom for the few is translated through the development process into a freedom for all, especially for the members of the least privileged classes in the society, in order to broaden *every* individual's range of choices to achieve happiness.[26]

Notes

1. The discussion in this section is based on Naqvi (2002).
2. Thus, to produce a car in the United States requires the participation of no less than nine countries: 17½ per cent of the car's value goes to South Korea for assembly, 17½ to Japan for components and advanced technology, 7½ per cent to Germany for design, 4 per cent to Taiwan and Singapore for minor parts, 2½ per cent to the United Kingdom for advertising and marketing service, and 1½ per cent to Ireland and Barbados for data processing, etc. (WTO 1998).
3. It has been noted that for identical books and CDs the price differential between online retailers may be as large as 50 per cent!
4. No less than 1,60,000 patents, which grant a 20-year monopoly to their holders, were taken out in 1999 in the US alone, and a lot of this activity is by no means 'productive': 'since so much value that a business creates lies in its patents, they are producing nothing but patents' (*The Economist* 2000d: p. 80). This is a striking example of unproductive rent seeking by *the private sector.*
5. The econometric studies done on the eve of the Uruguay Round agreement estimated that a major portion ($179 billion) of the total gains from the Round (about $200 billion) would accrue to the developed countries (World Bank 1995). But these potential gains have turned out to be vastly exaggerated mainly because the incidence of the anti-dumping duties and other trade restrictions by the developed countries has increased, not declined (UNCTAD 1999).
6. The GATT/WTO system has been able to secure a rapid expansion of world trade by a combination of the reciprocity principle and by the Most Favoured Nations Clause in order to multilateralize world trade. However, as Bhagwati (1990) shows, the departures from multilateralism have been frequent, and mostly in the wrong direction. The non-discrimination principle has been undermined by the virtual outbreak of regional blocs, especially in the 1990s, while the reciprocity principle is mercantilist in temperament (it treats 'trade liberalization as a cost rather than as a source of gain') and is being threatened by the 'aggressive unilateralism' of the US.
7. On an annual average, merchandise exports grew by 6 per cent in real terms from 1948 to 1997, compared to an annual average output growth of 3.7 per cent. Put differently, trade multiplied by the factor of 17, while GDP has grown six-fold during this period (WTO 1998).
8. An outstanding example of such financial disasters due to the much advertised merges is the ill-fated takeover of Digital Equipment by the super successful Compaq Computer in 1998, which was then growing at 38 per cent a year. However, in just one year 'Compaq is a shaken company with an uncertain future. It has lost more money since the merger than in all previous history: more than £2 billion in all' (*The Economist* 2000e: p. 73). Some mergers have worked relatively well, but the overall picture cannot be interpreted as efficient capitalism. However, it cannot be doubted that it has become 'redder in tooth and claw'.
9. This aspect of modern day capitalism has been made crystal clear in the trial of Bill Gates. The trial judge accused him of using his prodigious market power and huge profits to stifle innovation and risk-taking, and to harm both

consumers and any companies that dared to compete with it (*The Economist* 2000d).

10. IMB now takes out 10 patents a day! And as if that is not enough, such companies are also doing 'strategic patenting': 'firms are no longer merely patenting things they have already; they are using patents to colonise new areas of technology' because 'it is a gold-rush, and we have some wicked prospecting tools' (*The Economist* 2000d: p. 80).

11. The five firms controlling biotechnological research, based in the US and Europe, are investing the fruits of highly expensive genetic engineering products to transform agriculture in the *rich* countries (UNDP 1999).

12. For details of the highly restrictive assumptions, see Bhagwati (1965). Some of these are: linear, homogenous production functions in each good, diminishing returns along the isoquant, non-reversible and different factor intensities of the two goods at all relevant factor prices, perfect competition and valuation of factors according to their marginal product, zero transport costs, and incomplete specialization. What is even more peculiar is that the non-satisfaction of *any* one of these myriad assumptions (for e.g., zero transport costs) will guarantee that the HOS model described in the text will *not* work.

13. There is need to re-examine Article XVIII, and Sections A and C of GATT 1994 where the compensation requirements are so onerous as to nullify the very intent of the Article. Also, Part IV of GATT together with the 1979 Tokyo Round Enabling Clause can provide a good starting point to reform the UR Agreement (UNCTAD 1999: p. 132).

14. Successful convergence and orderly transformation can be achieved at a growth rate exceeding 3.5 per cent on a sustained basis. According to Naqvi (1995), the main developers in this category are Singapore, China, Thailand, Malaysia and South Korea. According to IMF (2000), the fast developers are China, Indonesia, Botswana, Korea, Malaysia, Mauritius and Thailand. Perhaps Singapore has been excluded from the IMF list because it is no longer in the low- and middle-income category. The estimation period in the former study is 1970–90, while it is 1970–98 in the latter.

15. Lewis (1954) assigns central importance to understanding the forces that make savings rise secularly in the process of economic growth: 'We cannot explain any industrial revolution (as the economic historians pretend to do) until we can explain why saving increased relatively to national income.' (in Agarwala and Singh [1963]: p. 416).

16. It may be noted that contrary to common perception, the *constancy* of the agricultural wage and it being equal to the marginal or average product is not at all essential for the validity of the Lewis's model. This clarification should set at rest criticism of the validity of development economics, which proves that a zero agricultural wage is its defining characteristic.

17. The studies of the fast-growing East Asian countries have found that: 'high rates of growth provided resources that could be used to promote equality, just as the high degree of equality helped sustain high rates of growth' (Stiglitz 1996a). Yet another set of factors helping growth and equity are related to the fact that the faster the share of labour force in agriculture tends to decline, the higher will be the growth of agricultural output, so that agricultural productivity will rise very quickly among the fast growers than among the slow growers.

(For an excellent analysis of the relationship between growth, inequality and poverty, see Bairoch [1975] and World Bank [2001], especially Chapter 3).

18. It may be noted that in Lewis's model, labour is not surplus in the sense that agricultural output will be unaffected if *any* amount of it was removed from agriculture. Also, the usual assumption that agriculture uses no capital but only labour (and land), while manufacturing uses capital and labour (but no land) is not at all central to Lewis's model. If that were so, it would be inconsistent with his emphasis on a strongly growing agriculture to support manufacturing activity. Further, such a sequence is not possible unless some capital use is allowed in the agriculture sector as well, though a lot of it is concentrated in manufacturing, as the growth process gets underway.

19. The exposition in the text draws liberally on Hahn and Mathews (1965).

20. Another counter-intuitive property of the neo-classical two-sector models is that the consumption goods sector must be *more* capital intensive than the capital goods sector to achieve a steady-state solution.

21. It is interesting that the authors of the endogenous growth theory do *not* recognize at all the contribution of development economics in emphasizing, much earlier than them, the importance of knowledge and human capital, of economies of scale, and of complementarities in the development process. This cannot possibly be attributed to an oversight on the part of the authors; one wonders whether it is yet another example of the neo-classical scientific hubris, which prevents them from looking for new ideas outside their own discipline.

22. For example, Sen (1984) notes: 'Not merely is it the case that economic growth is a means rather than an end, it is also the case that for some important ends it is not a very efficient means either.' Similar statements can be found in the successive UNDP reports. See Chapter 6 of this book on Sen's capability calculus and my remarks on the ends–means debate.

23. Thus, Sen (2000) is also opposed to attaching too much importance to the Human Development Index (*HDI*), which is UNDP's rival as the real income indicator.

24. A recent study finds that in a sample of 80 countries, 'income of the poor rises one-for-one with overall growth' (Dollar and Kray 2000). See also Naqvi (1995) and World Bank (2001) on these matters.

25. Difficulties also arise because the Gini Coefficients do not always accurately replicate the state of income distribution over the entire range. The required number of observations about the lowest and highest income points are not satisfactorily, if at all, covered by the Income and Household Surveys (for e.g., in Pakistan).

26. Sen (1992) points out that the tendency to link liberty to freedom is a 'category mistake': 'liberty is among the *fields* of application of equality, and equality among the *patterns* of distribution of liberty' (p. 22).

10

The Future of Development Economics

This final chapter is meant to put the discussion so far in a wider perspective. As should be clear by now, there can be no question regarding the clarity and reliability of the vision of development economics with respect to the broad purpose and strategy of economic development. This unbreakable linkage between the ideals and reality is central to the continued vitality of the former, which keeps alive the hope that the latter is possible, if not inevitable. One only has to look at the lively debate that has raged on the factors which have caused development successes and failures, and on what needs to be done to strengthen success and avoid failure to be convinced of the salience, reach, and vitality of development economics. Its *exclusive* claim to understanding the economic and social reality in the developing countries remains unchallenged by the neo-classical economics of Walrasian vintage. While the former worries about the perennially unfinished agenda of human existence, the latter remains blissfully unaware of any such thing and vainly seeks to make the real world conform to certain axiomatically derived rules of behaviour 'according to which an economy is to be understood as the maximization of a representative agent's utility over an infinite future' (Hahn 1991: p. 49). Once the mind is heavy with such heady stuff, it does not pay to bother about the oddities and non-convexities of reality. Rather, it is more comfortable to create a make-believe world, in which the 'right' prices are given, the production set is convex, the economic agents behave rationally (that is, selfishly and unsocially), and all markets clear. When all this happens, the residual problems of economic development must be solvable. In the neo-classical vision no (involuntary) unemployment is possible, and the problems of distributive justice arising from an unequal distribution of private property rights can be solved by defining these rights clearly and exchanging them at zero transaction cost in a mythical game-theoretic environment. And, if notwithstanding such gimmicks, unemployment rates still persist, inequalities of income and wealth continue to grow, and the shadows of poverty of the underclass do not stop lengthening, then these are regarded as necessary for achieving efficiency, which takes precedence over the pursuit of all other worthwhile social objectives. Needless to point out, it is patently irresponsible of neo-classical economists to insist on the relevance of such fairy tale (market-friendly) solutions to the problems of the developing countries, notwithstanding their growing unreality as the domestic and international markets become more and more complex and unpredictable in the wake of globalization. It would therefore, be appropriate that neo-classical economics gets back to 'where it belongs', that is, out of development.

The fact is that the developing countries cannot afford the luxury of such esoteric ideas which render neo-classical economics a 'soulless abstraction' not relevant to reality. Since these countries do not present the picture of 'well-ordered societies'—assumed to exist by neo-classical economics—development economics cannot fall for the ostrich-like posturing of the former. Rather, it *has* to remain engrossed full time with vital social problems—that is, of increasing the wealth of each nation and all nations, reducing poverty, social injustices, and the deprivation of the voiceless millions. In this context, an unbending belief in free-market regimes, in which the government does no better than guard the negative individual freedoms (of the rich), is obviously a misguided superstition because such regimes simply perpetuate a socially and politically unacceptable status quo. Instead, it is more realistic that a non-minimalist government takes on a substantial role in developing countries to maximize the social good. There is growing consensus now that rather than forcing the economic universe into the sub-reality of 'market friendliness', it is more natural for markets to be guided, though not suppressed, in order to become people friendly.

A dramatic manifestation of this consensus is the worldwide protest against world capitalism in general, and globalization in particular. Also, the rising concern for human development has highlighted a substantial role for the government and the need for a consequentialist moral perspective—one that goes beyond the applications of certain abstract rules and judges the worth of these rules by their consequences for the real world. Doing all this, development economics has emerged stronger and wiser from the purgatory of scientific neglect, even rejection. In the realm of theory, it has judiciously drawn on alternative development paradigms, which has enabled it to offer more complex explanations of rational behaviour, and recognize the influence of structural constraints and asymmetrical power relations on the development possibilities of the developing countries and on their prospects to benefit from international exchange (i.e., globalization). Furthermore, development economics is now more sensitive to the ethically motivated issues related to human development. Learning from the development experiences of the last 50 years, it is now better equipped to deal with the new challenge that developing countries face in the MNC-dominated globalized world of the 21st century. With an ample supply of relevant questions, which require a constructive and relevant response, the future of development economics seems secure.

Whither Development Economics?

The basic question we ask is, has development economics been entirely (or, even largely) successful in achieving what it aimed to achieve when it all began around the 1950s—when, measured by the intensity of expectations held at the time, 'to be young was very heaven'. Or have those rosy expectations, weighed down by conspicuous failures, turned to dust? By now, there is enough evidence to show that the developing countries, with only a handful of exceptions, did quite well in the 'sunny' decades of the 1950s and 1960s when the basic ideas of development economics commanded broad support. In particular, it was possible for these countries to have an interventionist government and still enjoy extremely rapid economic growth over a period of decades (World Bank 2000). Ironically, the exceptions to this rule are the countries located in Africa where the ideas of development economics were *never* put into practice! Thus, for instance, the (allegedly 'distortionary') import substitution strategy, which paid off splendidly in the East Asian Tiger countries and satisfactorily elsewhere, was never tried in Africa (Riddell 1990). Instead, the latter opted for an all-out export orientation. The result has been a bad case of Dutch disease and an excessive degree of vulnerability of these economies to adverse movements of the terms of trade.

The validity of development economics seems to be supported by the economic woes of the developing economies ever since the 'liberalist' ideas (for e.g., privatization, and 'big-bang' liberalization of trade and capital flows world-wide) began to be implemented in 1970s, with the full backing of the so-called Washington Consensus. The East Asian crisis of 1988–1999 may be the most dramatic illustration of the failure of such ideas, but the problem is a general one. It is a fact that most developing countries have failed to register any appreciable economic progress ever since liberalism became the intellectual fashion in 1970s around the globe. Thus, during 1970–1998, 44 developing countries, located in Africa and thoroughly inebriated by the wine of the free markets, grew at a rate between 0–2 per cent, while 32 countries of similar policy orientation actually regressed (IMF 2000a). In sharp contrast, 27 countries, all of which have sinned *against* the market in the past and still remain hesitant to embrace it wholeheartedly, have progressed!

Fortunately, however, the euphoria about the infallibility of the so-called marked-based and market-friendly solutions to development problems, which the 'liberalist' counter-revolution made fashionable, and is again doing so to pave the way for globalization, has by and large evaporated. The main reason for this detumescence is the essentially 'inhuman' nature of such solutions. No wonder, therefore, that we now hear about 'structural adjustment with a human face' and the 'humanizing' of globalization, the essential role of a non-minimalist state both at the national and global levels, and the need for a moral perspective to achieve the basic objectives of economic (and human) development. More and more peoples and countries in the West, weary of the Hayek–Friedman extreme rightism, are turning to the 'left of the centre' (or the Third Way). Is it, then, not somewhat quixotic that the developing world in these fateful times is once again being forced by international donors to ride the market bandwagon in a rush, and to entrust its fate to the twists and turns of an MNC-driven globalization—and this with the neo-classical assurances of an illusory reward in the long run, once the necessary sacrifices have been made by the (poor) people. Is this yet another illustration of public policies (those based on neo-classical economics) serving as a political and social cover for the exercise of corporate influence and authority (Galbraith 1991: p. 43); or is it the case of the reassertion of an orthodoxy when it is in the throes of its last twitches and gasps? Let us hope that the latter is the case.

It is, then, only rational that the developing countries, having had the bitter taste of the market medicine in the last 30 years or so, take a second look at a resurgent development economics, whose broad message remains valid; a message that development policy must retain its mixed-economy character and its ethical nature to regain its cutting power. Indeed, these aspects will need greater emphasis in the future because the challenges of the 21st century may turn out to be even more difficult in some crucial respects than those of the preceding century. Fortunately, there has emerged a consensus around some of the basic recommendations of development economics.

Elements of an Emerging Consensus

Looking back to the early 1970s, it appears that the initial response of development economists to the liberalist attack did not reflect enough self-confidence on their part. Hence, many prematurely issued obituary notices. Thus, some vital territory was relinquished in a state of disarray; the Invisible Hand (the market) was allowed to win for itself a much greater role as a regulator of the economic universe than is necessary, little realizing that an unbounded faith in the unimprovability of unregulated markets is not consistent with the inherent logic of development economics![1] We now know that market regimes are not context-free, and it is a dangerous fallacy to think that all that is necessary to create a modern industrial economy is deregulation. The task before development economists, therefore, is to search for feasible combinations of effective state intervention and markets in specific contexts of time and space. The fact is, not only in practice, but also in theory things have not gone badly for development economics. For instance, the many neo-classical versions of growth theory (in particular, the endogenous growth theory) have not made a net contribution to our knowledge beyond what is already known: invest enough in *human* capital and knowledge creation.[2] By contrast, Lewis's theory of economic development, which accords centrality to the universally true growth-promoting process of structural transformation and explicitly features inter-sectoral shifts of resources from the low-productivity to high-productivity sectors, firmly holds the field. Also, as if to pay homage to the founding fathers of our discipline, development plans are still in vogue in developing countries and the no-plan periods are still considered an oddity in the annals of policy-making, despite warnings to the contrary by agnostics like Bauer (1972). Even more, the focus of development policy still is on problems of poverty, inequality and income redistribution, even though some of the remedies offered to solve these problems remain tainted with liberalist confusion. Even more important, in the light of 50 years of experience with managing the development process, there has come about a broad agreement regarding some of the basic contentions of development economics. This recaptures the highlights of the discussion of these issues in the preceding chapters.

Reassertion of a Non-minimal State

The liberalist assertion of the state not being upto any good to the society, so that the less we have of it the better, has proved to be essentially wrong-headed and illogical; wrong-head because there is a large area of social life where state intervention is obligatory, and illogical because a state not doing development work cannot help economic progress through the market either. True, the traditional sentimental view of the state which always acts as a conscience of the society will also have to be modified to recognize that the state, to some extent, does reflect the interests of various lobbies and pressure groups (Becker 1983); but this fact actually warrants an effective socially oriented government intervention to regulate the illegal pressurizing of public officials by private lobbies. In general, the assertion that the government can do no better than the market is simply false because market solutions can almost always be improved by sensible government intervention (Greenwald and Stiglitz 1986). At the global level, the rising inequalities of income, wealth and opportunities between nations, fed by globalization, bespeak a 'systemic malfunction' of the world economic system, which 'the free operation of unregulated markets' cannot repair (Malinvaud 1991: p. 66). A global effort is, therefore, required to redistribute resources from the rich nations to the poor nations, which, in fact, has been the concern of development economics since the 1950s.

This is all the more so because the heated debates about the historical superiority of free-market solutions, and the corresponding ills that government must bring about, are not based on solid empirical or historical foundations. Thus, the widely held notion that 19th century England represented the Age of *Laissez Faire* is not correct. Samuelson (1976) states that since the late 19th century, it has been understood that 'ours is a "mixed economy" in which both the public and the private institutions exercise economic control' (p. 41). Indeed the fact is that '*Laissez Faire* was not a maxim which determined the issue in any instance; but it played a notable role in contemporary lobbying and propaganda' (Gordon, cited in Coats [1971]: p. 126). Further, 'market capitalism has never been the basis of political economy in any country, at any time' (Hirsch 1977: p. 118). Rivlin (1987), in her Presidential Address before the American Economic Association, said: '... the arguments among economists about the merits of larger vs smaller governments too often revolve around anecdotes or, worse, misleading statistics quoted out of context.' True, developing countries (including India and Pakistan) have come to rely increasingly on the market (mostly under pressure from the multilateral donors and because of the lingering influence of discredited liberalist ideas); but this is neither to disprove the worth of development economics, nor is it a prescription for embracing neo-classical economics. It should be understood that the love of the free market that we hear so much about these days is not exclusively motivated by a concern for human freedom. Instead, as Hirschman (1988) has suggested, it is more like a *reaction* against the 20th century extension of the idea of citizenship in the social and economic spheres, which has meant that too little 'space' has been left for altruistic non-market activities, so vital for economic and human development. The main theoretical plank of this reaction is an extreme case of the Hayekian principle (1960) of the 'unintended social consequences of individual action', or the 'perverse-reaction' principle. According to this extremist formulation, every step taken by the government to improve the lot of human beings, especially of the poor, must always have the perverse effect of worsening it! Such a view of human nature—that humankind are simply unable to make correct decisions under conditions of uncertainty—is both unscientific and contrary to fact. Rather, the truth is that individuals learn by doing things, perhaps the wrong way at first, and they acquire in the learning process the capacity to forecast with a reasonable degree of accuracy. If this were not so, econometricians would have gone out of business long ago. Similarly, it would be incorrect to deny the government's ability to produce the intended effects of its decisions on economic variables as the rational expectationists would have us believe. The correct attitude on the matter is to look at the successes and failures of the market and government in the wider context of maintaining social justice in a strongly growing economy.

Thus, there is not much excuse to implement a socially irresponsible (non) policy of leaving it all to the market as a formula for turning a sow's ear into a silk purse. All the more so because there is ample room for the public and the private sectors to devise effective remedies together for such fundamental problems as slow growth, unemployment, poverty, illiteracy, inadequate supply of health services, etc. It is more reasonable to expect that both when the government and market fail and when they succeed in specific situations, remedial policy action does make a difference, and it would be market-based or interventionist (requiring some degree of development planning) depending on the magnitude of information costs involved in coordinating investment decisions—an attitude which is closer to the teachings of development economics than of neo-classical economics. To this end, we should focus on 'a mutually supportive structure of market and non-market institutions that best suits the requirements of economic development' (Datta-Chaudhri 1990). An area where such supportive institutions are required is in the context of the creation and propagation of knowledge, which is a kind of a public good (*WDR* 1999).

Emphasizing Egalitarianism

It is now common knowledge that egalitarianism is generally consistent with growth; indeed, high growth occurs relatively easily in equal societies than in unequal ones (World Bank 2001: p. 22). Further, no country that has made a success of economic development could ever have done so without first producing deep changes in the basic institutions of the society, especially those involving a redistribution of income and wealth. Harrod (1972), in his classic biography of Keynes, quotes him as saying that capitalism cannot be saved without the capitalist societies accepting a substantial curtailment of the institution of private property and an increasing role of the state in economic management. Adelman and Morris (1973) emphasize substantial structural changes in the existing pattern of the distribution of wealth, and Birdsall and Londono (1997) find that 'initial inequalities in the distribution of ... human capital have a clear negative effect on economic growth, and the effects are almost twice as great for the poor as for the population as a whole'! Relatively more 'incrementalist' egalitarian policies are proposed by Chenery (1975, 1983), and similar in temperament is the UNDP's prescription to increase social spending, which is given in its annual *Human Development Reports*. The basic motivation in each case is to reduce the unacceptable levels of economic inequalities, poverty and 'entrenched deprivation' found in the developing countries. Without such changes taking place, the existing income inequalities will increase 'explosively' over time. Myrdal (1984), reviewing his thinking on development problems, has concluded: 'what is needed to raise the miserable living levels of the poor masses is instead radical institutional reforms. These would serve the double purpose of greater equality and economic growth' (p. 154). Tinbergen (1959) advocated establishing some kind of an 'optimum regime', which would require substantial income transfers to correct the present income differences between the rich and the poor, which, in turn, are more unequal than is socially acceptable. And there is broad consensus now that as economic growth proceeds apace, using both physical and human capital, the relative share of the poorest in the GNP should increase, not fall. This latter condition must be met to prevent absolute poverty from getting any worse as a result of economic growth, which happens if the opportunity offered by growth is not seized by the government to increase social spending (for e.g., on education and health). It may be noted in this context that a tacit acceptance of the status quo is hardly ever a sign of its endorsement. Hence, to achieve social justice and enhance human happiness we need to create institutions that transmute the longing for a better world into a set of policies which *begin* by enhancing the welfare of the underclass.

The Asymmetrical Working of International Trade and Investment

In relating foreign trade and investment to growth, both the mercantilist protectionism and Smithian free-trade idealism have become even more inappropriate reference points in the post-UR world trading order than in the 1950s when the ideas of development economics commanded broad economic and political support. The fact is that the Singer–Prebisch scenario of an essentially defective international trade and investment mechanism now haunts the developing world because:

1. Both the barter and income terms of trade have moved against the developing countries in the last 30 years or so and the purchasing power of their exports has eroded;

2. The Uruguay Round (UR) Agreement has either discarded or undermined the 'old' approach underlying Part IV of GATT, and the Tokyo Round's Enabling Clause (together with Article XVIII and sections A and C of GATT 1997), which recognized the developing countries' endemic balance-of-payments problems and supported the need for infant industry protection;

3. Western protectionism is alive and well while the developing countries are having to liberalize *voluntarily* under pressure from the WTO and the multilateral donors;

4. The foreign capital flows have generally been destabilizing for the developing countries, which is a disturbing trend because their growth is now increasingly associated with higher current-account deficits, which, in turn, require a large inflow of a vanishing foreign capital into productive sectors; and

5. The meaning of the TRIPS Accord is being willfully distorted by the MNCs to the detriment of the developing countries.

All these factors strongly suggest that it would be naive to expect, without a substantial rewriting of the UR-Agreement, that developing countries can achieve high rates of growth mainly by accelerating their export activity, and by indulging in the very costly game of big-bang liberalization of trade and capital flows. It also follows that deceptively simple tricks like 'letting the prices come right', as if out of a state of inaction, cannot be the exclusive basis of development success. It would rather depend on the developing countries' ability to innovate (to some extent, by import-substituting knowledge rather than goods) and to improve the quantity and quality of exports. But doing this will require making greater government investment in R&D to take advantage of the knowledge 'spillovers', which is the main message of the endogenous growth theory. And it will also take accelerating the process of structural transformation to diversify the export structure at the same time as a propitious external environment is created, by making the WTO more responsive to the needs of the developing countries as advised by development economics. The moral of the story is that the post-UR world can probably be made beneficial to the developing countries if the weak chain of causation between trade liberalization, exports and growth is made stronger not by simply specializing more in the traditional (unskilled) labour-intensive industry, but by applying new scientific ideas to production processes to discover areas of (dynamic) comparative advantage. In this context, both efficient import substitution and export expansion remain relevant, partly to ensure gains from trade and investment, and partly because the former provides a firm basis for the latter. As Bruton (1998) has noted, both the strategies need to be refocused to make a contribution to the processes of learning and capital accumulation, which are the true sources of an accelerated rate of economic development. The secret of success, as in the case of the East Asian countries, is to make a speedy and efficient transition from one strategy to another in response to the changing conditions of the world demand, and to expand the tradable sector by making it increasingly knowledge-based.

The Importance of Morality

The concern for the least privileged in the society is now widely shared. But this requires that development economics explore systematically the question of how best to inject moral and ethical considerations into the main corpus of development theory and policy. This advice, which comes out quite strongly from Rawls's (1971) influential work, is even more relevant to developing countries than it is to the developed. A logical consequence of the acceptance of such advice is that considerations of equity on ethical grounds acquire at least as much significance as the positivist dictates of efficiency. This is because, as Boulding (1966) pointed out, 'no science of any kind can be divorced from ethical considerations', and such considerations have a bearing on the kind of questions asked and the quality of answers provided by positive economics.

Such an 'integrationist' exercise is worth undertaking. Moral constraints are recommended because: (a) the pursuit of self-interest may lead to non-optimal outcomes; (b) even if optimal outcomes do flow from the exercise of self-interest, these may not be the socially most desirable ones; and (c) an ostensibly moral motive, not informed by self-interest, (for e.g., gift exchanges, being honest, keeping trust) may lead to superior outcomes in terms of efficiency and equity. In addition, issues like globalization, human development and environmental degradation cannot even be formulated properly without an overarching moral vision of the ends of economic development. In development economics, such a task is not only intellectually challenging but also morally obligatory, and it will require a lot of soul-searching and intellectual commitment on the part of development economists to do this job satisfactorily. It is, therefore, widely understood that development economics need not be the high church of positivity that mainstream economics, which was itself born out of a marriage of philosophy and ethics, has pretended to be. The argument that the market-given freedom economizes on the use of scarce ethical resources (Arrow 1972) is true to some extent, but the fact remains that altruism is *not* a scarce resource; rather it increases with more frequent use (Hirschman 1985).[3]

This brings us to one of the central themes of this book: *the search for value-free or ethically neutral decision rules is both pointless and counter-productive* in evaluating the merits of a successful development policy. It is pointless because ethical considerations affect economic behaviour so that excluding these from the economic calculus will make the latter incomplete, even misleading, and because no such thing is possible. (Even the Pareto optimality rule is not entirely value-free as it involves a value judgement about preserving the status quo which is supposed to command unanimity.) Such an exercise is also counter-productive for the simple reason that keeping ethical norms alive and compelling by internalizing the sense of obligations reduces the cost of policing and monitoring the working of economic systems as well as checking the incidence of free riding in the society. The point here is that an excessive dose of self-interested behaviour (which is seen to be the hallmark of rational behaviour) weakens 'the crucial social underpinnings of market processes' (Hirsch 1977: p. 122). It follows that it is neither irrational to act morally nor immoral to act rationally.

But for development economists, the problem does not end once economic problems have been anlaysed from a moral point of view; it rather sets the stage to choose a set of moral values that are beneficial to society, that is, values which ensure distributive justice, within the context of a growing economy. Clearly, moral values which lead to the perpetuation of an unjust status quo in society cannot serve as appropriate points of reference for the making of a fruitful development policy—for example, the Pareto optimality rule, Nozickian non-consequentialism and the Buchanan–Hayek–Friedman uncompromising insistence on individual liberty. On the other hand, Harsanyi's equi-probability model of moral value judgements, Hare's principle of 'universality', the Suppes' grading principle, the Rawlsian conception of 'justice-as-fairness' and his maximin principle of justice, which aim to maximize the welfare of the worst-off individual(s) in society, and Sen's capability calculus which seeks to increase human well-being by enhancing personal freedom to make the 'right' choices for their own good are the type of ethical rules that development economics should take as its 'reference point' to evaluate the merits (or demerits) of alternative states of the economy.

A New Paradigm?

Keeping this emerging consensus in view, it is pertinent to ask as to what world-view has pushed development thinking and policy in this direction. The inevitable answer is that development economics is made of materials that are significantly different from those that form the core of neo-classical economics, which even at its dynamic best talks of stodgy, steady states. Thus, by virtue of the immiscibility of the former with the latter, the decaying remnants of liberalist ideology must be cleared out of the way for development economics to advance the cause of science. As shown at length in this book (especially, in Chapters 2 and 8), the claim of development economics to a distinctive paradigm rests on solid foundations. The following considerations are pertinent in this regard.

1. Development economics accepts, once and for all, the relativity of economics to the nature of the society, and understands that there is no pure theory that is immune to changes in social values or current policy problems (Deane 1983). In other words, it rejects as unwarranted the claim about the (unnatural) universality of neo-classical economics that leads the latter to keep churning out one-size, fits-all types of policy prescriptions.

2. It has kept in the forefront the problems of growth and development, and has recommended development policies that work. This contrasts sharply with the insouciance with which neo-classical economics has treated such vital issues.[4] Incredible as it may seem, the economic profession seemed to have all but lost interest 'in the theory of growth for nearly twenty years, from the late sixties to the late eighties' (Stern 1991: p. 122). And even when its interest did revive in the 1990s, it once again got lost in the pursuit of steady-state solutions with the help of the other-wordly one-sector and two-sector growth models, which display only the remotest concern for offering plausible policy prescriptions and which, for lack of policy motivation, leave little room for the growth-promoting inter-sectoral transfers of resources. The dynamic optimization exercises, though dynamic by definition, have contributed little to comprehend reality except when used as a tool of planning in developing countries. This intellectual void has been filled by development economics, which will continue to exercise its unchallenged monopoly in the realm of development policy in the 21st century, making an invaluable contribution to understanding the mechanics of economic development. The central hypotheses in this area are about the structural transformation and orderly transformation of low-income economies into middle- and high-income economies, which introduce hitherto unknown empirically verifiable (and verified) regularities and uniformities of the development process.

3.   Development economics enjoys undisputed monopoly with respect to dealing effectively with such vital issues as distributive justice, poverty and social-economic deprivation of the majority of humankind. Once again, this is because neo-classical economics (even welfare economics), weighed down by esoteric worries—for example, Arrow's Impossibility Theorem, Pareto optimality, the impossibility of making inter-personal comparisons of utilities— *cannot* deal with such issues and still remain scientific. Major advances in development thinking have changed this veritable riot of confusing (and confused) ideas into a more disciplined mode of thought, which makes it possible to be sensitive to the interests of a diverse population, especially of the least assertive ones among them (Sen 1999).

4.   In the light of some development-related research done in developing countries (for e.g., by Stiglitz, Akerlof and others), the Arrow–Debreu (A–D) synthesis on which it rests is making way to a post-A–D research programme, which, however, still 'looks fragmentary, complicated, and incomplete' (Eatwell *et al.* 1989: p. xii). All this shows that development economics is by no means a 'basket case' in the realm of ideas; quite the contrary, it has made a net contribution to economic knowledge by asking the right questions about economic development as well as giving the right answers. An important example of such a contribution is the modification of the historical fixation of neo-classical economics with the sanctity and unimprovability of competitive market solutions (which are also Pareto optimal). It is now well known that when markets are incomplete and information is imperfect, which is almost always the case in the developing (and developed) countries, competitive solutions need neither be efficient nor unimprovable. It follows that efficient government intervention can always improve such solutions (Stiglitz 1991).

5.   Equally compelling is the point, to which the internal logic of economic development has led, that rational thinking is seldom antiseptically amoral and moral judgements need never be irrational. To maximize social welfare, self-interest behaviour must be supplemented by a sympathy for others and by the exhilaration that comes from contributing to the improvement of the lot of other individuals in society; from being in someone else's shoes. Thus,

moral rights, entitlements, liberty, and equality must feature in development economics to enhance its explanatory and predictive powers. These moral values are especially relevant in the developing countries where most traditional institutional structures are unjust and need a complete overhauling. Efficiency-oriented criteria (for e.g., Pareto optimality) alone cannot help explain, let alone solve, the difficult problems of want, poverty and human deprivation which darken the face of the developing countries. Indeed, a strong 'ethical understructure' is required to resolve the key problem facing development economists, even neo-classical economists—namely, 'how to reconcile social responsibility with the opposing mainstream of the market ethos' (Hirsch 1977: p. 143).

These considerations should be enough to convince oneself that development economics has a logic of its own which must be followed to frame a meaningful development policy. An implication of this statement is that the induction of elements contrary to this logic—for example, the universality of neo-classical economics, the inviolability of competitive-equilibrium solutions, the unadulterated rationality (read, amorality) of the economic calculus and its unbending neutrality with respect to the outcomes of specific policies—in the corpus of development policy will lead to irreconcilable contradictions. The development experience of the last 50 years also points to the same conclusion. True, there may have been some truth in the observation that development economics had shown at one time (maybe in the 1970s and 1980s) considerable vulnerability to the 'unlikely conjunction of distinct ideological currents' (Hirschman 1981c), but things have changed since then. There has been a reaffirmation of the basic 'message' of development economics, and it has been able to shed fresh light on old questions and offer new hypotheses of its own. All this has set in motion the evolution of our discipline to meet the new challenges of the 21st century.

'The Road Less Travelled By'

Ideas influence human lives, for good or for evil, and this is illustrated best by the rapidity with which reactionary 'liberal' thought has spread all over the world since the 1970s. Armed with no more dangerous a weapon than the power of a basically incorrect idea repeated infinitely, the so-called liberalist philosophy has, in one country after another, pulled down welfare states, promoted high unemployment rates, and widened the chasm between the rich and the poor within and between countries—without quite fulfilling its promise to promote efficiency. As noted at the outset of this chapter, the developing countries, which faithfully followed the routine and compulsory advice to dismantle their governments, and give free rein to the often-unhelpful Invisible Hand (of the vested inter-ests)—which the liberalist enthusiasts perceive to be everywhere, yet nowhere—have generally suffered from slow growth, rising in-equality and deepening poverty. On the other hand, those which regulated the market intelligently (without suppressing it altogether) have done well, some of them spectacularly.

The unfolding of the events in the wake of the UR-Agreement has also shown the unwisdom of those developing countries which hoped to attain economic *nirvana* by an overwhelming reliance on the access to foreign (OECD) markets. It has been estimated that the developing countries could have gained $700 billion in extra export earnings if the developed had been relatively freer (UNCTAD 1999), but the latter have chosen not to become less protectionist. Thus, the OECD protection of *their* agriculture (the annual cost of which in 1996–98 was double the level of agricultural exports from all developing countries taken together during those three years) remains in full force and is likely to continue till Kingdom come, and the notorious Multi-fibre Agreement (MFA) is yet to be dis-mantled (indeed, there has been wilful backtracking here). Further, the tariffication exercise (i.e., the conversion of non-tariff barriers into tariff barriers) has resulted in extremely high tariffs, much above the pre-UR Agreement level, and, perhaps worst of all, the frequency of the imposition of anti-dumping duties on frivolous grounds has increased, rather than decreased in the post-UR world (World Bank 1999). And more bad news is likely to come if the developed countries have their way, as they probably will, in the Millennium Round—in the form of securing greater protection for their 'sunset' industries by enviro-restrictions and labour and human-rights related constraints. The sheer magnitude of such pres-sures—the intensity of which is likely to grow in the decades to come—on the domestic producers seems to have had an unintended pulverizing effect on their capacity to innovate new low-cost production processes and compete internationally. Their difficulties have been further aggravated because the MNCs are taking out monopolies not only in the production of goods and services, but also in respect of the creation of new ideas. Moreover, the asymmetrical mobility of capital and labour (the former having been set free while the latter is still in chains), and a disproportionate (and increasing) concentration of economic power in the developed countries have made the world a more unequal and insecure place to live—and the more uncertain too because the volatility of the financial markets has already crossed 'safe limits'. All of this adds up to an impressive case for effective 'policing' at the domestic and global levels.

The analysis presented in this book makes clear that a guide to the road of economic progress, which contains directions only about efficiency, and nothing of substance about growth and equity, cannot be recommended for development economics. What should be recommended, instead, is that the development process be looked at, a là Rawls, as one that requires a rearrangement of the basic structure of society, which is 'fair', 'just', and focuses on the needs of the least privileged in the society; and further, a là Sen, as one that enhances people's well-being by strengthening their capabilities to convert resources into personal happiness and well-being. By the same token, the standard neo-classical prescription—get the prices right, let the markets do their job unhindered, ensure personal freedom (mainly of the rich) even though other worthwhile social objectives wither—has turned out to be, by and large, wrongheaded. As development economics has always warned, the vast problems and privations of the millions residing in the developing countries cannot be waived aside by airy free-market generalizations. However, this does not mean that markets should be abolished, suspended or weakened; nor does it imply that the developing countries should, like Canute, attempt to roll back the waves of the future and bar the door on their prosperity by turning inwards. Thus, for instance, the challenge of globalization in the 21st century must be met by the developing countries; but to succeed in this venture they should accept, understand and change it: *accept* it as an inevitable event of the history of the future; *understand* it as an essentially de-equalizing and dehumanizing force, run by powerful MNCs which make money even in the darkest hour of human survival; and *change* it by growing faster and more equitably—all lessons that development economics has consistently taught. Such domestic efforts by the developing countries must supplement international efforts to rectify the inbuilt inequities of the world trading system, and strengthen the global governance mechanisms in order to mitigate the damaging fallout of globalization—a demand which has grown so pressing and urgent as to force even the high priest of capitalism, Michael Camdessus, on the verge of his retirement from the IMF, to plead for 'reinvigorating multilaterism with a view to 'humanizing globalization' (IMF 2000b). Also, institutions like the Commission on Global Governance—constituted in 1995—need to be strengthened because the price of failure is going to be prohibitively high: 'without strong governance, the dangers of global conflicts could be a reality—trade wars, promoting national and corporate interests, uncontrolled financial volatility setting off civil conflicts, untamed global crime infecting neighbourhoods and criminalizing polities, business and the police' (*HDR* 1999: p. 8).

If we propagate the great virtues of individual freedom that the market supposedly protects, we must honestly reflect on whether it is a freedom for only a privileged few or freedom for all. The litmus test that all theories and institutions need to pass should establish their contribution to, and relevance for, ensuring economic growth with social justice. The Rawlsian homily to social philosophers is apt: 'A theory, however elegant and economical, must be rejected or revised if it is untrue; likewise, laws and institutions, no matter how efficient, must be reformed or abolished if they are unjust' (Rawls 1971: p. 3). This sound advice should also inform public policy. But the real world sometimes moves away from the path of justice and fairness. Free-market economics, and now its reincarnation in the garb of globalization, has made societies poorer by benumbing their sense of social responsibility and gradually depriving them of compassion. And, under its influence, social scientists, which is what economists are basically supposed to be, have become insensitive to the rising tide of unemployment and the widening gulf between the rich and the poor. Development economics must, however, resist such ideas and relate, as it must by its nature, to reality. For development economics is nothing if it is not relevant to policy, not sensitive to human suffering and not explicitly geared to raising social welfare by invoking the altruistic urges of humankind. Indeed, the momentum of institutional transformation that drives economic development cannot be sustained without ensuring a modicum of equality among the citizens, a just assignment of rights and duties, and active participation of the least privileged in the society who sullenly endure what they are powerless to change. True, the job of a major restructuring of unjust social institutions is daunting, sometimes even disruptive; but it must be done to change the world for the better. The key to success, however, lies elsewhere: it is in accepting that 'the major advances in civilizations are processes that all but wreck the societies in which they occur' (Whitehead 1927), and still pushing ahead with the historical task of transforming and enriching poor societies while the candle of hope flickers. To this end, these societies must conquer the fear of the unknown and the unconventional and venture to tread the 'road less travelled by'. They should also be ready to catch the first rays when the sun of economic prosperity actually rises in the East. This is what development economics is all about.

Notes

1. In this context, it is pertinent to quote Leontief (1983) in full: 'To an insightful observer, such as Adam Smith was, the entire national economy appears to be guided and protected by an Invisible Hand. But neither the classical nor the present-day mathematical economists seem to have realized that the effective operation of the automatic price mechanism depended critically on the nature of the nineteenth-century technology, which brought an unprecedented rise in total output, but at the same time it maintained and even strengthened the dominant role of human labour in most kinds of productive processes—thus automatically securing for labour a large and, in many instances, a gradually increasing share of total national income.' However, Leontief warned that such a happy confluence of economic growth and income distribution will not hold, even in advanced countries, with the increasing importance of labour-saving computer technology which has permeated all sectors of developed economies.

2. Thus Stern (1991) states: 'Whilst growth theory has contributed to our understanding of how growth is determined and how it may be influenced, it has in many ways missed some of the crucial issues for developing countries' (p. 129).

3. What we are arguing in the text is not contrary to the Arrowian view that ethically motivated altruism is a scarce resource which should not be 'used up recklessly'. This is because our recommendation is not to substitute ethics for self-interest behaviour across the board; it is rather to combine the two to run the economic system more efficiently and equitably.

4. Not only has neo-classical economics deviated from the original 'cause' of economics (i.e., an enquiry into the causes of the increase in the wealth of nations), but it has also let the Smithian Revolution be undermined in another respect. It

has abandoned 'attempts to understand the central question of our subject: how do decentralized choices interact and perhaps get coordinated in favour of a theory according to which an economy is to be understood as the outcome of maximization of a representative agent's utility over an infinite future'? (Hahn 1991: p. 49).

Select Bibliography and References

Abramovitz, Moses (1986), 'Catching up, Forging ahead, and Falling behind', *Journal of Economic History*, 46:2, 385–406.

Adelman, Irma (1978), 'Redistribution Before Growth: A Strategy for Developing Countries', Inaugural Lecture for the Cleveringa Chair, Leiden University, The Hague: Martinus Nijhof.

_____ and Cynthia T. Morris (1973), *Economic Growth and Social Equity in Developing Countries*, Stanford: Stanford University Press.

_____ (1997), 'Development History and Its Implications for Development Theory (Editorial)', *World Development*, 25:6, 831–40.

Agarwala and Singh (1963), *The Economics of Underdevelopment*, New York: Oxford University Press.

Aghion, Philippe, Eve Caroli, and Cecilia Garcia-Penalose (1999), 'Inequality and Growth Theories', *Journal of Economic Literature* (December) 37, 1615–60.

Ahluwalia, Montek S. (1976), 'Inequality, Poverty and Development', *Journal of Development Economics*, 6, 307–342.

Akerlof. G. (1970), 'The Market for Lemons', *The Quarterly Journal of Economics*, August, 488–500.

_____ (1983), 'Loyalty Filters', *The American Economic Review*, 73:1, 54–63.

Alamgir, Mohiuddin (1980), *Famine in South Asia*, Boston: Oelgeschlager, Gunn and Hain.

Alesina, Alberto and Dani Rodrik (1994), 'Distributive Politics and Economic Growth', *The Quarterly Journal of Economics*, 109:2, 465–90.

Amin, Samir (1976), *Unequal Development*, Sussex: Harvester Press.

Anand Sudhir and Amartya K. Sen (2000), 'The Income Component of the Human Development Index', *Journal of Human Development*, 1:1, 83–106.

Arrow, Kenneth J. (1951), *Social Choice and Collective Values*, New York: Wiley.

_____ (1972), 'Gifts and Exchanges', *Philosophy and Public Affairs*, 1:4, 343–63.

_____ (1974), 'Limited Knowledge and Economic Analysis', *The American Economic Review*, 61:1, 1–10.

_____ (1977), 'Current Developments in the Theory of Social Choice', *Social Research*, 44:4, 607–622.

Arrow, Kenneth J. (1979), 'The Property Rights Doctrine and Demand Revelation under Incomplete Information', in Michael J. Boskin (ed.), *Economics and Human Welfare: Essays in Honor of Tibor Scitovsky*, New York: Academic Press Inc., pp. 23–39.

Aturupane, H., Paul Glewwe and Paul Isenman (1994), 'Poverty, Human Development, and Growth: An Emerging Consensus', *The American Economic Review*, (Papers and Proceedings), 84:2, 244–49.

Bairoch, P. (1975), *The Economic Development of Third World Since 1900*, Berkeley: University of California Press.

Balassa, Bela (1971), *The Structure of Protection in Developing Countries*, Baltimore: The Johns Hopkins University Press.

——— (1978), 'Exports and Economic Growth: Further Evidence', *Journal of Development Economics*, 5:2, 181–89.

Baran, Paul (1952), 'On the Political Economy of Backwardness', *Manchester School*.

——— (1957), *The Political Economy of Growth*, New York: Monthly Review Press.

Bardhan, Pranab (1988), 'Alternative Approaches to Development Economics', in Hollis B. Chenery and T.N. Srinivasan (eds.), *Handbook of Development Economics: I*, Oxford: North-Holland, pp. 39–71.

——— (1993), 'Economics of Development and Development Economics', *Journal of Economic Literature*, 7:2, 129–42.

Barro, Robert, J. (1992), *Determinants of Economic Growth: A Cross-Country Empirical Study*, Cambridge, Ma: The MIT Press.

——— (1997), *Determinants of Economic Growth: A Cross-Country Empirical Study*, NBER Working Paper No. 5698, Cambridge, Ma: National Bureau of Economic Research.

Bator, Francis M. (1958), 'The Anatomy of Market Failure', *The Quarterly Journal of Economics*, 72:3, 351–79.

Bauer, Peter T. (1972), *Dissent on Development: Studies and Debates in Development Economics*, Cambridge, Ma: Harvard University Press.

——— (1984), *Reality and Rhetoric: Studies in the Economics of Development*, Cambridge, Ma: Harvard University Press.

——— (1984a), 'Remembrance of Studies Past: Retracing First Steps', in Gerald M. Meier and Dudley Seers (eds.), *Pioneers in Development*, New York: Oxford University Press, pp. 27–43.

Bauer, Peter and B.S. Yamey (1957), *The Economics of Underdeveloped Countries*, Chicago: University of Chicago Press.

Baumol, William J. (1991), 'Towards a Newer Economics: The Future Lies Ahead', *The Economic Journal*, 101:404, 1–8.

Becker, Gary S. (1960), 'An Economic Analysis of Fertility in Universities', in National Bureau Committee for Economic Research (ed.), *Demographic and Economic Change in Developed Countries*, Princeton, NJ: Princeton University Press.

——— (1962), 'Investment in Human Capital: A Theoretical Analysis', *The Journal of Political Economy*, 70:5 (Part 2), 9–49.

——— (1964), *Human Capital: A Theoretical and Empirical Analysis with Special Reference to Education*, New York: National Bureau of Economic Research and Columbia University Press.

——— (1983), 'A Theory of Competition among Pressure Groups for Political Influence', *The Quarterly Journal of Economics*, 97:3, 371–400.

Bell, Clive (1987), 'Development Economics', in Eatwell, Milgate and Newman (eds.), *The New Palgrave: A Dictionary of Economics*, I: (A–D), London: MacMillan

Bell, Daniel and Irving Kristol (1981), *The Crisis in Economic Theory*, New York: Basic Books Inc.

Benabou, Roland (1996), 'Inequality and Growth', *NBER Economics Annals*, 11, 11–74.

Bennet, Anthony, (ed.) (1997), *How Does Privatization Work?* London: Routledge.

Berlin, Isaiah (1969), 'Two Concepts of Liberty', in *Four Essays on Liberty*, Oxford: Oxford University Press.

Berry, R. Albert and William R. Cline (1979), *Agrarian Structure and Productivity in Developing Countries*, Baltimore: The Johns Hopkins University Press.

Bhagwati, Jagdish (1958), 'Inmiserising Growth: A Geometrical Note', *Review of Economic Studies*, 23:3, 201–205.

_____ (1965), 'The Pure Theory of International Trade', in American Economist Association and Royal Economic Society, *Surveys of Economic Theory (Growth and Development)*, Surveys V-VIII, New York: St Martin's Press, 156–239.

_____ (1968), 'Distortions and Immiserizing Growth: A Generalization', *Review of Economic Studies*, 35:104, 481–85.

_____ (1971), 'The Generalized Theory of Distortion and Welfare, in Bhagwati, et al. (eds.) *Trade, Balance of Payments and Welfare and Growth*, Amsterdam: North-Holland, pp. 69–90.

_____ (1978), *Anatomy and Consequences of Exchange Control Regime*, Cambridge, Ma: Ballinger.

_____ (1982), 'Directly Unproductive Profit-seeking (DUP) Activities', *The Journal of Political Economy*, 90:5, 988–1002.

_____ (1984), 'Development Economics: What Have We Learned?', *Asian Development Review*, 2:1, 23–38.

_____ (1985), 'Growth and Poverty', Occasional Paper No.5, Michigan State University: Center for Advanced Study of International Development.

_____ (1990), 'Departures from Multilateralism: Regionalism and Aggressive Unilateralism', *The Economic Journal*, 100:404, 1304–17.

_____ and Padma Desai (1970), *India: Planning for Industrialization*, London: Oxford University Press.

_____ and V.K. Ramaswami (1963), 'Domestic Distortions, Tariffs and the Theory of Optimum Subsidy', *Journal of Political Economy*, 71, Feb, 44–45.

_____ and Sukhamoy Chakravarty (1969), 'Contributions to Indian Economic Analysis: A Survey', *The American Economic Review*, 59:4 (Part 2), 2–73.

_____ and T.N. Srinivasan (1982), 'The Welfare Consequences of Directly Unproductive Profit-seeking (DUP) and Lobbying Activities: Prices versus Quantity Distortions', *Journal of International Economics*, 12:1/2, 33–44.

_____ Richard A. Brecher and T.N. Srinivasan (1984), 'DUP Activities and Economic Theory', in David C. Collander (ed.) *Neoclassical Political Economy: An Analysis of Rent-Seeking and DUP Activities*, Cambridge: Ballinger Publishing Co., pp. 17–32.

Binswanger, Hans P., and Vernon Ruttan (1978), *Induced Innovation: Technology, Institutions and Development*, Baltimore: The Johns Hopkins University Press.

Birdsall, Nancy (1988), 'Economic Approaches to Population Growth', in H.B. Chenery and T.N. Srinivasan (eds.), *Handbook of Development Economics*, 1, New York: North-Holland and Elsevier Science Publishers.

Birdsall, Nancy and J.L. Londono (1997), 'Asset Inequality Matters: An Assessment of the World Bank's Approach to Poverty Reduction', *The American Economic Review*, 87:2, 32–37.

Blaug, Mark (1976), 'Kuhn versus Lakatos *or* Paradigm versus Research Programmes in the History of Economics', in Spiro J. Latsis (ed.) *Method and Appraisal in Economics*, Cambridge: Cambridge University Press, pp. 149–80.

———— (1983), *The Methodology of Economics, or How Economists Explain*, Cambridge: Cambridge University Press.

Bosworth, Barry and Susan M. Collins (1996), 'Economic Growth in East Asia: Accumulation Versus Assimilation', *Brookings Papers on Economic Activity*, No.2, 135–203.

Boulding, Kenneth (1966), 'The Economics of Knowledge and the Knowledge of Economics', *The American Economic Review*, 56:2, 1–13.

Bowles, Samuel (1985), 'The Production Process in a Competitive Economy: Walrasian, Neo-Hobbesian, and Marxian Models', *The American Economic Review*, 75:1, 16–26.

Borensztein, E., M. Khan, C. Reinhart and P. Wickham (1994), 'The Behaviour of Non-oil Commodity Price', IMF Occasional Paper 112, Washington DC: IMF.

Bradford, J., De Long, and L.H. Summers (1991), 'Equipment, Investment and Economic Growth', *The Quarterly Journal of Economics*, 106:2, 445–502.

Brahmanand P.R., and C.N. Vakil (1956), *Planning for an Expanding Economy*, Bombay.

Brandt, Willy (1980), *North-South: A Programme for Survival*, London: Pan Books.

Brenner Robert (1990), 'Feudalism', in Eatwell, Milgate and Newman, *Marxian Economics*, (*The New Palgrave*), London: MacMillan.

Brock, William A. and Stephen P. Magee (1984), 'The Invisible Foot and the Waste of Nations: Redistribution and Economic Growth,' in David C. Collander (ed.), *Neoclassical Political Economy: An Analysis of Rent-Seeking and DUP Activities*, Cambridge: Ballinger Publishing, pp. 177–86.

Bruton, Henry (1998), 'A Reconsideration of Import Substitution', *Journal of Economic Literature*, 36:2, 903–36.

Buchanan, Allen (1985), *Ethics, Efficiency, and the Market*, Littlefield, USA: Rowman and Allenheld.

Buchanan, James M. (1986), *Liberty, Market, and State: Political Economy in 1980s*, Sussex: Wheatsheaf Books Ltd.

———— and W.C. Stubblebine (1962), 'Externality', *Economica*, 29, 371–84.

———— and G.Tullock (1962), *The Calculus of Consent: Logical Foundation of Constitutional Democracy*, Ann Arbor: The University of Michigan Press.

Buchanan, N.S. and H.S. Ellis (1995), *Approaches to Economic Development*, New York: Twentieth Century Fund.

Calabresi, G. (1968), 'Transaction Costs, Resource Allocation and Liability Rules: A Comment', *Journal of Law and Economics*, 11, 67–73.

Cardoso, F.H. (1972), 'Dependency and Development in Latin America', *New Left Review*, 74, 83–95.

Chakravarty, Sukhamoy (1969), *Capital and Development Planning*, Cambridge, Ma: The MIT Press.

———— (1984), 'Aspects of India's Development Strategy for the 1980s', *Economic and Political Weekly*, 19:20 & 21, 845–52.

Chakravarty, Sukhamoy (1987), *Development Planning: The Indian Experience*, Delhi: Oxford University Press.

Chang, Ho-Joon (1994). 'State, Institutions and Structural Change', *Structural Change and Economic Dynamics*, 5:2, 293–313.

Chenery, Hollis B. (1965), 'Comparative Advantage and Development Policy', in American Economic Association and the Royal Economic Society, *Survey of Economic Theory: Growth and Development, II*, Surveys V–VIII, New York: St. Martin's Press and London: MacMillan.

_____ (1975), 'The Structuralist Approach to Development Policy', *The American Economic Review* (Papers and Proceedings), 65:2, 310–16.

_____ (1983), 'Interaction between Theory and Observation in Development', *World Development*, 11:10, 853–61.

_____ and Syrquin (1975), *Patterns of Development, 1950–1970*, London: Oxford University Press.

_____ S. Robinson and M. Syrquin (1986), *Industrialization and Growth: A Comparative Study*, Washington DC: The World Bank.

_____ and T.N. Srinivasan (eds.) (1988), *Handbook of Development Economics, I*, New York: Elsevier Science Publishers.

_____ and T.N. Srinivasan (eds.) (1989), *Handbook of Development Economics, II*, New York: Elsevier Science Publishers.

_____ Montek S. Ahluwalia, C.L.G. Bell, John H. Duloy and Richard Jolly (1974), *Redistribution with Growth*, London: Oxford University Press.

Chow, C. Steven and Gustav F. Papanek (1981), 'Laissez-faire, Growth and Equity', *Economic Journal*, 91:362, 466–485.

Clark, Colin (1940), *The Conditions of Economic Progress*, London: MacMillan.

_____ (1984), 'Development Economics: The Early Years', in Gerald M. Meier and Dudley Seers (eds.), *Pioneers in Development*, New York: Oxford University Press.

Coale, A.J. (1973), 'Demographic Transition Reconsidered', *Proceedings*, Leige: The International Union for Scientific Study of Population.

_____ and Edgar M. Hoover (1958), *Population Growth and Economic Growth in Low Income Countries*, Princeton, N.J.: Princeton University Press.

Coase, R.H. (1960), 'The Problem of Social Cost', *Journal of Law and Economics*, 3, 1–44.

Coats, A.W. (1971), *The Classical Economists and Economic Policy*, London: Methuen.

Cohen, Suleiman I. (1978), *Agrarian Structures and Agrarian Reform*, Leiden and Boston: Martinus Nijhoff.

_____ (1980), 'Two Attempts to Extend Economic Model to Socio-political Issues and Realities', *The Pakistan Development Review*, 24:4, 281–310.

Collandar, David C. (1984), *Neoclassical Political Economy: The Analysis of Rent-seeking and DUP Activities*, Cambridge, Ma: Ballinger Publishing Co.

Corden, W.M. (1966), 'The Structure of a Tariff System and Effective Protection Rate', *The Journal of Political Economy*, 74:3, 221–37.

Cornwall, John (1977), *Modern Capitalism: Its Growth and Transformation*, London: Martin Robertson.

Crook, Clive (1989), 'The Third World: Trial and Error: Poor Man's Burden', *The Economist*, 23–29 September.

Dahrendorf, Ralf (1989), 'Liberalism', in Eatwell, Murray Milgate and Peter Newman (eds.), *The Invisible Hand (The New Palgrave)*, London: MacMillan.

Datta-Chaudhri, M (1990), 'Market Failure and Government Failure', *Journal of Economic Perspectives*, 4:3, 25–39.

Deane, Phyllis (1983), 'The Scope and Method of Economic Science', *The Economic Journal*, 93:369, 1–12.

Debreu, Gerard (1959), 'Theory of Value: An Axiomatic Analysis of Economic Equilibrium', Cowles Foundation, Monograph No. 17, New York: John Wiley.

_____ (1987), 'Mathematical Economics', in Eatwell, Murray and Peter Newman (eds.), *The New Palgrave: A Dictionary of Economics, (K-P)*, London: MacMillan pp. 399–403.

_____ (1991), 'The Mathematization of Economic Theory', *The American Economic Review*, 81:1, 1–6.

Deininger, Klaus and Lyn Squire (1998), 'New Ways of Looking at Old Issues: Inequality and Growth', *Journal of Development Economics*, Supplement to Vol. 57, 259–87.

Denison, Edward F. (1962), *The Sources of Economic Growth in the United States and the Alternatives Before US,* New York: Committee for Economic Development.

_____ (1967), *Why Growth Rates Differ: Post-War Experience in Nine Western Countries,* Washington DC: Brookings Institution.

_____ (1985), *Trends in American Growth, 1929-1982,* Washington DC: Brookings Institution.

Dollar, David and Art Kray (2000), 'Growth *is* Good for the Poor', Development Research Group, Washington, DC: World Bank.

Domar, Evsey D. (1946), 'Capital Expansion, Rate of Growth, and Employment', *Econometrica*, 14, 137–47.

_____ (1957), *Essays in the Theory of Economic Growth,* Westport, Ct: Greenwood.

Dowrick, Steve and Norman Gemmel (1991), 'Industrialization, Catching up and Economic Growth: A Comparative Study Across the World's Capitalist Economies', *The Economic Journal*, 101:405, 263–75.

Drèze, Jean and Amartya K. Sen (1989), *Hunger and Public Action*, Oxford: Oxford University Press.

_____ (1995), *Economic Development and Social Opportunity*, Delhi and New York: Oxford University Press.

Dutt, A (1985), 'Stagnation, Income Distribution and Monopoly Power', *Cambridge Journal of Economics*.

Dworkin, R. (1981a), 'What is Equality? Part I: Equality of Welfare', *Philosophy and Public Affairs*, 10:3, 185–246.

_____ (1981b), 'What is Equality? Part II: Equality of Resources', *Philosophy and Public Affairs*, 10:4, 283–345.

Duesenberry, James (1952), *Income, Saving and Theory of Consumer Behaviour*, Cambridge, Ma: Harvard University Press.

Eatwell, John, Murry Milgate and Peter Newman (1989), *Allocation, Information and Markets (The New Palgrave)* UK: The MacMillan Press Ltd.

Edlin Aaron and J.E. Stiglitz (1992), 'Discouraging Rivals: Managerial Rent-seeking and Economic Inefficiencies', Stanford University, California: Department of Economics.

Edwards, Sebastian (1993), 'Openness, Trade, Liberalization and Growth in Developing Countries', *Journal of Economic Literature*, 31:4, 1358–93.

El-Feki, Shereen (2000), 'Agriculture and Technology', *The Economist* (March 25), 3–16.

Emmanuel, Arghiri (1972), *Unequal Exchange: A Study of the Imperialism of Trade*, New York and London: Monthly Review Press.

Fei, John C.H. and Gustav Ranis (1963), 'Innovation, Capital Accumulation and Economic Development', *The American Economic Review*, 53:3, 283–313.

Feldman, Alan M. (1991), 'Welfare Economics', in Eatwell, Milgate and Newman, *The World of Economics, (The New Palgrave)* London: MacMillan.

Ferreira F.H.G. (1999), 'Inequality and Economic Performance: A Brief Overview of the Theories of Growth and Distribution', Text for World Bank's Site on Inequality, Poverty and Socio-economic Performance.

Findlay, Ronald (1979), 'Economic Development and the Theory of International Trade', *The American Economic Review*, 69:2, 186–90.

———— (1988), 'Trade, Development and the State', in Gustav Ranis and T. Paul Schultz (eds.), *The State of Development Economics*, New York: Basil Blackwell, 78–95.

Fishlow, Albert (1972), 'Brazilian Size Distribution of Income', *The American Economic Review*, 62, 391–402.

Frankel, A Jeffrey and David Romer (1999), 'Does Trade Cause Growth?' *The American Economic Review*, 89:3, 379–99.

Friedman, Milton (1953), *Essays in Positive Economics*, Chicago: University of Chicago Press.

———— (1962), *Capitalism and Freedom*, Chicago: University of Chicago Press.

———— (1968), 'The Role of Monetary Policy', *The American Economic Review*, 58:1, 1–17.

Furubotn, Eirik G., and Svetozar Pejovich (1972), 'Property Rights and Economic Theory: A Survey of Recent Literature', *The Journal of Economic Literature*, 10:4, 1137–62.

Galenson, Walter, and Harvey Leibenstein (1955), 'Investment Criteria, Productivity, and Economic Development', *Quarterly Journal of Economics*, 69:3, 343–70.

Galbraith, John Kenneth (1991), 'Economics in the Century Ahead', *The Economic Journal*, 101:404, 41–46.

Galor, O and J. Zeira (1993), 'Income Distribution and Macroeconomics', *Review of Economic Studies*, 60, 35–52.

Gerschenkron, Alexander (1962), *Economic Backwardness in Historical Perspective: A Book of Essays*, Cambridge, Ma: Harvard University Press. Also published in 1952 in B. Hoselitz (ed.) *The Progress of Underdeveloped Countries*, Chicago: Chicago University Press.

Gilder, George (1981), *Wealth and Poverty*, New York: Basic Books.

Gillis, D.H., M.R. Roemer and D. R. Snodgrass (1983), *Economics of Development*, New York: Norton.

Goodwin, R.M. (1990), *Chaotic Economic Dynamics*, Oxford: Oxford University Press, p. 198.

Graaff, J. De V. (1989), 'Social Cost', in Eatwell, Milgate and Newman (eds.), *The Invisible Hand (The New Palgrave)*, London: MacMillan.

Greenwald, Bruce and J.E. Stiglitz (1986), 'Externalities in Economies with Imperfect Information and Incomplete Markets', *The Quarterly Journal of Economics*, 101:2, 229–64.

Griffin, K.B. and J.L. Enos (1970), 'Foreign Assistance: Objectives and Consequences', *Economic Development and Cultural Change*, 18:3, 313–27.

Grossman, Gene M. and Elhanan Helpman (1994), 'Endogenous Innovation in the Theory of Growth', *Journal of Economic Perspectives*, 8:1, 23–44.

Haberler, Gottfried (1950a), 'Some Problems in the Pure Theory of International Trade', *The Economic Journal*, 60. Reproduced in Richard E. Caves and Harry Johnson (eds.) (1968), *Readings in International Economics*, Illinois: Richard D. Irwin, pp. 213–29.

_____ (1950b), *International Trade and Economic Development*, Cairo: National Bank of Egypt. Later published in 1980 with a new Introduction, San Francisco: International Center of Economic Growth.

_____ (1980), 'Notes on Rational and Irrational Expectation', Report No. III, Washington, DC: American Enterprise Institute.

Hahn, Frank (1987), 'Neo-classical Growth Theory', in Eatwell, Milgate and Newman, *The New Palgrave: A Dictionary of Economics, 3: (K-P)*, London: The MacMillan Press Ltd.

_____ (1991), 'The Next Hundred Years', *The Economic Journal*, 101:104, 47–50.

_____ and R.C.O. Mathews (1965), 'The Theory of Economic Growth: A Survey', in *Surveys of Economic Theory (Growth and Development)*, London: MacMillan.

Hanmer, Lucia, John Healey and Felix Naschod (2000), 'Will Poverty Halve by 2015?' *ODI Poverty Briefing*, 8 (July), 1–4.

Haq, Mahbub ul (1963), *The Strategy of Economic Planning: A Case Study of Pakistan*, Karachi: Oxford University Press.

_____ (1995), *Reflections on Human Development*, New York: Oxford University Press.

Hardin, G (1968), 'The Tragedy of Commons', *Science*, 162, 1243–48.

Hare, R.M. (1963), *Freedom and Reason*, Oxford: Oxford University Press.

_____ (1982), 'Ethical Theory and Utilitarianism', in Sen and Williams, *Utilitarianism and Beyond*, Cambridge: Cambridge University Press.

Harris, John R. and Michael P. Todaro (1970), 'Migration, Unemployment and Development: A Two-sector Analysis, *The American Economic Review*, 60:1, 125–42.

Harrison, Ann (1991), 'Openness and Growth', Working Paper 809, Office of the Vice-President, Development Economics, World Bank, Washington DC.

Harrod, R.F. (1939), 'An Essay in Dynamic Theory', *Economic Journal*, 49:193, 14–33.

_____ (1970), *Towards a Dynamic Economics: Some Recent Developments of Economic Theory and their Application to Policy*, London: MacMillan.

_____ (1972), *The Life of John Maynard Keynes*, London: Penguin Books (first published in 1951).

Harsha, A., P. Glewwe and P. Isenman (1994), 'Poverty, Human Development, and Growth: An Emerging Consensus?', *The American Economic Review* (Papers and Proceedings), 84:2, 244–49.

Harsanyi, John C. (1977a), 'Morality and the Theory of Rational Behaviour', *Social Research*, 44:4, 623–56.

Harsanyi, John C. (1977b), *Rational Behaviour and Bargaining Equilibrium in Games and Social Situations*, Cambridge: Cambridge University Press.

———— (1982), 'Morality and the Theory of Rational Behaviour', in Sen and Williams (eds.) (1982), *Utilitarianism and Beyond*, Cambridge: Cambridge University Press.

———— (1991), 'Value Judgements', in Eatwell, Milgate and Newman (eds.), *The New Palgrave (The World of Economics)*, London: The MacMillan Press.

Hausman, Daniel and Michael S. McPherson (1993), 'Taking Ethics Seriously: Economics and Contemporary Moral Philosophy, *Journal of Economic Literature*, 37:2, 671–731.

Hayek, F.A. (1960), *The Constitution of Liberty*, London: Routledge and Kegan Paul.

Heckscher, E.F (1933), 'The Effect of Foreign Trade on the Distribution of Income', in Ellis, H.S. and L.A. Metzler, *Readings in the Theory of International Trade*, Philadelphia: Blackiston.

Heilbroner, Robert L. (1980), *The Worldly Philosophers*, (Fifth Edition), New York: Simon and Schuster.

———— (1990), 'Analysis and Vision in the History of Modern Economic Thought', *Journal of Economic Literature*, 28:3, 1097–114.

Hicks, John (1965), *Capital and Growth*, New York: Oxford University Press.

———— (1976), 'Revolution in Economics', in Spiro J. Latsis (ed.), *Method and Appraisal in Economics*, London: Cambridge University Press (reprinted in 1978), pp. 207–18.

Hirsch, Fred (1977), *Social Limits to Growth*, London: Routledge and Kegan Paul.

Hirschman, Albert O. (1958), *The Strategy of Economic Development*, New Haven, Ct: Yale University Press.

———— (1981a), *Essays in Trespassing: Economics to Politics and Beyond*, Cambridge: Cambridge University Press.

———— (1981b), 'Morality and the Social Sciences: A Durable Tension', in Albert O. Hirschman (ed.), *Essays in Trespassing Economics to Politics and Beyond*, Cambridge: Cambridge University Press.

———— (1981c), 'The Rise and Decline of Development Economics', in Albert O. Hirschman (ed.), *Essays in Trespassing: Economics to Politics and Beyond*, Cambridge: Cambridge University Press.

———— (1984), 'A Dissenter's Confessions: The Strategy of Economic Development Revisited', in Gerald M. Meier and Dudley Seers (eds.), *Pioneers in Development*, New York: Oxford University Press (for the World Bank). pp. 87–111.

———— (1985), 'Against Parsimony: Three Easy Ways of Complicating some Categories of Economic Discourse', *Economic Philosophy*, 1:1, 7–12.

———— (1988), 'Two Hundred Years of Reactionary Rhetoric: The Case of the Perverse Effect', in Grethe B. Peterson (ed.), *The Tanner Lectures on Human Values, X*, Salt Lake City: University of Utah Press.

———— and Michael Rothschild (1973), 'Changing Tolerance for Income Inequality in the Course of Economic Development', *The Quarterly Journal of Economics*, 87:4, 544–66.

Hurwicz, L (1960), 'Optimality and Informational Efficiency in Resource Allocation Processes', in K.J. Arrow, S. Karlin and Suppes, *Mathematical Methods in Social Science*, Stanford: Stanford University Press.

Iqbal, Mohammad (1936), *The Reconstruction of Religious Thought in Islam*, also published by Lahore: Institute of Islamic Culture in 1986.

IMF (2000a), *World Economic Outlook*, Washington, DC: IMF.

_____ (2000b), *IMF-Survey*, Washington, DC: IMF.

Johnson, Harry (1957), 'Factor Endowments, International Trade, and Factor Prices', *The Manchester School of Economic and Social Studies*, 25:3, 270–83.

_____ (1964a), 'Tariffs and Economic Development: Some Theoretical Issues', *Journal of Development Studies*, 1, 3–30.

_____ (1964b), 'Optimal Trade Intervention in the Presence of Domestic Distortions', in Cave, Johnson and Kenen, *Trade Growth and Balance of Payment*, Chicago: Rand McNally and Company.

_____ (1969), 'The Theory of Effective Protection of Preferences', *Economica*, 36:142, 119–39.

Johnston, Bruce F. and John W. Mellor (1961), 'The Role of Agriculture in Economic Development', *The American Economic Review*, 51:4, 566–93.

Jones, L.P. and I. Sakong (1980), *Government, Business and Entrepreneurship in Economic Development: The Korean Case*, Cambridge, Ma: Harvard University Press.

Jones, Ronald (1993), 'The New Protectionism and the Nature of World Trade', *The Pakistan Development Review*, 32:4, 398–408.

Kaldor, Nicholas (1955), 'Alternative Theories of Distribution', *Review of Economic Studies*, 23.

Kalecki, M. (1971), *Selected Essays on the Dynamics of the Capitalist Economy*, Cambridge: Cambridge University Press.

Kanbur, Ravi and K. McIntosh (1990), 'Dual Economies', in Eatwell, Milgate and Newman, *Economic Development (The New Palgrave)*, London: MacMillan, pp. 114–21.

Karni, Edi (1989), 'Fraud', in Eatwell, Milgate and Newman (eds.), *Allocation, Information and Markets (The New Palgrave)*, London: MacMillan, pp. 117–19.

Kelly, A.C. (1980), 'Interactions of Economic and Demographic Household Behaviour', in R.A. Easterlin (ed.), *Population and Economic Change in Developing Countries*, Chicago: University of Chicago Press.

Kemp, Murray. C (1962), 'The Gains from International Trade', *The Economic Journal*, December, 32, 903–19.

Kemp, Murray C. and Michihiro Ohyama (1978), 'On the Sharing of Trade Gains by Resource-poor and Resource-rich Countries', *Journal of International Economics*, 8:1, 93–115.

Kendrik, J.W. (1961), *Productivity Trends in United States*, Princeton: Princeton University Press.

Keynes, John M. (1932), *Essays in Persuasion*, New York: Harcourt Brace.

_____ (1936), *The General Theory of Employment, Interest and Money*, New York: Harcourt Brace.

Khan, M. Ali (1979), 'Relevance of Human Capital Theory of Fertility Research: Comparative Findings for Bangladesh and Pakistan,' in Ismail Sirageldin (ed.), *Research in Human Capital and Development: 1*, Greenwich, Ct: JAI Press Inc.

_____ (1980a), 'The Harris–Todaro Hypothesis and the Heckscher–Ohlin–Samuelson Trade Model: A Synthesis', *Journal of International Economics*, 10:4, 527–48.

_____ (1980b), 'Dynamic Stability, Wage Subsidies and the Generalized Harris–Todaro Model', *The Pakistan Development Review*, 19:1, 1–24.

Khan, M. Ali (1987a), 'Harris–Todaro Model', in Eatwell, Milgate and Newman, *The New Palgrave: A Dictionary of Economics, 2: (E-J)*, London: MacMillan, 592–94.

———— (1987b) 'Perfect Competition', in J. Eatwell Milgate and Newman, *The New Palgrave: A Dictionary of Economics, 3 (K-P)*, New York: MacMillan.

———— (1989), 'In Praise of Development Economics', *The Pakistan Development Review* (Papers and Proceedings), 28:4 (Part 1), 337–78.

———— (1991), 'On the Languages of Markets', *The Pakistan Development Review*, 30:4 (Part I), 503–45.

———— and Y. Sun (1990), 'On a Reformulation of Cournot–Nash Equilibria', *Journal of Mathematical Analysis and Application*, 146, 442–60.

Khan, Mahmood Hasan (1975), *The Economics of the Green Revolution in Pakistan*, New York: Praeger Publishers.

———— (1983), 'Classes and Agrarian Transition in Pakistan', *The Pakistan Development Review*, 22:3, 129–62.

Klamer, Arjo (1984), *The New Classical Macro-economics: Conversations with the New Classical Economists and their Opponents*, Sussex: Wheatsheaf Books Ltd.

Klein, Lawrence R. (1978), 'The Supply Side', *The American Economic Review*, 68:1, 1–7.

———— (1983), *The Economics of Supply and Demand*, Oxford: Basil Blackwell.

———— (1985), 'Reducing Unemployment without Inflation', *America*, 4 May, 262–65.

———— (1994), 'Development Economics: A New Paradigm: A Review', *Pakistan Development Review*, 191–93.

Kneese A.V. and James L. Sweeney (eds.) (1985), *Handbook of National Resources and Energy Economics* (Vols. 1 & 2), Amsterdam: North-Holland.

Koopmans, T.C. (1957), *Three Essays on the State of Economic Science*, New York: McGraw-Hill.

———— T.C. (1965), 'On the Concept of Optimal Growth', *Pontificia Academia Scientiarum*, 225–88.

Krugman, Paul (1987), 'Is Free-Trade Passé', *Journal of Economic Perspectives*, 1:2, 131–44.

———— (1992), 'Towards a Counter-Revolution in Development Theory', Annual World Bank Conference on Development Economics.

Kreps, D. (1990), *Micro-economic Theory*, Princeton, NJ: Princeton University Press.

Krishna, Raj (1963), 'Farm Supply Response in India-Pakistan: Case Study of the Punjab Region', *The Economic Journal*, 73:3, 477–87.

Krueger, Anne O. (1974), 'The Political Economy of the Rent-seeking Society', *The American Economic Review*, 64:3, 291–303.

———— (1978), *Liberalization Attempts and Consequences*, Cambridge, Ma: Ballinger.

Kuhn, Thomas (1962), *The Structure of Scientific Revolutions*, Chicago: University of Chicago Press.

Kuznets, Simon (1955), 'Economic Growth and Income Inequality', *The American Economic Review*, 45:1, 1–28.

———— (1971), *Economic Growth of Nations: Total Output and Production Structure*, Cambridge, Ma: Harvard University Press.

Lakatos, Imre (1970), 'Falsification and Methodology of Scientific Research,' in Imre Lakatos and A. Musgrave (eds.), *Criticism and Growth of Knowledge*, Cambridge: Cambridge University Press.

Laffont, J.J. (1991), 'Externalities', in Eatwell, Milgate, and Newman (eds.), *The Invisible Hand (The New Palgrave)*, London: MacMillan.

Laffont, J.J., eds. (1979), *Aggregation and Revealed Preferences*, Amsterdam: North-Holland.

Lal, Deepak (1983), *The Poverty of Development Economics*, London: Institute of Economic Affairs, Hobart Paperback 16.

Lange, Oscar (1936–37), 'On Economic Theory of Socialism', *Review of Economic Studies*.

Leibenstein, Harvey (1957), *Economic Backwardness and Economic Growth*, New York: John Wiley.

Leontief, Wassily (1983), 'Technological Advance, Economic Growth and the Distribution of Income', *Population and Development Review*, 9:3, 403–10.

Lewis, W. Arthur (1954), 'Economic Development with Unlimited Supplies of Labour', *Manchester School*, 22, 139–91.

———— (1955), *The Theory of Economic Growth*, London: Unwin University Press.

———— (1980), 'The Slowing Down of the Engine of Growth', *The American Economic Review*, 70:4, 555–64.

———— (1984a), 'The State of Development Theory', *The American Economic Review*, 74:1, 1–10.

———— (1984b), 'Development Economics in the 1950s', in Gerald M. Meier and Dudley Seers (eds.), *Pioneers in Development*, New York: Oxford University Press.

———— (1988), 'The Roots of Development Theory', in H.B. Chenery and T.N. Srinivasan (eds.) *Handbook of Development Economics*, *1*, New York: Elsevier Science Publishers, 27–37.

Lewis, Stephen R., Jr. (1969), *Economic Policy and Industrial Growth in Pakistan*, London: George Allen and Unwin.

Linder, Staffan B. (1961), *An Essay on Trade and Transformation*, New York: John Wiley.

———— (1996), *An Essay on Trade and Transformation*, New York: John Wiley.

Little, Ian M.D. (1982), *Economic Development: Theory, Policy and International Relations*, New York: Basic Books.

————, Tibor Scitovsky and Michael Scott (1970), *Industry and Trade Regimes in Some Developing Countries*, London & New York: Oxford University Press.

Lowe, A (1977), 'On Economic Knowledge', cited in Chakravarty Sukhamoy (1987), *Development Planning*, Delhi: Oxford University Press.

Lucas, Robert E., Jr. (1972), 'Expectations and Neutrality of Money', *Journal of Economic Theory*, 4, 103–24.

———— (1988), 'On the Mechanics of Development', *Journal of Monetary Economics*, 22:1, 3–42.

———— (1993), 'Making a Miracle', *Econometrica*, 61:2, 251–72.

———— and Thomas Sargent (1978), 'After Keynesian Macroeconomics', in *After the Phillips Curve: Persistence of High Inflation and High Unemployment*, Boston: Federal Reserve Bank of Boston, 49–72.

Luce, R.D. and H. Raiffa (1958), *Games and Decisions*, New York: John Wiley.

Machlup, Fritz (1956), 'Rejoinder to a Reluctant Ultra-empiricist', *Southern Economic Journal*, 22, 483–93.

Maddison, Angus (1970), *Economic Progress and Policy in Developing Countries*, London: George Allen and Unwin.

Maddison, Angus (1991), *Dynamic Forces in Capitalist Development*, Oxford, UK: Oxford University Press.

Mahalanobis, P.C. (1953), 'Some Observations on the Process of Growth of National Income', *Sankhya*, 12:4, 307–12.

Malenbaum, Wilfred (1962), *Prospects for Indian Development*, London: George Allen and Unwin.

Malinvaud, Edmond (1969), 'Capital Accumulation and Efficient Allocation of Resources', first published in *Econometrica*, 1953, reprinted in Kenneth J. Arrow and T. Scitovsky (eds.), *Readings in Welfare Economics*, London: George Allen and Unwin, 645–81.

———— (1984), *Mass Unemployment*, New York: Basil Blackwell.

———— (1989), 'Decentralization', in Eatwell, Milgate, and Newman (eds.), *Allocation, Information and Markets*, London: MacMillan.

———— (1991), 'The Next Fifty Years', *The Economic Journal*, 101:404, 64–68.

Marshall, Alfred (1969 [1920]), *Principles of Economics*, 8th edition, London: MacMillan.

Marshall, T.H. (1950), *Citizenship and Social Class*, Cambridge: Cambridge University Press.

Marx, Karl (1967 [1867]), *Capital*, New York: International Publishers.

Meade, James (1983), 'Impressions of Maynard Keynes', in D.Worswick and D. Trevithick (eds.), *Keynes and the Modern World*, Cambridge: Cambridge University Press.

Meier, Gerald M. (1984a), *Emerging from Poverty: The Economics that Really Matters*, New York: Oxford University Press.

———— (1984b), 'The Formative Period', in Meir and Seers (eds.), *Pioneers in Development*, New York: Oxford University Press, pp. 3–22.

Mellor, John W. (1986), 'Agriculture on the Road to Industrialization', in John P. Lewis and V. Kallab (eds.), *Development Strategies Reconsidered*, USA: Transaction Books.

———— and Bruce F. Johnston (1984), 'The World Food Equation: Inter-relations Among Development, Employment and Food Consumption', *Journal of Economic Literature*, 22:2, 531–74.

Metzler, Loyd. A. (1949), 'Tariffs, the Terms of Trade, and the Distribution of National Income', *Journal of Political Economy*, 47:1, 1–29.

Michaely, Michael (1977), 'Exports and Growth: An Empirical Investigation', *Journal of Development Economics*, 4:1, 49–53.

Milgrom, Paul and John Roberts (1990), 'Bargaining and Influence Costs and Organization of Economic Activity', *The American Economic Review*, 80:3, 511–29.

Miliband, R. (1983), 'State Power and Class Interests', *New Left Review*, 138.

Mincer, J. (1962), 'Market Prices, Opportunity Costs, and Income Effect', in C. Christ *et al.* (eds.), *Measurement in Economics: Studies in Mathematical Economics and Econometrics in Memory of Yehuda Grenfeld*, Stanford: Stanford University Press.

Modigliani, Franco (1977), 'The Monetarist Controversy, or Should We Forsake Stabilization Policies', *The American Economic Review*, 67:2, 1–19.

Morris, M.D. (1979), *Measuring the Condition of the World's Poor: The Physical Quality of Life Index*, New York: Pergamon Press.

Mueller, Dennis C. (1979), *Public Choice*, Cambridge: Cambridge University Press.

Musgrave, R.A. (1959), *The Theory of Public Finance*, New York: McGraw-Hill.

Myint, Hla (1958), 'The Classical Theory of International Trade and the Underdeveloped Countries', *The Economic Journal*, 68:270, 317–37.

Myrdal, Gunnar (1956a), *Development and Underdevelopment*, Cairo: National Bank of Egypt.

_____ (1956b), *An International Economy: Problems and Perspectives*, Westport, Ct: Greenwood Press.

_____ (1984), 'International Inequality and Foreign Aid in Retrospect', in Gerald M. Meier and Dudley Seers (eds.), *Pioneers in Development*, New York: Oxford University Press.

Naqvi, Syed Nawab Haider (1964), 'Import Licensing in Pakistan', *Pakistan Development Review*, 4:1, 51–68.

_____ (1966), 'The Allocative Biases of Pakistani Commercial Policy', *Pakistan Development Review*, 4:4, 465–89.

_____ (1969), 'Protection and Economic Development', *Kyklos*, 22 (Fasc.1), 124–54.

_____ (1971), 'On Optimizing "Gains" From Pakistan's Export Bonus Scheme', *Journal of Political Economy*, 79:1, 114–27.

_____ (1981), *Ethics and Economics: An Islamic Synthesis*, Leicester: The Islamic Foundation.

_____ (1982), 'The "Policy Gaps", Allocative Inefficiencies and Self Reliance', in Heinz Ahrens and Wolfgang Peter Zingel (eds.), *Towards Reducing the Dependence on Capital Imports*, Weisbaden: Franz Steiner Verlag.

_____ (1993), *Development Economics: A New Paradigm*, New Delhi: Sage Publications.

_____ (1994), *Islam, Economics and Society*, London: Kegan Paul.

_____ (1995), 'The Nature of Economic Development', *World Development*, 23:4, 543–56.

_____ (1996), 'The Significance of Development Economics', *World Development*, 24:6, 975–87.

_____ (1999), 'The Rise of Development Economics', *Asia-Pacific Development*, 6:1, 108.

_____ (2000), *The Crisis of Development Planning in Pakistan: Which Way Now*, Islamabad: Institute of Policy Studies.

_____ (2002 [forthcoming]), 'Globalization and Human Development', in *Encyclopedia of Life Support Systems (EOLSS), Human Development Theme*, Paris and Oxford: UNESCO-EOLSS. (Also available on the internet).

_____, Ashfaque H. Khan, Nasir Khilji and Ather Maqsood Ahmed (1983), *The P.I.D.E. Macro-econometric Model of Pakistan's Economy, 1*, Islamabad: Pakistan Institute of Development Economics.

_____ and Asghar Qadir (1985), 'Incrementalism and Structural Change: A Technical Note', *The Pakistan Development Review*, 24:2, 87–102.

_____ and Ather Maqsood Ahmed (1986), *Preliminary Revised P.I.D.E. Macro-econometric Model of Pakistan's Economy*, Islamabad: Pakistan Institute of Development Economics.

_____ and Peter A. Cornelisse (1986), 'Public Policy and Wheat Market in Pakistan', *The Pakistan Development Review*, 25:2, 99–126.

_____, Mahmood Hasan Khan and M. Ghaffar Chaudhry (1989), *Structural Change in Pakistan's Agriculture*, Islamabad: Pakistan Institute of Development Economics.

Naqvi, Syed Nawab Haider and A.R. Kemal (1991), *Protectionism and Efficiency in Manufacturing: A Case Study of Pakistan*, San Francisco: ICS Press.

―――― and A.R. Kemal (1994), 'Structural Adjustment, Privatization, and Employment in Pakistan', in Rizwaul Islam, *Social Dimensions of Economic Reforms in Asia*, New Delhi: International Labour Office (ILO).

―――― and A.R. Kemal (1997a), 'Privatization, Efficiency and Employment in Pakistan', in Anthony Bennet (ed.), *How Does Privatization Work*, London: Routledge, 228–49.

―――― and A.R. Kemal (1997b), 'The Structure of Protection and Industrial Efficiency in Pakistan's *Journal of Economic Cooperation Among Islamic Countries*, 18:3, 47–70.

Nelson, Richard and Edmund Phelps (1996), 'Investment in Humans, Technological Differences and Economic Growth', *The American Economic Review*, 56:2, 69–75.

North D. (1984), 'Three Approaches to the Study of Institutions', in David C. Collander (ed.), *Neoclassical Political Economy: The Analysis of Rent-seeking and DUP Activities*, Cambridge, Ma: Ballinger, 33–40.

Nozick, Robert, (1974), *Anarchy, State and Utopia*, Oxford: Basil Blackwell.

Nurkse, Ragnar (1953), *Problems of Capital Formation in Underdeveloped Countries*, New York: Oxford University Press.

Ohlin, B (1933), *Inter-regional and International Trade*, Cambridge, Ma: Harvard University Press.

Ohlin, P.G. (1959), 'Balanced Economic Growth in History', *The American Economic Review*, 49:2, 338–53.

Okhawa, K, B.F. Johnston and H. Kaneda (eds.) (1970), *Agriculture and Economic Growth: Japan's Experience*, Princeton, NJ: Princeton University Press.

Olson, M., Jr. (1965), *The Logic of Collective Action: Public Goods and the Theory of Groups*, Cambridge, Ma: Harvard University Press.

Pack, Howard (1994), 'Endogenous Growth Theory: Intellectual Appeal and Empirical Shortcomings', *Journal of Economic Perspectives*, 8:1, 55–72.

Pack, Howard, and Larry E. Westphal (1986), 'Industrial Strategy and Technological Change: Theory versus Reality', *Journal of Development Economics*, 22:1, 87–128.

Papanek, Gustav F. (1967), *Pakistan's Development: Social Goals and Private Incentives*, Cambridge, Ma: Harvard University Press.

―――― (1972), 'The Effect of Aid and other Resources on Savings and Growth in Less Developed Countries', *Economic Journal*, 82:327, 934–50.

―――― and Oldrich Kyn (1986), 'The Effect of Income Distribution of Development, the Growth Rate, and Economic Strategy', *Journal of Development Economics*, 23:1, 55–66.

Park, Se-H (1996), 'East Asian Industrial Policy: Its Relevance and Lessons for Developing Countries', in ESCWA, *Industrial Strategies and Policies, Management Entrepreneurial Skills under Conditions of Global and Regional Change*, Bahrain, 361–86.

Pastoral Letter (1985), *Catholic Social Teaching and the US Economy*, Washington, DC: National Conference of Catholic Bishops.

Perroux, F.(1955), 'Note on the Notion of Poles of Growth' (French), *Economic Appliquee*, 8, Series D, Jan–June.

Pigou, A.C. (1932), *The Economics of Welfare*, London: MacMillan.

Popper, Karl R. (1980 [1959]), *The Logic of Scientific Discovery*, tenth (revised) edition, London: Hutchinson.

Prebisch, Raul (1950), *The Economic Development of Latin America and Its Principal Problems*, New York: Department of Economic Affairs, The United Nations.

_____ (1959), 'Commercial Policies in Underdeveloped Countries', *The American Economic Review*, 49:2, 251–73.

_____ (1984), 'Five Stages in My Thinking on Development', in Meier and Seers (eds.), *Pioneers in Development*, New York: Oxford University Press.

Pritchett, Lant (1997), 'Divergence, Big Time', *Journal of Economic Perspectives*, 11, 3.

Putnam, H. (1990), *Realism with a Human Face*, Cambridge, Ma: Harvard University Press.

Ranis. G. (1988), 'Analytics of Development Dualism', in H.B. Chenery and T.N. Srinivasan, (eds.), *Handbook of Development Economics I*, New York: Elsevier Science Publishers.

_____ 'Labour Surplus Countries', in Eatwell, Milgate and Newman (eds.), *The New Palgrave (Economic Development)*, London: MacMillan.

Ranis, G. and Frances Stewart (2000), 'Strategies for Success in Human Development', *Journal of Human Development* 1:1, 49–69.

Rapoport, A. (1991), 'Prisoner's Dilemma', in Eatwell, Milgate and Newman, *The New Palgrave (The World of Economics)*, London: MacMillan.

Rawls, John (1971), *A Theory of Justice*, Cambridge, Ma: Harvard University Press, and Oxford: Clarendon Press.

_____ (1985), 'Justice as Fairness: Political not Metaphysical', *Philosophy and Public Affairs*, 14:3, 223–51.

_____ (1990), *Political Liberalism*, New York: Columbia University Press.

_____ (1998), 'Priority of Rights and Ideas of Good', *Philosophy and Public Affairs*, 17, (cited in Sen (1992).

Reynolds, Loyd G. (1977), *Image and Reality in Economic Development*, New Haven, Ct: Yale University Press.

Riddell, Roger C. (1990), *Manufacturing Africa*, London: James Currency.

Rivlin, Alice M. (1987), 'Economics and the Political Process', *The American Economic Review*, 77:1, 1–10.

Robbins, Lionel, (1932), *An Essay on the Nature and Significance of Economic Science*, London: MacMillan.

Robinson, Joan (1973), *Economic Philosophy*, England: Penguin Books.

_____ (1979), *Aspects of Development and Underdevelopment*, Cambridge: Cambridge University Press.

Roemer, John (1986), 'Equality of Resources Implies Equality of Welfare', *The Quarterly Journal of Economics*, 100:4, 751–84.

Roemer, Michael and Mary K. Gugerty (1997), 'Does Growth Reduce Poverty', HID Technical Papers, Cambridge, Ma: Harvard Institute of International Development.

Romer, Paul A (1986), 'Increasing Returns and Long-run Growth', *Journal of Political Economy*, 94:5, 1002–37.

Rodrik, Dan (1997), *Has Globalization Gone Too Far*, Washington, DC: Institute for International Economics.

Rosenstein-Rodan, P.N. (1943), 'Problems of Industrialization of Eastern and Southeastern Europe', *The Economic Journal*, 53:210, 202–11.

Rosenstein-Rodan, P.N. (1984), 'Natura Facit Saltum: Analysis of Disequilibrium Growth Process', in Meier and Seers (eds.), *Pioneers in Development*, New York: Oxford University Press.

Rostow, W. W. (1956), 'The Take-off into Self-sustained Growth', *The Economic Journal*, 66:261, 25–48.

—————— (1971), *Stages of Economic Growth*, second edition, Cambridge: Cambridge University Press.

Rozenzweig, Mark R. (1989), 'Labour Markets in Low-income Countries', in Chenery and Srinivasan (eds.), *Handbook of Development Economics, I*, New York: Elsevier Science Publishers.

Ruttan, Vernon W. (1982), *Agricultural Research Policy*, Minneapolis: University of Minnesota Press.

—————— and Yujiro Hayami (1970), 'Factor Prices and Technical Change in Agricultural Development: The United States and Japan 1880–1960', *Journal of Political Economy*, 78:5, 1115–141.

Sachs, Jeffery (1999), 'Helping the World's Poorest', *The Economist*, August 14th to 20th, 17–20.

Samuelson, Paul A. (1939), 'The Gains from International Trade', *The Canadian Journal of Economics and Political Science*, 5, 195–205

—————— (1949), 'International Factor Price Equalization Once Again', *The Economic Journal*, 59 (June) 181–97.

—————— (1966), 'A Brief Survey of Post-Keynesian Development', in Joseph E. Stiglitz (ed.), *The Collected Scientific Papers of Paul A. Samuelson, II*, Cambridge, Ma: MIT Press, pp. 1534–550.

—————— (1990), 'Pure Theory of Public Expenditure and Taxation', in J. Margolis and H. Guitton (eds.), *Public Economics*, New York: St. Martin's Press.

—————— (1976), *Economics*, tenth edition, New York: McGraw-Hill.

Sappington, David and Joseph Stiglitz (1987), 'Privatization, Information and Incentives', *Journal of Policy Analysis and Management*, 6:4, 567–82.

Sargent, Thomas J. and Neil Wallace (1975), '"Rational" Expectations, the Optimal Monetary Instruments and the Optimal Money Supply Rule', *The Journal of Political Economy*, 83:2, 241–54.

Sato, R. (1963), 'Fiscal Policy in a Neo-classical Growth Model: An Analysis of Time Required for Equilibrating Adjustment', *Review of Economic Studies*, 30:82, 16–23.

Schleifer, Andrie and Robert W. Vishny (1989), 'Management Entrenchment: The Case for Manager-specific Investment', *Journal of Financial Economics*, 25, 123–29.

Schmalensee, Richard (1991), 'Continuity and Change in the Economics Industry, *The Economic Journal*, 101:404, 115–21.

Schultz, Theodore W. (1962), 'Reflections on Investment in Man', *Journal of Political Economy*, 70:5 (Part 2), 1–8.

—————— (1964), *Transforming Traditional Agriculture*, Chicago: The University of Chicago Press.

—————— (1970), *Investment in Human Capital: The Role of Education and Research*, New York: MacMillan and Free Press.

—————— (1981a), 'The Economics of Being Poor' in Theodore W. Schultz (ed.), *Investing in People: The Economics of Population Quality*, Berkeley and Los Angeles: University of California Press.

Schultz, Theodore W. (1981b), *Investing in People: The Economics of Population Quality*, Berkeley and Los Angeles: University of California Press.

———— (1987), 'Education and Population Quality', in George Psacharopoulos (ed.), *Economics of Education: Research and Studies*, New York: Pergaman Press.

Schumpeter, Joseph A. (1934), *The Theory of Economic Development*, Cambridge, Ma: Harvard University Press.

Scitovsky, Tibor (1954), 'Two Concepts of External Economics', *Journal of Political Economy*, 17:2, 143–51.

———— (1987), 'Balanced Growth', in Eatwell, Milgate and Newman (eds.), *The New Palgrave: A Dictionary of Economics, I (A-D)*, New York: MacMillan.

Sen, Amartya K. (1967), 'Surplus Labour in India: A Rejoinder of Schultz's Test', *The Economic Journal*, 77:305, 163–65.

———— (1970a), 'The Impossibility of the Paretian Liberal', *Journal of Political Economy*, 78, 152–57. Reprinted in A.K. Sen (1983), *Choice, Welfare and Measurement*, Oxford: Basil Blackwell, pp. 285–90.

———— (1970b), *Collective Choice and Social Welfare*, San Franciso: Holden-Day Inc.

———— (1979), 'Personal Utilities and Public Judgements: Or What's Wrong with Welfare Economics?', *The Economic Journal*, 89:355, 537–58.

———— (1981a), *Poverty and Famine: An Eassay on Entitlement and Deprivation*, Oxford: Clarendon Press.

———— (1981b), 'Public Action and the Quality of Life in Developing Countries', *Oxford Bulletin of Economics and Statistics*, 43:4, 287–319.

———— (1983a), 'Development: Which Way Now?', *The Economic Journal*, 93:372, 745–62.

———— (1983b), 'Equality of What?', in A.K. Sen, *Choice, Welfare and Measurement*, Oxford: Basil Blackwell, pp. 353–69, (First published in *Tanner Lectures on Human Values, 1* [1980]).

———— (1983c), 'Poverty: An Ordinal Approach to Measurement', in A.K. Sen, *Choice, Welfare and Measurement*, Oxford: Basil Blackwell, pp. 373–87.

———— (1984), *Resources, Values and Development*, Oxford: Basil Blackwell.

———— (1985), Review of Kenneth J. Arrow's *Social Choice and Justice, Journal of Economic Literature*, 23:4, 1764–76.

———— (1987), *On Ethics and Economics*, Oxford: Basil Blackwell.

———— (1988), 'The Concept of Development', in Chenery and Srinivasan (eds.), *Handbook of Development Economics, I*, New York: Elsevier Science Publishers.

———— (1991), *Commodities and Capabilities*, Oxford: Oxford University Press.

———— (1992), *Inequality Re-examined*, New York: Clarendon Press.

———— (1999), 'The Possibility of Social Choice', *The American Economic Review*, 89:3, 349–78.

———— (2000), 'A Decade of Human Development', *Journal of Human Development*, 1:1, 17–23.

Shapiro, Carl and Joseph E. Stiglitz (1984), 'Equilibrium Unemployment as a Worker Discipline Device', *The American Economic Review*, 74:3, 433–44.

Sidgwick, H. (1874), *The Methods of Ethics*, London: MacMillan.

Simon, Herbert A. (1983), *Reason in Human Affairs*, Oxford: Basil Blackwell.

Singer, Hans W. (1950), 'The Distribution of Gains between Investing and Borrowing Countries', *The American Economic Review* (Papers and Proceedings), 40:2, 473–85.

Singer, Hans W. (1952), 'The Mechanics of Economic Development', *Indian Economic Review*, Vol. 1.

_____ (1984), 'The Terms of Trade Controversy and the Evolution of Soft Financing: Early Years in the UN', in Gerald Meier and Dudley Seers, *Pioneers in Development*, New York: Oxford University Press, pp. 275–303.

Singer, Hans W. and Patricia Gray (1988), 'Trade Policy and Growth of Developing Countries', *World Development* 16:3, 395–403.

Sirageldin, Ismail, (1966), *Non-market Components of National Income*, Ann Arbor: University of Michigan.

_____ (1979), 'United Naitons/UNFPA Export Group Meeting on Demographic Transition and Socio-economic Development', in *Demographic Transition and Socio-economic Development*, with United Nations Secretariat, the United Nations Department of International Economic and Social Affairs, 5–30.

_____ (2001), 'Sustainable Human Development in the 21st Century: An Evolutionary Perspective', *Encyclopedia of Life Support Systems*, Paris: UNESCO.

_____, James Morgan and Nancy Baerwaldt (1966), *Productive Americans*, Ann Arbor: Survey Research Center, University of Michigan.

Skinner, Andrew S. (1989), 'Adam Smith', in Eatwell, Milgate and Newman (eds.), *The Invisible Hand: The New Palgrave*, London: MacMillan.

Smith, Adam (1976 [1776]), *An Enquiry into the Nature and Causes of the Wealth of Nations*, reprinted by R.N. Campbell and A.S. Skinner, Oxford: Clarendon Press.

Solow, Robert M. (1957), 'Technical Change and the Aggregate Production Function', *Review of Economics and Statistics*, 39:3.

_____ (1980), 'On Theories of Unemployment', *The American Economic Review*, 70:1, 1–11.

_____ (1988), 'Growth Theory and After', *The American Economic Review*, 78:3, 307–17.

_____ (1994), 'Perspectives on Growth Theory', *Journal of Economic Perspectives*, 8:1, 45–55.

Spraos, J. (1980), 'The Statistical Debate on the Net Barter Terms of Trade between Primary Commodities and Manufactures', *The Economic Journal*, 90 (March), 107–28.

Sraffa, Pierro (1975), *Production of Commodities by Means of Commodities*, London: Cambridge University Press.

Srinivasan, T.N. (1985), 'New-classical Political Economy, the State and Economic Development', *Asian Development Review*, 3:2, 39–58.

_____ (1988), 'Introduction to Part 1', in H.B. Chenery and T.N. Srinivasan, *Handbook of Development Economics, I*, New York: Elsevier Science Publishers.

_____ (1994), 'Human Development: A New Paradigm or Reinvention of the Wheel?' *The American Economic Review*, 84:2, 238–43.

Stern, Nicholas (1989), 'The Economics of Development: A Survey', *The Economic Journal*, 99 (September), 597–685.

_____ (1991), 'The Determinants of Growth', *The Economic Journal*, 101:404, 122–33.

Stigler, George J. (1965), 'The Economist and The State', *The American Economic Review*, 55:1, 1–18.

Stigler, George J. (1981), 'Economics or Ethics?' in Sterling McMurrin (ed.), *Tanner Lectures on Human Values, II*, Cambridge: Cambridge University Press, pp. 145–91.

Stiglitz, Joseph P. (1985), 'Information and Economic Analysis: A Perspective', *The Economic Journal*, 95 (Supplement), 21–41.

———— (1986), 'The New Development Economics', *World Devleopment*, 14:2, 257–65.

———— (1988), 'Economic Organization, Information, and Development', in Chenery and Srinivasan (eds.), *Handbook of Development Economics, I*, New York: Elsevier Science Publishers.

———— (1991), 'Another Century of Economic Science', *The Economic Journal*, 101:404, 134–141.

———— (1996a), 'The Role of Government in Economic Development', Paper presented at the Annual World Bank Conference on Development Economies.

———— (1996b), 'Some Lessons from the East Asian Miracle', *The World Bank Research Observer*, 11:2, 151–77.

Stolper, W, and P.A. Samuelson (1941), 'Protection and Real Wages', *Review of Economic Studies*, 9 (July).

Streeten, Paul (1959), 'Unbalanced Growth', *Oxford Economic Papers*, 11:2, 167–90.

———— (1980), 'Basic Needs in the Year 2000', *The Pakistan Development Review*, 19:2, 129–41.

———— (1981), *Development Perspectives*, London: MacMillan.

———— (1984), 'Development Dichotomies', in Meier and Seers, *Pioneers in Development*, New York: Oxford University Press.

———— (1985), 'Comments by Paul Streeten' (on a paper by Anne O. Krueger, in *Hard Bargaining Ahead: US Trade Policy and Developing Countries*, Edited by Ernest H. Preeg, US). Third World Policy Perspectives, No. 4, Washington, DC Overseas Development Council, pp. 58–60.

———— (1989), 'International Cooperation', Chenery and Srinivasan (eds.), *Handbook of Development Economics, I*, New York: Elsevier Science Publishers.

———— (1993), 'Markets and States: Against Minimalism', *World Development*, 21:8, 1281–98.

———— (1998), 'Globalization: Threat or Opportunity', *Pakistan Development Review*, 37:4, 51–85.

———— , J. Burki and M. Haq (1981), *First Things First: Meeting Basic Human Needs in the Developing Countries*, New York: Oxford University Press.

Sudgen, Robert (1993), 'Welfare, Resource, and Capbilities: A Review of Inequality Re-examined by Amartya Sen', *Journal of Economic Literature*, 31:4, 1947–962.

Syrquin, Moshe (1988), 'Patterns of Structural Change', in Hollis B. Chenery and T.N. Srinivasan (eds.), *Handbook of Development Economics, I*, New York: Elsevier Science Publishers, pp. 203–273.

Temkin, Larry S. (1986), 'Inequality', *Philosophy and Public Affairs*, 15:2, 99–121.

The Economist (2000a), 'Europe's New Capitalism', *The Economist*, January 12th to18th, 75–78.

The Economist (2000b), 'The World's View of Multinationals', *The Economist*, January 29th to February 4th, 19–20.

The Economist (2000c), 'Europe's New Left', *The Economist*, February 12th to 18th, 19–21.

The Economist (2000d), 'The Knowledge Monopolies', *The Economist*, April 8th to 14th, 79–82.

The Economist (2000e), 'Merger Brief', *The Economist*, July 22nd to 28th, 73–74 (see also 'How Mergers Go Wrong').

The Economist (2001), 'Africa's Elusive Dawn', *The Economist*, February 24th to March 2nd, 17–28.

Thirlwall, A.P. (1999), *Growth and Development*, (6th Edition), London: MacMillan.

Thurow, Lester C. (1983), *Dangerous Currents: The State of Economics*, London: Oxford University Press.

———— (1990), 'How Supply-side Myths Warp the Political Process', *International Herald Tribune*, Paris, 10 October.

———— (1990a), 'The Supply-side Destination is a Frail Plutocracy', *International Herald Tribune*, Paris, 11 October.

Timmer, Peter (1988), 'The Agricultural Transformation', in Chenery and Srinivasan (eds.), *Handbook of Development Economics*, New York: Elsevier Science Publishers, pp. 275–331.

Tinbergen, Jan (1959), 'The Theory of Optimum Regime', in L.H. Klassen, L.M. Kyock and J.H. Witteveen (eds.), *Jan Tinbergen: Selected Papers*, Amsterdam: North-Holland, pp. 264–304.

———— (1977) *On the Theory of Economic Policy*, Amsterdam: North-Holland.

———— (1982), 'Ways to Socialism', *Coexistence*, 19:1.

———— (1985), *Production, Income and Welfare: The Search for an Optimal Social Order*, Brighton, Sussex: Wheatsheaf Books.

Titmuss, Richard (1971), *The Gift Relationship: From Human Blood to Social Policy*, New York: Random House.

Tobin, James (1985), 'Unemployment, Poverty and Economic Policy', *America*, 4 May, 359–62.

Todaro, Michael P. (2000), *Economic Development*, seventh edition, New York: Addison-Wesley Longman Inc.

Tullock, Gordon (1986), *The Economics of Wealth and Poverty*, Brighton, Sussex: Wheatsheaf Books.

UNCTAD (1998), *Trade and Development Report (TDR), 1998*, New York: United Nations.

———— (1999), *Trade and Development Report (TDR), 1999*, New York: United Nations.

UNDP (1990), *Human Development Report (HDR), 1990*, New York: Oxford University Press.

———— (1991), *Human Development Report (HDR), 1991*, New York: Oxford University Press.

———— (1996), *Human Development Report (HDR), 1996*, New York: Oxford University Press.

———— (1999), *Human Development Report (HDR), 1999*, New York: Oxford University Press.

———— (2000), *Human Development Report (HDR), 2000*, New York: Oxford University Press.

———— (2000), *Overcoming Human Poverty*, New York: United Nations.

UNIDO (1996), *Industrial Development Global Report, 1996*, Vienna: Oxford University Press.

Uzawa, H. (1961), 'On a Two-sector Model of Growth, Part I', *Review of Economic Studies*, 1:29, 40–47.

———— (1963), 'On a Two-sector Model of Growth, Part II', *Review of Economic Studies*, 30, 105–18.

Valen, Leigh Von (2000), 'How the Left Got Darwin Wrong', (A Review of Peter Singer's *A Darwinian Left*), *Scientific American*, June, 110–11.

Van Praag B., T. Goedhart and A. Kapteyn (1978), *The Poverty Line: A Pilot Survey in Europe*, Leiden: Centre for Research in Public Economics, Leiden University.

Varian, Hal (1974), 'Equity, Envy, and Efficiency', *Journal of Economic Theory*, 9:1, 63–91.

Veblen, Thorstein B. (1973), *The Theory of the Leisure Class: With an Introduction by John Kenneth Gabraith*', London: Houghton.

Viner, Jacob (1952), *International Trade and Economic Development*, Glenwe, Illinois: Free Press.

Walters, Alan A. (1989), in Eatwell, Milgate and Newman (eds.), *The New Palgrave (Economic Development)*, London: MacMillan, 59–60.

Waterston, Albert (1965), *Development Planning*, Baltimore: Johns Hopkins University Press.

Westphal, Larry E (1990), 'Industrial Policy in an Export-Propelled Economy: Lessons from South Korean Experience', *Journal of Economic Perspectives*, 4:3, 41–59.

Whitehead, Alfred, N. (1972), *Symbolism: Its Meaning and Effect*, New York: Capricorn Books.

Wicksell, K. (1958), 'A New Principle of Just Taxation', reprinted in R.A. Musgrave and A.T. Peacock (eds.), *Classics in the Theory of Public Finance*, New York: MacMillan.

World Bank (1978), *World Development Report (WDR) 1978*, New York: Oxford University Press.

———— (1982), *World Development Report (WDR)*, New York: Oxford University Press.

———— (1986), *Poverty and Hunger*, Washington, DC: The World Bank.

———— (1991), *World Development Report (WDR) 1991, (The Challenge of Development)*, New York: Oxford University Press.

———— (1993), *The East Asian Miracle*, 'London: Oxford University Press.

———— (1995), *World Development Report (WDR) 1995*, New York: Oxford University Press.

———— (1999), *World Development Report (WDR), Knowledge For Development*, New York: Oxford University Press.

———— (2000), *World Development Report (WDR), Entering the 21st Century*, New York: Oxford University Press.

———— (2001), *World Development Report, Attacking Poverty*, New York: Oxford University Press.

World Trade Organization (WTO) (1998), *Annual Report, 1998*, France: WTO.

Yotopoulos, Pan A. (1985), 'Middle-income Classes and Food Crises: The New Food-feed Competition', *Economic Development and Cultural Change*, 33:3, 463–83.

Index

About the Author

Syed Nawab Haider Naqvi is currently President of the Institute for Development Research, Islamabad. After completing his masters from Yale University, he obtained his doctorate from Princeton University and undertook post-doctoral work at Harvard. During a rich and distinguished career, Professor Naqvi has been OECD Consultant and Visiting Professor at the Middle East Technical University, Ankara (1972–75); Visiting Professor, Heidelberg University, (1977); Professor of Economics and Chairman, Department of Economics, Quaid-i-Azam University, Islamabad (1975–79); and National Professor of Economics, Pakistan (1993–1996). He has also served as Director of the Pakistan Institute of Development Economics, Islamabad (1979–1995) and is the founder-president of the Pakistan Society of Development Economists.

Professor Naqvi has been closely involved with the formulation of Pakistan's economic policy and served as Chief, Economic Affairs Division, Government of Pakistan (1971–72). Subsequently, he was a member or chairman of a number of key committees including the Pakistan Planning Commission (1979) and the strategy-formulating Working Group for the Fifth Five Year Plan. In recognition of his services to the economics profession, Professor Naqvi was awarded the prestigious Sitara-I-Imtiaz by the Government of Pakistan, the first Pakistani economist to be thus honoured.

A prolific author, Professor Naqvi has published 47 books and monographs, and around 100 articles in the areas of macro-econometric modelling, trade policy, development and agricultural economics, and comparative economic systems. He has served on the Editorial Boards of 14 national and international journals, and was the Editor of the Pakistan Development Review from 1979 to 1995.

DATE DUE